Re-Imaging Modernity

American Society of Missiology Monograph Series

THE ASM MONOGRAPH SERIES provides a forum for publishing quality dissertations and studies in the field of missiology. Collaborating with Pickwick Publications—a division of Wipf and Stock Publishers of Eugene, Oregon—the American Society of Missiology selects high quality dissertations and other monographic studies that offer research materials in mission studies for scholars, mission and church leaders, and the academic community at large. The ASM seeks scholarly work for publication in the Series that throws light on issues confronting Christian world mission in its cultural, social, historical, biblical, and theological dimensions.

Missiology is an academic field that brings together scholars whose professional training ranges from doctoral-level preparation in areas such as scripture, history and sociology of religions, anthropology, theology, international relations, interreligious interchange, mission history, inculturation, and church law. The American Society of Missiology, which sponsors this series, is an ecumenical body drawing members from Independent and Ecumenical Protestant, Catholic, Orthodox, and other traditions. Members of the ASM are united by their commitment to reflect on and do scholarly work relating to both mission history and the present-day mission of the church. The ASM Monograph Series aims to publish works of exceptional merit on specialized topics, with particular attention given to work by younger scholars, the dissemination and publication of which is difficult under the economic pressures of standard publishing models.

Persons seeking information about the ASM or the guidelines for having their dissertations considered for publication in the ASM Monograph Series should consult the Society's website—www.asmweb.org.

Members of the ASM Monograph Committee who approved this book are:

Michael A. Rynkiewich, retired from Asbury Theological Seminary
Paul V. Kollman, CSC, University of Notre Dame
James R. Krabill, Mennonite Mission

PREVIOUSLY PUBLISHED IN THE ASM MONOGRAPH SERIES

Christopher L. Flanders, *About Face: Rethinking Face for the 21st Century Mission*

W. Jay Moon, *African Proverbs Reveal Christianity in Culture: A Narrative Portrayal of Builsa Proverbs Contextualizing Christianity in Ghana*

E. Paul Balisky, *Wolaitta Evangelists: A Study of Religious Innovation in Southern Ethiopia, 1937–1975*

Stephen Pavey, *Theologies of Power and Crisis: Envisioning/Embodying Christianity in Hong Kong*

Re-Imaging Modernity

A Contextualized Theological Study of Power and Humanity within Akamba Christianity in Kenya

GREGG A. OKESSON

American Society of Missiology
Monograph Series

VOL. 16

☙PICKWICK *Publications* • Eugene, Oregon

RE-IMAGING MODERNITY
A Contextualized Theological Study of Power and Humanity within Akamba Christianity in Kenya

American Society of Missiology Monograph Series 16

Copyright © 2012 Gregg A. Okesson. All rights reserved. Except for brief quotations in critical publications or reviews, no part of this book may be reproduced in any manner without prior written permission from the publisher. Write: Permissions, Wipf and Stock Publishers, 199 W. 8th Ave., Suite 3, Eugene, OR 97401.

Pickwick Publications
An Imprint of Wipf and Stock Publishers
199 W. 8th Ave., Suite 3
Eugene, OR 97401

www.wipfandstock.com

ISBN 13: 978-1-61097-741-8

Cataloguing-in-Publication data:

Okesson, Gregg A.

Re-imaging modernity : a contextualized theological study of power and humanity within Akamba Christianity in Kenya / Gregg A. Okesson.

American Society of Missiology Monograph Series 16

xxiv + 250 pp. ; 23 cm. Includes bibliographical references and index.

ISBN 13: 978-1-61097-741-8

1. Power (Christian theology). 2. Kamba (African people) 3. Christianity—Kenya. I. Title. II. Series.

BR1443 K4 O452012

Manufactured in the U.S.A.

*I dedicate this book to those who have
most intimately nurtured my humanity.*

*To my children, Isaiah and Anna:
Thank you for being patient when I was hidden
in my office writing, or out in the churches.
You are God's most wondrous gifts in my life;
eternal treasures of God's beauty.*

*And pre-eminently, to my wife, Kimberly:
You have saturated these years with never-ceasing
words of encouragement, sacrifice, and quiet acts of service.
You are the image of Christ to me, and the very representation
of divine power manifested within my humanity.*

Contents

Acknowledgments / ix
Abbreviations / xi
Foreword by Kevin Ward / *xiii*
Introduction / xv

1. Themes of Discourse and Methodological Issues / 1
2. Images of Power / 47
3. Africa Inland Church: Secularization and Rationalization / 79
4. Africa Brotherhood Church: Self-Reliance and Development / 115
5. Redeemed Gospel Church: Individualism and Materialism / 145
6. Power and the Image of God: A Contextualized Theological Proposal / 181

Conclusions / 221

Bibliography / 229
Index / 247

Acknowledgments

I WISH TO THANK many people, to whom this book is indebted. From the beginning, Kevin Ward has been very gracious, provided sage guidance, and been the symbol of patience with my ruminations and (at times) embryonic ideas.

I further thank all the churches in Ukambani, and especially those individuals who sat with me, endured my questions, and generously shared their thoughts and theological contemplations. Justus Musila introduced me to some of the early leaders in the RGC. I am grateful to the Rt. Rev. Bishop Timothy Ndambuki and Bishop Paul Mutua for generously welcoming me to understand their respective denominations. The ABC congregation in Bomani invited my family to become regular members in fellowship with them. Foremost, to the administration, faculty, and students at Scott Theological College, who often served as sounding boards to my thoughts: you have shaped my life more than I can possibly imagine.

I thank Paul Mbandi for reading chapter 2, and correcting some of my Kikamba; and Moses Mollombe for translating certain documents into English. I am especially indebted to the labors of Stella Munyao, George Kiasyo, Dionysius Malusi and David Mutiso for the valuable interviews and qualitative research they undertook during the final year of field study, as well as for all students in my Africa Initiated Churches, Cultural Anthropology, and Foundations of Leadership courses.

I trust that this study accurately reflects the many people who have graciously shared their thoughts and lives with me, and hence presents an authentic (albeit, hardly exhaustive) picture of the intricate beauty found within Akamba Christianity.

Abbreviations

AACC	All Africa Council of Churches
ABC	Africa Brotherhood Church
ACB	African Christian Brotherhood
ACK	Anglican Church of Kenya
ACCS	Africa Christian Church and Schools
ACU	Akamba Christian Union
AEA	Association of Evangelicals in Africa
AIC	African Initiated Churches
AICK	Africa Inland Church (Kenya)
AIM	Africa Inland Mission
AJET	*Africa Journal of Evangelical Theology*
ACC	Area Church Council
BEE	Bible Education by Extension
CBM	Canadian Baptist Ministries
CCC	Central Church Council
CHE	Commission for Higher Education
CIM	China Inland Mission
CMS	Anglican Church Missionary Society
CU	Christian Union
DCC	District Church Council
DRC	Democratic Republic of Congo
EAK	Evangelical Alliance of Kenya
FOCUS	Fellowship of Christian Unions
GFF	Gospel Furthering Fellowship
IMF	International Monetary Fund
JEPTA	*Journal of the European Pentecostal Theological Association*
KJV	King James Version

Abbreviations

LCC	Local Church Council
MOU	Memorandum of Understanding
MP	Member of Parliament
NCCK	National Council of Churches of Kenya
NEGST	Nairobi Evangelical Graduate School of Theology
NGO	Non-Governmental Organization
NIST	Nairobi International School of Theology
NIV	New International Version
NKJV	New King James Version
PACU	Pan Africa Christian University
PCEA	Presbyterian Church of East Africa
PEFA	Pentecostal Evangelical Fellowship of Africa
RC	Roman Catholic
RGC	Redeemed Gospel Church
SA	Salvation Army
SDA	Seventh Day Adventist
STC	Scott Theological College
UBC	Ukamba Bible College
WCC	World Council of Churches

Foreword

I WARMLY RECOMMEND THIS book. It is a profound and illuminating search concerning the human condition, human agency and vulnerability, love and power. The focus is on Africa and on the way in which these fundamental human issues are articulated in an African context. The book looks at the ways in which Africans have related to spiritual forces, to divinity, and to the ambiguities of political and cultural authority, both historically and in response to the contemporary forces of modernity. The book is a work of Christian anthropology, grappling with the way in which Christ speaks to these human concerns, both questioning human aspiration and enhancing human potentiality. Okesson shows how the contemporary Christian churches in African can and must (if they are true to their calling) critically address the problems of the power structures of post-independent Africa, but also how they themselves are vulnerable, as institutions of power in their own right.

Gregg Okesson speaks from an Evangelical tradition. He addresses the legacy of Evangelical faith and life, both in the period of missionary power and under African leadership, with critical insight and warm appreciation. He is warmly appreciative, too, of African traditional cultures and of other Christian traditions. He has read extensively in the literature on African theology as it has developed since the 1960s, and reflects upon it in illuminating ways. But Okesson also utilizes his "local" knowledge, specifically of Akamba Christianity in Kenya. He admirably contextualises his theology, to show how structures and ideologies of power, both culturally and institutionally, in society and in the church community, are articulated and have life-enhancing or life-diminishing impact. This is contextual theology of a high order, full of insights, in its weaving of local, national and continental debates. Okesson focuses on three churches of significance in Ukambani: the Africa Inland Church, the Africa Brotherhood Church, and the Redeemed Gospel Church. The three churches represent traditional conservative, African independent, and Pentecostal traditions. The case studies are valuable for their own

Foreword

sake, full of fascinating detail and insight. But are also admirably integrated into the large narrative, providing important themes of more general concern for the construction of an African theology of power.

Okesson's work, precisely because if its critical acumen and constructive theological debate, is a fine tribute to the pioneering work of his own Africa Inland Mission. It also underlies the contemporary importance of the Africa Inland Church as one of the major Christian traditions in Kenya, and recalls us again to the fascination and insights of Kamba culture and its Christian heritage. In the first years of independence, John Mbiti showed how significant were the Akamba for establishing themes of relevance to African theology generally. In the early years of the twenty-first century, Okesson has finely continued this excellent tradition.

Kevin Ward
Leeds, UK

Introduction

IN THIS STUDY I attempt to show how ecclesiastical communities in Africa *reimage modernity* through theological resources. Divine power occupies center stage in this discussion. I will show how *power* provides an overarching, unifying hermeneutic that makes it possible for humans to invoke (*tap into*) God's nature for sociological expression; specifically, for *life*. This is consistent with African worldviews, where divine power relates to temporal concerns (within an integrative cosmos). Human agents (and in this case, ecclesiastical communities) function as central agents in these processes as they draw upon God's power, within the webs of power-relations that constitute life, leading to generative and world-shaping implications. The result of these dynamics, I propose, represents unique forms of modernity arising on the continent.

A few points of clarification are necessary. I have lived in Machakos since 2001 as an American missionary working in theological education at Scott Theological College (STC).[1] Besides teaching on subjects such as leadership and theology, I have been involved in administration at the University and developed relationships with many different churches in the region. I began my research with interest in how evangelical denominations in Machakos organize themselves in relation to power, thinking that the natural trajectory for this inquiry would lead toward the development of leadership patterns amongst the various churches. Through my teaching (in leadership courses, but no less in theological subjects) I have seen the importance of looking at *power* theologically and sociologically, and especially in relation to sacralizing and/or secularizing currents at play within contemporary societies. Thus, from the onset, I was curious how theological topics lend themselves to the development of sociological themes. My interactions with different leaders from surrounding denominations further bolstered my interest in this subject, eager to discover similarities and differences from a variety of churches in Ukambani.

1. A private, chartered Kenyan University sponsored by the Africa Inland Church.

Introduction

The area surrounding Machakos (Ukambani) has been strategic for the development of Christianity in Kenya, as it represents one of the first places where Western missionaries settled, and boasting a strong history of ecclesiastical creativity (with various *independent* churches arising during the years leading up toward independence). Yet very little has been written on Akamba Christianity.[2] From 2005–2009 I undertook qualitative field research within three evangelical denominations in the Machakos area, listening to ecclesiastical leaders and *washiriki* (literally, *fellowshippers*) from within the different churches. I asked simple, open-ended questions such as, "Where does power come from?" "Who has it?" and "What does it do?" expecting that their answers would largely relate to leadership characteristics. Instead, I found respondents talking about power in largely sociological ways, and often through modernity-related language (e.g., *development, autonomy, self-reliance,* and *education*). During the three-plus years of participatory observation (attending many different churches, visiting a variety of different ministries, and sitting with pastors, lay leaders, and *washiriki*), I was able to discern other themes of modernity prevalent within the churches (such as *secularization, individualization,* and *materialism*). These topics rarely display direct correspondence with Western varieties, helping to explain the title of this book, in which Akamba Christianity contributes a leading role toward *reimaging modernity*.

I approach the subject with the basic presupposition that modernity is not something that should be disregarded, ignored, or vilified, but rather nurtured from within ecclesiastical communities (and through employment of theological resources). I am hesitant to look at African societies as inextricably *premodern,* as if implying that they need to chart a course according to certain preordained Western trajectories. Yet with this said, Western varieties do influence the following discussion, and so the ensuing inquiry seeks a more integrative understanding of modernity, drawing upon global and local characteristics.

I do not offer this study as a sociological exploration of the themes, but as a contextual theology of power and humanity within Akamba Christianity. My interests are therefore pre-eminently theological (with due acknowledgement to the many ways that theology and sociology overlap within African worldviews). Precisely because of the importance given to divine power within African societies, I see the necessity of

---

2. Notable exceptions include Mbiti, *New Testament Eschatology;* and Sandgren, "Kamba," 167–95.

Introduction

developing a theological framework with which to guard churches from abuses related to how they interact with God's power. This study therefore focuses on the image of God concept, which further highlights the play of words offered in the title. Very simply, churches in Ukambani (and perhaps other parts of the country/continent) invoke God's nature as a means of engaging in their contexts. God's power remains one of the primary ways in which they understand the divine, and with implications for how they function in society. Humans are the image of God insofar as they image God with authenticity within their worlds.

ECCLESIASTICAL VIGNETTES

Loud music reverberates from a tin structure in the center of Machakos town. Parishioners attending the Machakos Worship Centre stand with hands outstretched to the sky, while a few wander off to secluded spots near the walls, or in the corners, calling out to God. The preacher walks to the pulpit, microphone in hand, and the congregation become silent; he shouts, "You have been given power; you have also been given authority."[3] The people feed off these words, shouting affirmations, and later departing with an inspired vision for what they can accomplish as God's agents in the world.

In another congregation, dwelling on the outskirts of Machakos town, a pastor occupies one side of the pulpit while the elders (*wazee*) huddle together on the other side. Women have *kitambaa* (scarf) coverings on their heads, and men wear suits. Youth occupy the last five rows. Members of the Africa Inland Church (AICK) sing from the Kikamba hymnal, *Nukwenda uthew'e waku? Nthakame yake yi vinya—wa uu, Ni kana utw'ike mundu wake? Nthakame yi vinya wa uu* (Would you be free from the burden of sin? There's power in the blood, power in the blood; Would you o'er evil a victory win? There's wonderful power in the blood). The atmosphere is orderly and methodical with elders exchanging turns addressing congregants regarding various building projects, needs in the congregation, or pre-wedding preparations. Near the end of the service, one of the elders introduces the "man of God." The pastor rises, and preaches from 2 Timothy 4:2–5, admonishing members to guard themselves against false teachers who come with various ideologies.[4] After the

---

3. Machakos Worship Centre, Redeemed Gospel Church, 17 September 2006, Machakos, Kenya.

4. Borrowed from different Africa Inland Church services I have attended in Kateve and Kasinga villages, Machakos, Kenya.

xvii

service, the *washiriki* stay for community meals and committee meetings before walking home by evening light.

Further from Machakos, I walk through the agricultural project of the Africa Brotherhood Church (ABC) and talk with various development experts. We pass grafted citrus orchards, a test plot in which church officials train community members in new farming techniques, a health clinic, and church building. I ask the reasons behind the project, and Millicent Manesa explains the desire "to change this place religiously."[5] Inside the church, parishioners follow a carefully orchestrated liturgy that combines Baptistic, Anglican, Salvation Army and Roman Catholic elements to form new meanings based upon their distinct "holistic Gospel." After the service, members meet in *self-help* groups to invest personal money in church-operated micro-credit schemes, care for less fortunate parishioners, and/or develop income-generating projects.

Each of these vignettes gives illustration to various ways that ecclesiastical communities in Ukambani organize themselves according to spiritual power. In giving explanation to important elements comprising African worldviews, Charles Nyamiti describes how proximity to God equips humans with essential powers for growing in life (where, nearness to the divine indicates heightened power; and thus, in a sense, with greater identity). He says, "God is, in the final analysis, behind all events in the world. He is the Fountain of life and power in which all participate and, as such He is the Foundation of human and cosmic solidarity, totality, and participation."[6] What Nyamiti and others[7] describe by means of traditional concepts and terminology, I would like to develop within contemporary categories, showing some of the ways that African ecclesiastical communities utilize divine power in order to image God within the world: expressive of a variety of *modernities* appearing on the continent.

This at once establishes a number of important presuppositions. Firstly, traditions are never static, but require reinterpretation within contemporary contexts in order to maintain efficacy; said in another way, "Humans do not just live in the world, but interpret the world by living in it."[8] As such, the forms and meanings that these *reinterpretations* take roughly correlate with emerging forms of African modernity. I will argue

5. Millicent Manesa, interview by author, Kibwezi, Kenya, Nov. 15, 2007.

6. Nyamiti, "Incarnation," 6.

7. In chapter 2, I will provide a brief overview of some of the ways that African scholars have utilized power as a theological category.

8. Nyamiti, "Incarnation," 6.

that modernity, as such, needs to be extricated from exclusive orientation (or, ownership) with the West. African forms of modernity—especially when viewed through the churches—have their own internal logic, and relate to an integrative cosmos built around participation with God's power. This should not indicate that African constructs are completely dislocated from Western varieties, since I will argue that ecclesiastical communities draw upon African and Western *traditions* in order to frame this encounter: showing elements of continuity and discontinuity; imaging and re-imaging. This further should not suggest that the forms of modernity appearing on the continent are always generative in nature. In as much as the churches invoke divine power in order to posture themselves favorably within the modern world, I seek to provide theological valuation to this process, highlighting the importance of looking at modernity as a theological category. I will frame this discussion within the image of God concept: demonstrating that humans represent God by representing his power within the world. The central argument is such that orientations with divine power should lead to generative and world-affirming manifestations (often expressed along sociological themes). Humans image God for the growth of the world around them.

"WHAT POWER? AND HOW DO THEY USE IT?"

Over thirty years ago, Adrian Hastings reflected upon the condition of African states and their relationship with the churches. Independence had been recently won and the churches were trying to figure out their relationship with the new governments: "There is plenty of power to be got and controlled in the many states of Africa today," he said. "The great question is: what is it used for? And how do the churches relate to it?... What power do they [the churches] have to influence courses of events and how do they use it?"[9] Discourses on power often imply some kind of association with politics or governance, but Hastings third and fourth questions suggest a different trajectory, where power may exist independent of the state and inherent within the churches. Many of these issues were of particular concern for scholars as they tried to understand the political theology of the emergent independent church movement. The outcome of these studies was largely ambiguous, with no definitive connection between the rise of new religious movements and protest against the colonial governments; however, Terence Ranger proposes that even

---

9. Hastings, *African Christianity*, 77–78.

Introduction

in such cases where the churches appeared apolitical, this should not discount any "form of politics."[10]

What kind(s) of power do churches have (to repeat Hastings earlier question) and how do they use such power? This study undertakes to show the life-enhancing power of ecclesiastical communities. As Ranger suggests, the churches display a "form of politics." But, perhaps because of disillusionment with the actual development of governance issues within the state, or due to certain traits in their theological heritage, the churches often turn away from directly attempting to influence political processes, and concentrate their attention, on the one hand, on the very local, and on the other hand, with global themes. I will explore these dynamics from the perspective of three evangelical churches in Ukambani, Kenya: the Africa Inland Church (AICK),[11] the Africa Brotherhood Church (ABC), and Redeemed Gospel Church (RGC).

EVANGELICALISM IN KENYA

Statistics show evangelicals (inclusive of Pentecostals/charismatics) to be the fastest growing segment of Christianity in Kenya, with annual growth rates of 2–3 percent and comprising approximately 67 percent of the entire population.[12] Missionaries brought various strains of evangelicalism to Africa in the late nineteenth and early twentieth centuries, but new varieties developed from the African response: sometimes reacting against missionary teaching, but more often through reframing the primary characteristics of the Gospel to relate to needs on the continent better. Therefore, what I am calling evangelicalism correlates with a missionary tradition that received new interpretations through its contact with African worldviews. However, making demarcations between evangelicals and non-evangelicals in Kenya often proves problematic, since all the churches draw upon shared faith commitments emanating from their Christian heritage,[13] and express themselves with conservative

---

10. Ranger, "Religious Movements," 4–5.

11. This abbreviation for the Africa Inland Church avoids confusion with the common acronym for African Independent Churches (AICs) and delineates the Africa Inland Church, Kenya, from its sister churches in countries such as Sudan and Tanzania.

12. Johnstone and Mandryk, *Operation World*, 381.

13. David Bebbington provides one of the most widely respected definitions of evangelicalism, describing the movement based upon four common characteristics: biblicism, crucicentrism, conversionism, and activism (see *Evangelicalism in Modern Britain*, 2–17).

credentials. The purpose of this study, therefore, is not to categorize the churches along highly tendentious lines, but to demonstrate the importance of divine power for ecclesiastical and social expression.

The three denominations highlighted in this study were chosen because of their origins in Ukambani and due to the ways they represent wider perspectives of evangelicalism in the region. These churches, together with Catholics, Orthodox and ecumenical Protestants, have contributed to the formation of a broad and pervasive conservatism within the religious and moral landscape of the country. The AICK arose from the work of the Africa Inland Mission (AIM) and exemplifies what may be called a "mainline," "mission-founded," or historic church.[14] The ABC broke away, in part, from the AICK/AIM in 1945 and falls into the category of an African *independent* or *initiated*[15] church. Finally, the RGC, founded in 1974, is representative of *newer* Pentecostal churches emerging in Kenya during the 1970s and 80s.[16] I am not suggesting that these are the only kinds of evangelical churches in Ukambani, or, that each is prototypical of its larger category (mainline, initiated, or newer Pentecostal);[17] only, that these three denominations provide a fair rendering of evangelicalism in the region, allowing me to draw wider implications for what may loosely be termed Akamba Christianity.

UKAMBANI

Ukamba is the traditional home of the Akamba people,[18] occupying the districts of Machakos and Kitui in the Eastern Province of Kenya. Some oral histories have them coming from the slopes of Kilimanjaro to settle in this region around the sixteenth century, while others place their origins along the coast. The Akamba are ethnically and linguistically North-East

---

14. I will be using these terms interchangeably.

15. I will be referring to these churches as *initiated* to emphasize their African origins. The older nomenclature of *independent* no longer carries the same meaning as it did prior independence, as currently Africans govern most historic or mission-founded churches. Scholars also refer to them as instituted.

16. Paul Gifford refers to these as "proto-Pentecostal" (*Christianity*, 128).

17. Recent developments in Ukambani suggest new varieties of *initiated* churches emerging in the region, including what I might call "neo-Ethiopian" (reacting against the historic churches) as well as more recent Pentecostal churches evolving from discontentment with the institutionalization of charismatic authority seen in newer Pentecostal denominations (such as the RGC). See note 24 in chapter 5.

18. The Akamba are sometimes referred to by the cognate, Kamba, but I will be using the more accurate Akamba to refer to them by name.

Introduction

Bantu, speaking Kikamba in the villages, while combining it with Kiswahili and English in town settings. They represent either the fourth or fifth largest ethnic group in Kenya, depending upon contemporary estimates.[19] Currently, ninety-five percent of the people living in Ukambani are Akamba, with smaller communities located in Nairobi and along the coast (particularly around Mariakani, Changamwe, and Shimba Hills). Machakos (also called Masaku)[20] is the largest city in Ukambani, located approximately 60 kilometres southeast of Nairobi. Most of the research for this study took place around Machakos town, while extending, as well, to Kangundo, Mbooni, Mukaa, Tawa, and Nzaui. I did travel as far away as Kibwezi, but this was unusual as I tried to limit my research to the Machakos district. (see Map B)

Most of the available research for the Akamba comes from the late nineteenth to mid-twentieth century, as colonial presence and early missionary activity encouraged the writing of various histories[21] and ethnographies.[22] After years of initial resistance, the Akamba turned to Christ in large numbers with Roman Catholics (RC) and the AIM among those most actively involved in missionary service in the region. The Anglican Church Missionary Society (CMS) had begun some early work, but conceded their original stations to the AIM, later turning their attention to the Kitui District. During the 1940s, three churches broke away from the AIM in Ukambani. One was the ABC, started by a group of Akamba Christians. The other was the African Christian Church and Schools (ACCS). And the last was the Gospel Furthering Fellowship (GFF), begun by the work of George Rhoads (an AIM missionary who left the mission to start his own organization). Many other churches have since come to Ukambani, including the Salvation Army (SA), Seventh Day Adventist (SDA), Presbyterian Church of East Africa (PCEA), and, more recently, numerous Pentecostal churches including the Pentecostal Evangelical Fellowship of Africa (PEFA) and RGC. Since independence, little has been written about Akamba Christianity. Yet, Ukambani remains strategic for understanding Christianity in Kenya due to its long

19. Updated statistics will be announced following the census, which occurred in August 2009.

20. The name Machakos comes from a distortion in how the colonial authorities pronounced the name of a prominent chief in the area, Masaku.

21. Krapf, *Travels*.

22. See Hobley, *Ethnography of the A-kamba*; Lindblom, *Akamba in British East Africa*; Middleton and Kershaw, *Kikuyu and Kamba*.

history of missionary activity and robust response to the Gospel. Nairobi is easily accessible to Wakamba living in Machakos district, which allows them to have a foot in urban and rural communities: carrying the influence of Akamba Christianity to their urban churches, while also acting as transmitters of urban Christianity back into Ukambani.

IMAGING POWER

Much of the early theological activity occurring in post-independent Africa focused on the central issue of relating theology to African traditions; in other words, trying to answer the question, "How African is our theology?" Future work depends on a more nuanced understanding of Africa and the West (particularly in regard to modernity-related themes), with greater attention given to the role of the divine for social construction.

This assumes a number of things fundamental for understanding the remainder of this study. Firstly, God's nature provides the underlying basis for interpreting the world, and more so that humans (as image-bearers) function as the central hermeneutical agents in these processes. Whether humans *are*, *have*, or *use* the *imago dei* is a topic that will come later in this study; at this stage, it is merely important to make connections between people's understanding of God and how they relate with the world. Moltmann says that humans function as "the image of God on earth insofar as they correspond to God and represent the invisible God in the visible world."[23] This underscores the relevancy of God's nature for how people associate with the world, with further implication for how humans utilize God's image in generative or world-shaping ways. Some social scientists speak of the role of religion in terms of "human projection";[24] yet another way of explaining it would be to borrow from theological language and talk about human imaging. Humans represent God within the world precisely because they are the image of God.

One of the main points I will make in this book is that people understand God as powerful, and relate to each other (and the world) in commensurate ways. Power is a fundamental component of reality. Martyn Percy argues that "power is one of the primary religious ideas; humanity's awareness of God is an awareness of him as powerful. It is seen as a fundamental attribute of God."[25] From my study of the churches

---

23. Moltmann and Moltmann-Wendel, *Humanity in God*, 63.
24. Berger, "Sociological and Theological Perspectives," 94–95.
25. Percy, *Words*, 23.

Introduction

in Ukambani, power serves as the primary attribute by which believers know and interact with God (subsequently, leading to how they engage with the world). God's power occupies prominence in the churches through choruses, prayers, and sermons, but no less on non-ecclesiastical stages, such as on *matatu* (public service vehicles), *duka* (shops), and in sociopolitical discourses.

Humans participate in God's image by representing and inculcating his attributes into the world: essentially utilizing the divine to make sense of the world around them and shape it in particular ways. This provides one of the primary bases for understanding power within human societies. On the one hand, God's power relates to human abilities (including those *mentalistic*, such as dreams and imagination); and on the other, it includes responsibilities and values whereby humans care, nurture, and govern the growth of God's nature within the world: quite literally with effect to the *spaces* existing within an integrative cosmos. Humans relate to God derivationally, as an image, or, as "representation."[26] They project God's nature into the world. The substance of God's power, therefore, can lead toward either domination or the enhancement of life, depending upon the accuracy of representation, and the ethical values associating humans with the image of God. This moves theological concepts into sociological categories, making it possible for theology to become an instrument of modernity, while also underscoring the need for ethical parameters to surround the employment of divine power within the world.

Chapter 1 will lay some of the theoretical foundations for connecting power with generative construction, while working to extricate modernity from exclusive orientation within Western societies. I will show that modernity has long served as an important theme for scholars of African religions trying to wrestle with the role of Christianity in contemporary society. Any reference to modernity, however, should not indicate polarity or detachment with traditional values; for, as stated earlier, traditions require re-interpretation within modern categories in order to maintain relevancy within contemporary stages. I will further develop a methodological approach in which theology and sociology work together to provide empirical "data" for theological reflection, while, simultaneously supplying the means by which theology serves for the development of sociological expressions (like *modernity*). Dual movement between the two disciplines provides much of the basis for an integrative approach.

---

26. Monga, *Anthropology of Anger*, 135.

1

Themes of Discourse and Methodological Issues

THIS CHAPTER LAYS THE theoretical framework for showing how ecclesiastical communities in Ukambani utilize divine power for generative life growth. Initially, I will explore some key thematic issues central to the thesis of this book, dealing with topics such as power, modernity, and the relationship between African traditions and modernity. These are highly convoluted matters, not easily fixed or established with neat boundaries. Furthermore, the particular shapes given to these topics remain dependent upon the contexts to which they appear. Power, for example, requires deeper investigation into the circumstances surrounding its appropriation: where power comes from, how it acts, who has it, and what it does. Modernity, likewise, I am arguing, assumes a myriad of forms with theological resources serving a leading role in its appearances. The second half of this chapter will give rationale to the particular methodological approach I employ, placing theology and sociology in dialogue with one another in order to offer an integrative understanding for how ecclesiastical communities utilize divine power for life growth.

THEMES OF DISCOURSE

Power

Power represents a multifaceted reality that extends into all domains of human existence; it is felt more than seen, and moves between people to fashion identities and bring meaning into the world.[1] James Mackey

---

1. Michel Foucault describes power with similar terminology, depicting it as "something which circulates, or rather as something which only functions in the form

1

describes it as "one of the original features or factors in the universe, so named because it affects things, or, more mildly put, because it enables states of affairs to come about."[2] While Martin Percy says,

> It is dispositional, in the form of ideas, manners, bonding and unity. It is also episodic, in the form of specific instances, interventions and moments. It is a phenomenon present within all epistemological and social frameworks, usually encountered via its agents rather than the source itself. Power is a *function* (emphasis in the original) of systems of social interaction.[3]

As such, power needs to be understood in context, and in action. It is more a verb than a noun,[4] and therefore requires empirical evidence to show how it functions on different stages.

Bureaucratic or institutional forms of power (often understood as "authority" and delineated by "permanence"[5]) provide important socio-religious information about *who* has power, *how* it is structured, and *what* relationship those in power have with people in the wider community. But I will go beyond defining it solely in terms of its organizational structures, to propose that *other forms* of power are available to the churches, especially when viewed through theological lenses: bringing the discussion back to Hastings challenge where more attention needs to be given to the *kinds of power* churches possess, and how they use it.

From his research into colonialism in South Africa, John Comaroff explains power from its "relative capacity to construct realities—to fashion human subjects and social forms, material value and truth-value, perception and intentions," further describing that it "always has interiorized and exteriorized, spoken and unspoken, private and public, *productive*

---

of a chain. It is never localised here or there, never in anybody's hands, never appropriated as a commodity or piece of wealth. Power is employed and exercised through a net-like organisation. Not only do individuals circulate between its threads; they are always in the position of simultaneously undergoing and exercising this power. They are not only its inert or consenting target; they are always also the elements of its articulation. In other words, individuals are the vehicles of power, not its points of application" (*Power/Knowledge*, 98).

2. Mackey, *Power*, 13.

3. Percy, *Words*, 20.

4. Laurenti Magesa makes a similar point in his chapter entitled, "'Power' in African Religion," 313–14.

5. Weber, "The Sociology," 245.

and repressive coordinates [italics mine]."⁶ Or, pertaining to political processes on the continent, Célestin Monga expresses how political actors create or manipulate symbols in order to fashion a form of reality; thus, for Monga, "power is above all representation."⁷ Each of these statements underscores the need for understanding power as it relates to social construction, where humans employ a wide variety of power-related resources in which to shape the world around them (with due acknowledgement to oppressive tendencies that color this dynamic).⁸

Recent theological activity has sought to explore some of these generative potentialities in order to better utilize power within human communities. Beverly Harrison, a feminist theologian, defines power as "the ability to act on and effectually shape the world around us,"⁹ while Larry Rasmussen describes it as "power of agency, human and non-human agency alike, in the vast web of this miracle called life, itself an expression of God's life."¹⁰ These ideas, taken collectively, seek to redeem the nature and practice of power from any "repressive coordinates" with a more specific aim of showing how people use God's nature in creative and generative ways.

As such, leaders are not the only ones capable of influencing social realities. People can assert power in the face of oppressive rule through strikes or public demonstrations (showing force without authority)¹¹ or affect entire communities by means of rumors or public opinion. Monga describes how political agents often fashion images for the representation of reality, but it should be acknowledged that followers have the ability to do the same by employing sacred or secular symbols for mounting political resistance.

Theological images, as they pertain to God's nature, provide one of the most accessible and strategic forms of power for Africans; where, in contradistinction with real or perceived dichotomies existing within Western cultures, greater cultural resources exist for Africans to integrate

---

6. Comaroff, "Governmentality," 123.

7. Monga, *The Anthropology*, 135.

8. Achille Mbembe is among these interpreting the post-independent state in terms of its oppressive and manipulative power; see "The Banality," 1–30.

9. Harrison, *Making the Connection*, 250, note 5.

10. Rasmussen, "Power Analysis," 9.

11. Mackey argues that power vacillates between its twin poles of "force" and "authority."

Re-Imaging Modernity

"sacred" and "secular" realities.[12] Stephen Ellis and Gerrie Ter Haar show this to be the case within the context of African political processes. They contend that spiritual power provides a framework for interpreting public affairs on the continent: "that it is largely through religious ideas that Africans think about the world today, and that religious ideas provide them with a means of becoming social and political actors."[13] Other studies have similarly chronicled how the Gospel furnishes Africans with resources in which to imagine themselves powerful within rapidly changing social contexts.[14] J. D. Y. Peel describes some of these processes for the Yoruba and their encounter with Christianity. He says, "Religions are not just ways of explaining and modifying experience but are formative of communities and the power structures with them."[15] Hence, whereas missionaries came with expectations for what the Gospel would bring to the hearers, Africans were active in appropriating these meanings for their own benefit. The resultant forms were often highly imaginative responses to the Gospel and customized to fit local contexts. Chapter 6 of this book builds on these ideas from a theological perspective, showing that humans image God into the world because they are the image of God. This moves the scope of imagination from fanciful introspection to willful intent (or, agency).

Not all associations with divine power, however, produce generative results. The earlier mentioned contributions of Comaroff, Monga, and Mbembe all highlight *oppressive coordinates* on the continent, while Kwame Bediako calls attention to dangers associated with *sacralization*. Although it is possible to talk about sacralization in many different ways, I am following Bediako in using the word to refer to an orientation that leaders have (or, perceived as having) with the divine: where power, because of its origin in the spirit world, tends to rest as a *divine entity* upon leaders due to their proximity with God.[16] By linking leaders with

---

12. See Turner, "Model for the Structure," 42–64. I will be using these words to denote distinct (but inseparable) ways of viewing reality. By *sacred* I mean to indicate an association with the divine, whereas *secular* refers to physical or material realities. Recent studies suggest that Western secularism contains implicit spiritual roots, thus requiring new interpretations of the sacred-secular dichotomy from within societies with an Enlightenment tradition; see C. Taylor, *Secular Age*.

13. Ellis and Haar, *Worlds of Power*, 2.

14. See D. Maxwell, *Christianity and the African Imagination*; Peterson, *Creative Writing*; Lonsdale, "'Listen While I Read.'"

15. Peel, *Religious Encounter*, 4.

16. Bediako, "Unmasking the Powers," 207–29.

this kind of spiritual power, there is little opportunity for people to hold them accountable, or question aspects of their governance. Therefore, my use of the term *sacralization* implies a pejorative reading, necessitating a theological response.[17] In a later work, Bediako defends the need for Africans to maintain their spiritual priorities, but in ways that avoid some of the pitfalls associated with sacralization.[18]

I will argue that the image of God provides a way of embracing the spiritual worldview found within African societies, while providing theological resources to govern its use. Monga and others accurately represent abusive tendencies within African political processes, highlighting how some agents attempt to harness God's power for personal gain. However, this should not be the only context for the discussion. I will offer a different perspective coming out from the voices of the people in the churches, where God's power relates to life growth. The image of God concept as found in the Bible provides ethical parameters for faith communities to appropriate divine power for social construction.

Modernity

My interest in modernity stems from linkages (I see) existing between power and life growth. In this section, I argue that the concept needs to be untangled from exclusive association with Western societies, by focusing in particular attention upon how theological material guides its manifestation on global stages.[19] Humans create modernity, and do so (among other means) through religious ideas.

The words *modern*, *modernity*, and what is being called *postmodernity* all relate to different perspectives on the human condition arising between the fifteenth and eighteenth centuries and extending either to the mid-twentieth century (for those who believe that modernity has run out of steam and given way to postmodernity) or continuing to the present. Some historians and/or sociologists locate the beginning of the modern period well before the Enlightenment, with the invention of the printing press and the discoveries of new world(s); while others are sceptical, referring to this as the early modern period and place more tangible

17. Okesson, "Are Pastors Human?" 19–39. I show how sacralization often blends with evangelical propensities toward deification to bring heightened and nuanced dynamics to this problem.

18. Bediako, *Christianity in Africa*, 246. Yet he fails to suggest how this is possible.

19. Ward argues something similar for understanding global forms of Anglicanism; see *A History of Global Anglicanism*, 317f.

starting points of modernity alongside the rise of the Enlightenment during the seventeenth and eighteenth centuries. There are vast differences of opinion on these topics, and further differentiated from within various schools of thought.

The word modern has the broadest meaning, either relating loosely to modernity or simply indicating something as contemporaneous. Societies everywhere can claim right of possession to things modern, despite the enduring image of a modern-traditional dichotomy that continues to linger in many African contexts.

Modernity typically carries more nuanced meanings, usually through association with the "intellectual and cultural heritage of the Enlightenment project"[20] and portraying a wide range of characteristics including the rise of capitalism, individualism, secularism, and rationalism (among others). Social scientists use the word to grapple with broader social systems; whether, giving rise to capitalistic forms of economic hegemony (Marx), freeing humans from ambiguous powers that were believed to fill the pre-modern world (Weber), or where complex divisions of labor associated with modern societies result in more organic solidarity among humans (Durkheim). Giddens provides a wide, sweeping definition to show some of the different ways of looking at modernity:

> At its simplest, modernity is a shorthand term for modern society or industrial civilization. Portrayed in more detail, it is associated with (1) a certain set of attitudes towards the world, the idea of the world as open to transformation by human intervention; (2) a complex of economic institutions, especially industrial production and a market economy; (3) a certain range of political institutions, including the nation-state and mass democracy. Largely as a result of these characteristics, modernity is vastly more dynamic than any previous type of social order. It is a society—more technically, a complex of institutions—which unlike any preceding culture lives in the future rather than the past.[21]

My own particular approach will more closely follow Gidden's first group of meanings, relating modernity to "a certain set of attitudes toward the world, the idea of the world as open to transformation by human intervention." Yet acknowledging that attitudes should also affect institutions (with the desire that the ideas set forth in this study would

20. Sampson et al., *Faith and Modernity*, 7.
21. Giddens, *Conversations*, 94.

promote the humanization of power for African Christianity, and thereby offer theological resources for the critique and transformation of African societies).

Concurrent to these dynamics, Western societies, are, themselves, undergoing changes that reveal characteristics at the same time contiguous and yet reactive to earlier forms of modernity. These involve, depending on one's perspective: increased suspicion pertaining to certainty and/or positivism, greater reflexivity of the self, movement away from individualism, and other components that raise awareness to how modernity may possibly be "turning upon itself."[22] Some sociologists refer to this as postmodernity, with the intention of demarcating a decisive shift away from many of the central affirmations of modernity, while others are less certain that Western societies have truly entered something *post* in its orientation to modernity. Gerard Delanty argues that scepticism has always been a fundamental characteristic of modernity, and that what we are seeing now is simply a different form of it appearing in the world.[23] Those scholars hesitant to endorse a clear break with modernity are likely to speak of *late, second,* or *high* modernity.

Zygmunt Bauman appears representative of this latter group. He explains the origins of modernity from the need to "liquefy" the premodern solids that stood for the previous order; including "traditional loyalties, customary rights and obligations which bound hands and feet, hindered moves and cramped the enterprise," making way for the rise of modernity with its "new and improved solids."[24] Bauman contends that the "new solids" appearing in the form of modernity eventually grew rigid in their own right, giving rise to what he refers to as "liquid modernity": a newer, "lighter" period of time that resists all permanent casts or moulds. This study will not enter into these broader, sociological discourses except to use some of these insights to argue for a more dynamic (liquid) conception of modernity evidenced within global contexts, and particularly where theological imagery provides important resources for articulating its varying shapes.

This fluid picture of modernity raises questions concerning the importance of the Enlightenment for explicating any subsequent development of modernity around the world. In one sense, the Enlightenment

---

22. Ulrick Beck, 1999 as cited in Bauman, *Liquid Modernity*, 6.
23. Delanty, *Modernity*.
24. Bauman, *Liquid Modernity*, 3.

was responsible for birthing the modern era, or at least providing its central logic, and therefore remains coterminous with it. The Enlightenment represents a set of attitudes toward the world that gave rise to the scientific and industrial revolution, promoting notions of progress, rationality, capitalism, secularization, and individualism. Advances in transportation, communication, and various aspects of global discourse (including the expansion of Christianity) subsequently propelled modernity-related themes around the world. David Bosch,[25] John and Jean Comaroff,[26] and others[27] have argued for the importance of the Enlightenment in understanding the modern missions movement, and especially its impact upon global forms of evangelicalism.[28] It is for such reasons that Stanley states, "We are all post-Enlightenment people now."[29]

Yet one of the dangers of limiting modernity (especially in Africa) to strict association with the Enlightenment is that such a conjecture assumes that these characteristics circulated along homogeneous lines, or where the receptors (in this case, the Africans) were passive in the process. Neither of these points can be sustained from the context of mission history. This study will show how the primary agents introducing Christianity in Ukambani promoted both modern and antimodern characteristics. The missionaries often functioned as representatives of an evangelical heritage on the one hand indebted to Enlightenment thinking, yet on the other distrustful of the culture it spawned. An example would be how the Africa Inland Mission (AIM) brought natural solutions to what Africans believed to be spiritual problems. At the same time, however, these missionaries were reacting against modernism[30] (with its perceived antisupernatural underpinnings), and therefore brought heightened forms of supernaturalism to Africa in response to the naturalism they saw taking

---

25. Bosch, *Transforming*, 262ff.; 349ff.
26. Comaroff and Comaroff, *Of Revelation and Revolution*, 11–12.
27. See Stanley, *Christian Missions*.
28. See Noll, *A History*, 154–57.
29. Stanley, *Christian Missions*, 5.
30. The term *modernism* will not appear prominent in this study, except when related to these missionaries. In the first half of the twentieth century the term was often associated with a theological evaluation of liberal forms of Christianity, where fundamentalistic forms of evangelicalism saw modernism (also used interchangeably with *liberalism*) as undermining the legitimacy of the Christian faith by questioning the trustfulness of Scripture by means of rationalistic inquiry.

place in the West. Therefore, the AIM's trajectory with Enlightenment influences was hardly uniform.[31]

It may be helpful at this point to provide a working definition for how I will be using modernity. Because of my interest in how humans image God in their societies (especially through power), I want to describe modernity in terms of generative, social construction: something that ecclesiastical actors envision (with intent) for their world. Humans create modernity as they attend to linkages between God, human communities, and nature. Modernity, therefore, relates to progress or, more accurately (in African contexts), to life. This does not presume some fanciful high ground in which to wrestle with modernity away from the thorny issues that entangle it with the Enlightenment (or more recent issues related to globalization). I wish merely to begin where the primary actors of this study are starting, with how they imagine or image modernity in their local contexts. Lawrencia Kwark advocates modernity be studied as "a working definition and as a tool of analysis" instead of as "a theory of the evolution of history";[32] while for her work among the Yoruba, Hermione Harris suggests modernity be treated as "a cluster of attributes to which individuals aspire, rather than an objective socio-economic state."[33] The sociological issues remain in the forefront of such a methodology, but instead of defining modernity strictly according to the confines of Western historical or sociological discourse, the scope of research extends to local ecclesiastical stages: specifically how churches in Ukambani engage in modernity-related themes, with linkages between power (understood primarily along theological lines) and sociological expressions. Modernity, in this light, carries strong associations with divine power (especially within an integrative cosmos) and relates to life growth.

This should not infer that it is possible for modernity to be completely extricated from its Western ancestry, for such a bifurcation is not possible within the modern world. Western themes of modernity will continue to feature in the following chapters, since, as the editors of *African Modernities* postulate, "the surmise that Africa is the counter-image

---

31. These dynamics will be explored in greater detail in chapter 3.

32. Kwark, "The Reinvention," 128.

33. Harris, "Missionaries," 312. However, one of the recommendations I will be making is that ecclesiastical communities need to go beyond conceptualising modernity only with regard to attitudes, and consider how they can affect socioeconomic issues and even the very structures that represent power within modern societies, thus humanizing the world before God.

of Western assumptions of modernity also works the other way around; that is, the West is an image of African ideas of modernity."[34] I want to show, however, that Western forms of modernity are not determinative for Africans, but where actors (faith communities) retain sufficient space or freedom in which to reimage modernity within their specific contexts and in ways that express the generative nature of divine power.

Modernity and Traditions

Any discussion of modernity (especially in the context of African studies) necessitates a clear understanding of its relationship with traditions. These two words are often set against each other: *tradition* as an image of a pure and unyielding African past and *modernity* as representing an enlightened and rapidly changing West. These stereotypes are problematic for the reason they fail to show how traditions are re-interpreted within contemporary circumstances, or how visions of modernity adjust to fit local traditions.

Africa has never been isolated from global influences. Yet in the late nineteenth and early twentieth centuries this contact became more pronounced (albeit one dimensional) through the era of colonialism and Western missions. Whereas before, Africans had dealings with a diverse array of peoples, but with the advent of colonialism the interactions developed a predisposition toward Europe and America. Western agents often approached African traditions with ambiguous attitudes: sometimes presenting them as "backward" and in need of "civilization"; other times endorsing certain traditions (to create more favorable conditions of governance, or in reaction to what missionaries saw taking place in the West); and still in other instances introducing new traditions altogether.[35] In each case, African traditions became the convenient *other* to Western modernity. Many of these trajectories have continued to the present, despite repeated entreaties for a cessation to this dichotomy. Birgit Meyer contends, "The fact that this dualism appears to be continuously called upon in contemporary debates does not prove its theoretical usefulness, but does testify to its persistence as a discursive frame."[36]

---

34. Probst et al., *African Modernities*, 2.

35. A point illustrated by Terence Ranger in "The Invention of Tradition in Colonial Africa." In Hobsbaum and Ranger, *Invention of Tradition*, 211–62.

36. Meyer, "Mediating Tradition," 275–76.

Themes of Discourse and Methodological Issues

African theologians are among those frequently drawing upon this dichotomy to correct what they perceive to be noxious influences of missionary teaching and/or globalizing influences; however, such a dualism runs the risk of idealizing (or, romanticizing) traditional values by relating them to a glorified past.[37] Elevating traditions in this manner creates greater contrast with modernity (alternatively with the West), and presents an ideal with no empirical basis. Bruce Berman makes a similar point:

> In particular, the dominant image of traditional society as highly integrated, stable, relatively unchanging, and largely free of disruptive internal conflict has been challenged by increasing evidence of the fluidity of political boundaries and ethnic identities and the significant levels of internal conflict revealed in contemporary historical research.[38]

Nineteenth century Africa represents a time in which people "moved in and out of multiple identities,"[39] thus displaying fluid social interactions. Much of this mobility continues to the present, albeit manifested in different ways. The enduring presence of "modern-traditional" dichotomies, therefore, reveals important themes related to the discursive of modernity, whether expressing the need for better understanding how traditions adjust within contemporary contexts, or by focusing upon the imaginative importance of the past for Africans.[40]

The years surrounding African independency brought new efforts to reclassify and reinterpret traditions into modern frames of discussion. Robin Horton promoted such a project by comparing and contrasting African traditions with similar points of reference within Western modernity.[41] Some scholars have accused Horton of constructing false dichotomies (between such concepts as modern/traditional, open/closed, or static/dynamic) but his work is more convincing than these charges

---

37. Gifford highlights some of these predispositions in "Africa's Inculturation Theology," 18–34.
38. Berman, "Nationalism," 186.
39. Ranger, "The Invention," 248.
40. See Kombo where he implores Africa theologians to wrestle with contemporary problems in ways that incorporate the importance of the past; see "The African," 3–24.
41. Horton, "African Traditional Thought," 131–71.

would suggest, since Horton's purpose was to provide greater integration between these concepts.⁴²

In recent years the dialogue has continued, enriched in part by the contribution of African philosophers. Many of these writers advocate resurgence in African traditional thought: seeking to extricate it from polarity with the West, and envisioning some sort of assimilation between the two. An example would be Kwame Gyekye. He approaches the topic by trying to disassociate modernity from its exclusive affiliation with the West, appealing to its "common human goals"⁴³ and arguing that all societies around the world share in its commitments. His work features a "critical evaluation of values and practices of traditional culture"⁴⁴ with an aim of showing how these are reinterpreted into modern contexts: ultimately wanting to show that "Modernity is created for humanity and not humanity for modernity."⁴⁵

To proceed in this direction, Gyekye argues that only those traditions evaluated and accepted by subsequent generations can claim "authority" within present frames of reference.⁴⁶ "Tradition does not have an automatic objective authority, one that is self-determined and or internal to itself or a feature of itself, standing as an eternal monolith to which successive generations bow in reverent obeisance."⁴⁷ He maintains that ancestors do not transmit traditions to their descendants as prepackaged and self-contained units, but rather with outstretched arms. "Subsequent generations may, on normative or other rational grounds, either accept, refine, and preserve them or spurn, depreciate and, then, abandon them."⁴⁸ The dynamic nature of cultural transmission highlights the important role humans contribute in processes pertaining to the transference of traditions, bringing the discussion out of the past and into the present by focusing on the evaluative powers of Africans to situate themselves "most favourably in the social, political, and intellectual formation of the contemporary world."⁴⁹

42. See also, Horton, *Patterns of Thought*.
43. Gyekye, *Tradition*, 279.
44. Ibid., vii.
45. Ibid., 297.
46. Ibid., 229.
47. Ibid.
48. Ibid., 221.
49. Ibid., 24–25.

Themes of Discourse and Methodological Issues

In like manner, Gyekye asserts that modernity also needs to be evaluated, as no culture has exclusive ownership to any particular idea or expression:

> To identify an idea or value as part of the cultural tradition of a people is not by any means to imply that that idea or value was necessarily originated by those people; nor is it to imply that a particular set of ideas or values . . . uniquely belongs to the tradition of that people.[50]

Topics such as progress, individualism or technology have points of reference in every culture, and the years of interaction with trader, colonist, and missionary have enabled Africans to imagine a modernity "creatively . . . forged from the furnace of the African cultural experience."[51] Gyekye's work contributes to this study by providing an integrative framework for traditions and modernity, while focusing upon the evaluative powers of Africans to fashion forms of modernity conducive to their contexts: employing all available resources to these ends.

MODERNITY AND THE CHURCHES

Gyekye's work highlights the dynamic nature of modernity on the continent, especially as it relates to African traditions and Western artefacts. Churches, I am arguing, play a central role in this process. Presently, I will provide an overview of how scholars have interacted with mainline, initiated, and *newer* Pentecostal churches along modernity-related themes, with an aim of sketching in broad lines the relationship between ecclesiastical actors and sociological currents.

Modernity and "Mainline" Churches

Limited research has been devoted to *mainline* or mission-founded churches in Kenya. More attention has been given to the rise of indigenous or initiated churches, excepting for a brief time when scholars concentrated on mission-founded responses to the politics and practices of Moi's government during the 1970s and 80s.[52] Since that time, mainline churches only seem to factor into scholarly discussions as the "other" to

---

50. Ibid., 227.
51. Ibid., 280.
52. See Sabar-Friedman, "Church and State," 25–52; Lonsdale, "Emerging Pattern," 267–84.

popular religions, creating a kind of polarity between the two, and with predispositions to view these churches through hegemonic associations with state leaders.[53] This kind of antithesis creates the impression that mission churches have endured only because of their political linkages, while failing to explain the considerable growth they experienced since independence. I will examine the broader reasons for their increase and postulate that it may have less to do with proximity to political authorities and more in how they orient human communities with power.

In order to accomplish this, I will begin by summarizing certain features of missionary encounters with Africans, especially pertaining to the subject of cultural transmission and modernity. During the nineteenth century, interactions between Africans and missionaries tended to be relatively loose and informal, with missionaries living in close proximity to Africans and often exhibiting aptitude in local languages.[54] Over time, the flexibility of these relationships gave way to formal, structured living arrangements on mission stations or compounds. Robert Strayer describes these places as "centres of social reintegration in very fluid and changing circumstances"[55] where Africans and missionaries shared cultural information through social and religious discourse. Usually, what is emphasized in this process is how the missionary imparted religio-cultural dictates to the African, leading to the adoption of features commonly associated with Western modernity. However, to make this argument, one would need to assume passivity in the Africans: something not supported by historical records and communicating a paternalistic reading of the encounter. In fact, Africans often found the instruments of Western modernity advantageous for engaging with missionary and colonist alike, and usually on their own terms. Such was the case for Western clothing,[56] literacy,[57] education, and/or other means of social advancement. This "active answering back"[58] to the artefacts and rituals of Western culture involves important elements of power essential for diagnosing resultant forms of modernity in Africa.

---

53. See Haynes, "Popular Religion," 89–108.
54. Ward, "Africa," 221.
55. Strayer, *Making of Mission Communities*, 59, 157.
56. Ibid., 20.
57. See Harries, "Missionaries," 405–27.
58. I am borrowing this term from Frederiksen, "Popular Culture," 210.

Themes of Discourse and Methodological Issues

Before coming to this, however, it may be helpful to take a step back and examine if the missionaries were the only ones affecting the progression towards modernization. The assumption that missionaries acted alone yields a form of reductionism and disregards the fluid relationships Africans had with ethnic groups, traders, and colonists. Robin Horton advances this point in what he calls a "thought experiment" where African societies were already making adjustments to increased exposure from outside influences prior the arrival of the missionaries. One of these adaptations, he argues, focuses upon a "high god" rather than on "lesser deities."[59] Terence Ranger provides a similar argument, positing the existence of a religious spectrum where Christianity provided one notable influence among many, showing the diversity and complexity of influences affecting African societies and casting new light on the relationships between church, state and modernization.[60] He says,

> The various mission churches in Africa had a great deal of authority; they were allocated monopolistic spheres of influence by the colonial regimes; they imposed upon their converts an ecclesiastical discipline long since defunct in Europe itself. But always below the surface was the seething of innovation and the movement of people to and from along the spectrum.[61]

These comments illustrate the artificiality of speaking exclusively about the impact of missionary *or* African religion, since it is often a combination of these together. The result was either the formation of new, indigenous churches; or, more frequently, creative innovation occurring within mission-founded churches.

Returning to the earlier discussion, the various interactions between missionary, state, traditions, and other religious beliefs produced a myriad of responses: sometimes in reaction to the missionary, other times with them, and more often through reinterpretations from the encounter. It has been common to portray the rise of ecclesiastical independency in contradistinction to mission-founded churches, but Adrian Hastings cautions against placing too much in such a reading and ignoring how the African clergyman who remained with his church often had greater influence than the one who started something new.[62] The reasons for this

---

59. Horton, "African Traditional Thought," 131–71.
60. Ranger, "Churches, the Nationalist," 492.
61. Ibid., 501.
62. Hastings, *History of African Christianity*, 118.

are many, and often connected with how Africans negotiated through the forms and rituals of Western cultural (and religious) practice in order to gain spiritual (and material) benefit. Robert Strayer makes this point for the Anglican Church Missionary Society (CMS) in Kenya. He argues for a new perspective on the missionary encounter, with greater attention upon how mission churches provided opportunities for change and development:

> With a foot in both worlds, then, mission communities represented an important arena for the making of a new African culture. Despite the many strains and tensions which accompanied the process, they remained in many cases and for many people institutions of sufficient flexibility and responsiveness to ensure their continuity to the present day.[63]

This helps explain the contemporary relevance of mission-founded churches. Even at the height of the independent church movement, most Africans remained loyal to their historic churches, and did so for important reasons.

In order to unpack some of these motivations, I will give brief deliberation to a few of the primary agents in the process. John and Jean Comaroff depict the relationship between missionaries and Africans as a "two-sided historical process"[64] that seems to recognize reciprocal flows of cultural information. However, their research is mostly directed toward how Europeans acted as purveyors of Enlightenment thought. Yet, if the two-sided historical process is, in fact, an accurate representation of engagements with modernity than more research should be given to how the missionary changed and/or adjusted through the encounter. Brian Stanley provides a corrective in this direction. His article, "Conversion to Christianity"[65] addresses common misconceptions arising from interactions between missionaries and Africans, and shows how scholars such as Mudimbe and the Comaroffs tend to misinterpret this encounter (and the very topic of conversion) by expressing it with paternalistic undertones: essentially viewing Africans as passive receptors in the process and the missionaries as unmoved mover. In response, Stanley discusses the other side, where through the process of engagement with another cul-

---

63. Strayer, *Making of Mission Communities*, 159; see also Strayer, "Mission History," 1–15.

64. Comaroff and Comaroff, *Of Revelation and Revolution*, 54.

65. Stanley, "Conversion to Christianity," 315–31.

Themes of Discourse and Methodological Issues

ture, and its people (in the context of the Gospel), missionary convictions and beliefs were constantly reshaped. Rather then distorting the purity of the Gospel, this understanding contributes to a richer and fuller perspective by insisting upon the Holy Spirit as primary agent within conversion, affecting both evangelist and proselyte alike.

What is more, even if one were to accept the notion of missionary as purveyor of Western culture, this should not imply that they consistently embodied all its tenets: as if to communicate either a monolithic and unchanging Western culture; or a corresponding acceptance that they were passive conspirators behind these ideologies. Most missionaries were simultaneously modern and anti-modern in their beliefs. Furthermore, even when they attempted to control the process of religious transmission according to their own cultural presuppositions, their scarcity in numbers particularly in the rural areas inhibited any full-scale imperialistic enterprise and left ample space for Africans to negotiate change.[66]

These comments highlight the complexity of the topic relating to Africans, the missionaries, and the resultant churches. Chapter 3 will continue this discussion through the Africa Inland Church (AICK), and show with greater detail how this denomination (representative in some ways of mainline churches) navigated through the contemporary world by re-imaging elements from its missionary heritage.

Modernity and African "Initiated" Churches

Contrary to what was just shared about the scarcity of research among mainline churches, scholars have long found interest in exploring relationships between AICs and modernity. Harold Turner's article, "The Place of Independent Religious Movements in the Modernization of Africa" came shortly after many African countries experienced political independence and addresses the role that AICs may or may not have contributed to that process. Turner deals with such topics as nationalism, religious and continental partnerships, desacralization of politics, and progress. While admitting the complexity of the project, Turner sometimes falls into simplistic comparisons between open Western worlds and closed African societies. Despite these proclivities, however, his main contribution comes in highlighting the role that Christianity made within traditional communities:

---

66. Isichei, *History of Christianity*, 238.

Re-Imaging Modernity

> Into this repetitive, conservative society there came the view that life is tied neither to the past nor to the levels of the present, but can progress to a paradisal consummation in the future. This is the revolution in the world-view represented in secular form by schemes of development for underdeveloped nations, and in religious forms not only by the explicit millennialisms but also by the ordinary evangel and achievements of the independent and older churches. The widespread penetration of this outlook accounts for the mounting demand for the better human existence that so many Africans see should and can be theirs.[67]

Turner's view that religion, and Christianity in particular, provides a progressive outlook leads him to extrapolate these findings for the transformation of African worldviews, suggesting multiple forms of modernization. Yet he is quick to add that any resultant modernity should not be equated directly with Western varieties; for, as a result of proximity with traditional and modern contexts, a "new culture and way of life [is] being born in Africa."[68]

Years later, G. S. Oosthuizen would take up similar issues.[69] Like Turner, he compares and contrasts primal religious worldviews with Western ones: especially in such areas as development, community, and future-orientation. He proceeds to show how AICs (specifically among the Zulu) display attitudes that directly relate to modernization. This involves a new conception of modern that corresponds to Africa, which emphasizes religiosity, human values and dignity, without *capitalist* or other distinctly Western cultural baggage. In the end Oosthuizen says, "The AIC is thus a movement towards adaptation to a modern secular society without discarding the deep religious disposition which was basic to the African worldview. Progress and religion go for them hand in hand."[70] His work, thus, highlights how spiritual power contributes a leading role in the development of African conceptions of modernity.

More recently, other studies have looked at comparable issues, notable among them Dawid Venter's edited collection, *Engaging Modernity*.[71] This book, and especially Lawrencia Kwark's contribution, emphasizes a growing sense of integration barely seen in Turner's earlier study, but now

---

67. Turner, "Place of Independent Religious Movements," 56.
68. Ibid., 57.
69. G.C. Oosthuizen, "AIC and the Modernisation Process," 223–45.
70. Ibid., 240.
71. Venter, *Engaging Modernity*.

fully recognized. In her chapter "The Reinvention of Tradition," she reacts against the common perception, evidenced to some degree in the two earlier studies, where tradition and modernity are polarized. In response to this dichotomy, she argues that "Africanness and modernity relate to one another in a complex solidarity"[72] and that it is precisely within this complexity that researches should look for contributions that AIC's make to re-conceptualising modernity. Like Turner and Oosthuizen, she posits that religion and spirituality provide the essential ingredients for any African modernity. This was especially the case during the height of Apartheid, illustrating how "black South Africans engaged modernity through religious activities."[73] Her study proceeds to demonstrate how traditions (closely linked in her definition with religion) function as the primary means for Africans to actively engage in the contemporary era. However, she tends to limit traditions to the cultural past—focusing on the cult of ancestors, orality, and magic—instead of recognizing new traditions coming from years of interaction with Christianity. My own research will place more emphasis upon these new traditions, exploring in detail how the contributions of the Africa Brotherhood Church (ABC) and their *holistic Gospel* lead to resultant forms of modernity in Ukambani.

Modernity and Newer Pentecostal Churches

Finally, and perhaps most problematic, is the relationship between the newer Pentecostal churches and modernity. The reasons for the difficulty become apparent when trying to discern points of continuity or discontinuity with Western (and particularly American) forms of Pentecostalism. David Maxwell explains the early origins of the movement arising from the "profusion of Holiness and Faith Missions, which entered Africa at the end of the nineteenth century, and whose strands, along with revivalist tendencies, came together in the first decade of the twentieth century to create Pentecostalism."[74] In the years that followed, Pentecostal missionaries established new churches, while at the same time charismatic influences were simmering within the mainline churches, such as the Holy Spirit (or Roho) movement in Western Kenya, and the later East African Revival. The combination of Western Pentecostalism with indigenous revivals occurring within mainline denominations proved

---

72. Kwark, "The Reinvention," 127.
73. Ibid., 134.
74. D. Maxwell, "Christianity and the African Imagination," 18–19.

advantageous for the rise of independent, Zionist (or Spirit) churches.[75] While these forms of ecclesiastical independency had clear points of origin from within Western Pentecostalism, they differed significantly from them in other respects, emphasizing healing through prophets, and sourcing much of their internal logic from within African traditions.[76] Many of these Spirit churches continued to maintain prominence (albeit in heterogeneous ways) until the 1960s,[77] when they gradually gave way to what Kalu calls "the third response by Africans to the missionary message"[78] or what Anderson describes as "newer" Pentecostals.

Anderson classifies these newer Pentecostals (of which the RGC is representative) as a "continuation" of the older AICs. He argues for this based upon their African governance, the fact that most of their financial base comes from within the continent, and how they view things through the lenses of an integrative, spiritual cosmos.[79] Kalu likewise insists they be interpreted as "a strand in the element of continuity between African traditional religion and Christianity."[80] Yet these points of correspondence are not always clear. During the 1980s, Western preachers proliferated Kenyan cities with a message of *prosperity*. Since that time there has been a steady stream of American, Pentecostal churches coming to Kenya in order to partner alongside these newer churches. Gifford contends that the rise of Pentecostalism in Africa coincided with the economic decline during the 1980s, leading to a dependency scenario with the West, and ultimately to what he implies to be an "Americanization" of Christianity in Africa.[81] Any attempt to locate these newer Pentecostal churches from within primal African spirituality, on the one hand, and global influences, on the other, proves to be highly problematic. On the surface, African Pentecostal leaders disavow any association with the older AICs, and particularly interpret traditions through association with demons and spiritism. Bishop Paul Mutua of the RGC explained that his church has nothing to do with Akamba traditions (but then later softened his stance and talked about efforts to reintroduce Akamba marriage dowry

---

75. Ibid.
76. Anderson, *Introduction to Pentecostalism*, 104–5.
77. Kalu, "African Christianity," 206–7.
78. Kalu, *Power, Poverty and Prayer*, 104–5.
79. Anderson, "Evangelism and the Growth," 20.
80. Kalu, *Power*, 104.
81. Gifford, *African Christianity*, 318–19.

back into the practices of his church).⁸² Formally, these newer Pentecostal churches are resolute in their polemics against spirits and ancestral worship, but appear to be gradually becoming more receptive to some of the values (and practices) associated with their traditional past.

To what extent are these churches "sourced from the interior of African spirituality," as suggested by Kalu; or, on the other hand, focused upon modern and/or global frames of reference? The answer to this question is not entirely clear, and most likely includes a sometimes integrative, sometimes conflicting combination of the two. Anderson emphasizes the contemporary viability of newer Pentecostals as they offer a "radical reorientation to a modern and industrial, global society,"⁸³ while Martin states that the "prime appeal of Pentecostalism (and associated movements) was to groups who were anxious to share in what modernity has to offer but through the lens of a spiritual and inspired understanding."⁸⁴ Spiritual language occupies a central role in these churches. Images of power appear prominent through singing, healing, or casting out demons, and often correspond with primal African needs for control and/or protection against ambiguous forces within an integrative cosmos. However, their use of media, technology and global inter-relationships conveys a modern ideology that positions these churches favorably within contemporary needs and aspirations. Maxwell warns against tendencies for the "prosperity gospel" to inculcate values indicative of "liberal capitalism,"⁸⁵ whereas Lonsdale regrets the ways that they alleviate personal responsibility in the name of faith in God.⁸⁶

Perhaps one way out of this morass is by acknowledging both global and local elements of modernity within these churches. Marshall-Fratani makes this point in her study of Pentecostalism in Nigeria. Her research focuses upon how Pentecostal churches utilize media to "connect local actors to global networks" while taking advantage of "local appropriations of these images."⁸⁷ Both processes, she argues, occur simultaneously, where global media often represents "islands of modernity in a sea of local 'artisanal' culture," and local actors take advantage of global

82. Paul Mutua, interview by author, Machakos, Kenya, Sept. 3, 2007.
83. Anderson, "Evangelism," 21.
84. Martin, *Pentecostalism*, 133.
85. Maxwell, "Christianity without Boundaries," 23.
86. Lonsdale, "Kikuyu Christianities," 189.
87. Marshall-Fratani, "Mediating," 280.

media to fashion "an alternative vision of modernity."[88] The process of interpreting modernity within these churches involves paying attention to the *externality* of the churches, particularly in relationship to American forms of prosperity gospel, while acknowledging creativity and imagination as local actors re-interpret and adjust these global images for their local contexts. The modernity of the Pentecostals, thus, involves important elements of continuity and discontinuity, "in which global images, ideas and forms are locally appropriated and used in the creation of new subjectivities and collectivities whose forms and activities appear to reflect a new role for the imagination in changing the everyday lives of individuals."[89] The degree of appropriation may therefore depend upon the physical location of the church, with urban congregations exhibiting greater degrees of externality while rural congregations show more local initiative. I will seek to bring greater definition to these ideas by exploring how the Redeemed Gospel Church (RGC) utilizes spiritual power in order to situate itself most favorably within the modern world.

MODERNITY AS THEOLOGICAL DISCOURSE

This brief sketch illustrates some of the features associating African churches with modernity, suggesting not only that different forms of Christianity will appear through the process of engagement with sociological themes, but also that local actors are likely to fashion distinct forms of modernity through their employment of theological imagery.

One way of describing this process is to speak of the role of theology in "social construction,"[90] or where it leads to the creation of a "spiritual landscape."[91] God's nature furnishes humans with resources in which to inculcate his attributes into the world, providing the means for growth (alternatively, oppression) within modern societies. Initially, this entails looking at culture as a process, something that humans create, rather than

88. Ibid., 295, 282.

89. Ibid., 311.

90. Schweiker and Welker define *social construction* by acknowledging that, "human beings continually face the great task of social life, that is, the demand to form cultures and civilizations to meet the necessities of life and to answer the human drive for meaning. Human beings are profoundly 'worldly' creatures in the sense that to be human is to exist in some socio-cultural world and to contribute to the continuation or destruction of that world in the process of world" (Rigby, *Power*, 5–6).

91. I thank Kevin Ward for these words that he used in response to one of my papers.

Themes of Discourse and Methodological Issues

some fixed entity. The propensity for East African theologians to wrestle predominantly with traditional concerns and attach "culture" with notions of a romantic and sacrosanct past further raises the importance of countering these proclivities with a theological assessment of modernity in Africa.[92] People like Mbiti (and more recently, Mugambi, Magesa, and Kanyandago) have built their scholarship around trying to explicate an understanding of Christianity in Africa by appealing to the traditional past. Yet, the dynamic relationship between modernity and traditions, combined with the mutability of culture, suggests that this may be a misdirected project.

Not all African theologians, however, share such disdain for things modern. Kä Mana provides one example of theological reflection in Africa that focuses upon themes of humanization and modernity. His theology of reconstruction begins with what he sees to be the initial step of deconstruction: lamenting how Africans have become captive to nature, to their own identity, and through association with the West. They have "lost the inventive power of Africa" and "lost the utopian energy of Africa,"[93] which is critical for them to construct an "African modernity," informed by "God's humanizing project for humankind through Christ."[94] Unlike other studies that begin with a similar tone of protest, Kä Mana does not fault colonialism, the World Bank, or globalization, but turns his polemics against Africans for how they have allowed passivity to rule their interactions with the West. He calls for theological activity on the continent to develop its African *imaginaire* (taken in regard to creativity and ideas) in order to explore new relationships with the West, with the end result being the creation of an "African modernity."[95] In this regard, Kä Mana provides new directions for African theological activity, where he places more attention upon global themes than trying to retrieve some primal and romanticized past.[96]

Similar shifts have taken place within Western theological discourse. Jürgen Moltmann is representative of scholars advocating theological reflection to take up "modern" issues. For example, he says,

---

92. See Gifford, "Africa's Inculturation Theology," 18–34.
93. Cited in Dedji, "The Ethical Redemption," 259.
94. Cited in Dedji, *Reconstruction and Renewal*, 111.
95. Ibid.
96. This is especially helpful if *traditions* are not rejected outright, but reinterpreted within contemporary frames of reference.

> The project of Western, scientific-technological civilization has become the destiny of humankind. We can neither continue as before without bringing about universal catastrophes, nor withdraw from this larger project and allow the world to come to ruin without us. Our only option is a thorough reformation of the modern world. *Hence, let us reinvent the modern world* [italics mine]!⁹⁷

Such a course of action redirects theology from its customary methodological trajectories into broader sociological currents of thought. This should not imply that theology needs to be reinvented, but expanded and integrated; where categories such as God, humans and creation move together and unite with more "worldly" ones, such as social systems, political constructs and economic policies. Miroslav Volf recommends something similar.

> [Theology cannot] just feed the pious souls in the church nor just delight the inquisitive minds in the academy. Beyond the church, beyond the academy, the horizon of theology is the world as the place of the coming reign of God. For the sake of the future of the world, that object of God's pain and God's delight, theology must be a public endeavor.⁹⁸

This returns the discussion to *who* undertakes theological activity. Paul Bowers contends that African theology has spent too much energy attending to the needs of the intelligentsia, and should become more active in listening to the Christian community and locating the contributions of Africans within the broader scope of ecclesiology; effectively answering the question: "How can we be more authentically Christian?"⁹⁹ In this study, I want to provide a corrective towards these ends, by listening to the voices of people in the churches and situating their concerns within the broader scope of African Christianity, looking specifically at how theological communities utilize spiritual power to engage in contemporary realities.

Initially, the subject of modernity and its attendant concerns arose from interviews I conducted with people in the churches. I began my research with the modest presupposition that power would relate

---

97. Moltmann, "Theology," 3, 21.

98. Volf, "Theology, Meaning and Power," 111.

99. Paul Bowers, (paper presented at Scott Theological College, Machakos, Kenya, Nov. 7, 2007); see also Bowers, "African Theology."

fundamentally with leadership or governance issues. However, it soon became apparent that the *washiriki* (literally, fellowshippers), along with most of the church leaders, viewed power in much larger, comprehensive, and modern categories. Pastors talked openly about God's power as it pertains to education, development, or financial concerns. Youth told me about how they wanted to be part of something "successful," and with commensurate "freedom" to engage in the modern world. Elders interspersed secular NGO-language with ecclesiastical terms, talking about "empowerment" or how God's blessings provide "value-added" benefits to people. Hence, it became clear that ecclesiastical communities were employing theological imagery for the purposes of social construction, where power was relating directly to issues such as education, development, progress, and prosperity.

INTEGRATIVE METHODOLOGY: SOCIOLOGY AND THEOLOGY

Andrew Walls makes the point that "when theological studies cut themselves off from other branches of learning, they lose opportunities to renew their own streams with fresh, clear water."[100] Innocuous as this statement appears, there are certain predispositions within Christianity where such integrative approaches to theology encounter varying degrees of resistance.

Evangelicals, in particular, have been tentative, and sometimes hostile, to any notion of theology needing renewal from outside. Some theologians might fear that this would be tantamount to saying that God is not sufficient for the needs of humans, questioning whether mixing theology with another discipline will inevitably compromise the role of God in society, leading to *secularism* or *syncretism*, or de-emphasizing the centrality of Scriptures. These concerns have historic points of origin stemming from evangelicalism's uneasy relationship with modernity, and especially liberal Christianity's accommodating posture with Western culture, from the nineteenth and early twentieth centuries. Evangelicals have often reacted against Enlightenment influences by turning greater attention toward supernatural affirmations (while concurrently adopting certain implicit Enlightenment-based assumptions).

Early AIM missionaries arriving in Ukambani carried these theological predilections. Meanwhile, the Africans adopted some of these

---

100. Walls, "Globalization," 78.

characteristics, rejected others, and made modifications to still others as they utilized the heritage of Western evangelicalism for their own benefit. One aspect that appealed to the Africans was the relevancy of God's nature for world application. The missionaries brought with them a doctrinal parentage that focused upon theology *from above* (in contradistinction to what they saw in liberal Christianity that took its origin *from below*); however, the Africans often held a much more nuanced relationship between God, humans, and nature due to ways their worldview integrated these facets into a more holistic reading of the cosmos. These cultural resources enabled the Africans to adopt the *supernaturalness* of the early missionaries and creatively apply these elements to make sense of their *natural* world. This study will illustrate some of these dynamics in order to show how Akamba Christianity draws upon God's power for dealing with contemporary realities. The presence of an *integrated* or *holistic* cosmology also highlights the need for a more integrated methodology.

Humanity represents one of the central subjects of enquiry for this study, with further clarification through the image of God concept. The particular focus upon contextual theology demands a certain amount of dialogue between theology and the social sciences, accepting that faith convictions correlate with lived experiences. I should initially make clear that this study does not propose to be a sociology of religion, a sociology of power, or a sociology of modernity; instead, it is a contextual theology which finds fresh streams within the thoughts and methods of sociology for investigating how faith communities utilize power in order to conceptualize themselves within the modern world. The chapters that follow will inevitably deal with common themes or borrowed discourses from the field of sociology, but I should make clear that my purposes are preeminently theological.

Sociology and theology may interrelate in countless ways. Robin Gill provides a typology for examining various possibilities for the encounter. He adds his voice to those of David Martin and Peter Berger who have likewise contributed to the growing body of knowledge in this area. After briefly discussing some of the ways that theology services sociology, Gill moves toward his greater interests, developing a methodology for how sociology assists with theological research. He presents three possibilities (ultimately suggesting that all three are inseparable, leading to "an interactionist approach").[101] The first option is to examine the social

---

101. Gill, "Three Sociological Approaches," 3–14.

Themes of Discourse and Methodological Issues

determinants of theological positions and explore ways that theologians are influenced by their society and how their thoughts can be examined in such a light. As such, he argues, that theology does not exist as some isolated sacred realm, impervious to personal, social, or cultural factors. Theologians are products of their contexts; they are historically and socially conditioned. A second possibility involves understanding the social significance of theological positions, which looks at the other side of the relationship and how theological perspectives impact society. This is roughly similar to the approach taken by Max Weber where he postulated that Calvinistic theology was partially responsible for the growth of capitalism in the West. This perspective promotes the frequently overlooked possibility that theology functions as independent variable. The third option, proposed by Gill, employs sociological methods for the service of exploring the social context of theology. In this case, sociology offers its tools and resources for explicating the social context around which theology operates. My research moves in similar directions, arguing that sociology and theology work together; firstly, by supplying theology with pertinent and grounded information based upon sociological methods; and secondly, by using theological positions to understand how the churches navigate, construct, and interpret themselves within the contemporary world (often expressed in profoundly sociological ways).

My own methodology roughly parallels the work of Agbonkhianmeghe E. Orabator, a Jesuit priest, who has undertaken innovative work on the church in Africa as it pertains to HIV/AIDs, refugees and poverty.[102] Orabator begins with the assertion that the complexity of what is usually understood as "church" demands a multifaceted and multidisciplinary methodology to probe and discover its hidden treasures. One of the reasons that theology often proves insufficient to these ends is that the church represents an entity with "two sides: one theological, the other social" or, further, where "the church's identity is such that it is simultaneously related to God and to the world."[103] Theology tends to employ its resources for the spiritual dimension, but often misses the more social or human aspect of how people relate to each other (and the world) within their ecclesiastical communities. Orabator contends that the church must be seen "an open human community of faith, that is, open to society, to its social environment,"[104] thus making vital the case for an empirical

---

102. Orabator, *Ecclesiology*.
103. Ibid., 14.
104. Ibid., 15.

approach for understanding how the church relates to (and is influenced by) wider societal issues. Human and divine elements need to be held together, in tension, since "the church's relationship to God can only be adequately understood as mediated in and through the world; and the church's relationship to the world or history can only be adequately understood on the basis of its relationship to God."[105]

Orabator's point of departure, thus, is with the visible church. This should not imply that empirical analysis can exhaustively disclose the *mysterious* or *divine* aspects of the church. Instead, he wants to argue that "what the church is doing in its social environment"[106] is critical for developing any subsequent theological analysis.[107] In a similar way, I will argue that the nature of humans as the image of God demands a more integrative methodology and one founded upon empirical research. Like the church, humans are oriented towards God and unto the world. This returns to the earlier discussion whether theology begins "from above" or "from below." I argue that this is an illegitimate question, or a false dichotomy, as it is people who are created in the *imago dei*: representing God within creation. Humans are the ones who think about God, and ponder his nature as a means for understanding and navigating through their respective societies; and that human communities are the ones who visibly represent the divine as the transformed image of Christ within the world. These affirmations, along with the holistic nature of African worldviews, provides the underlying rationale for an empirical analysis of human communities in order to probe theologically the significance of God's power for contemporary African societies.

Since humans are the primary theological agents in this research, particular emphasis will be given to the *washiriki* (fellowshippers) for how they think about and act upon the knowledge of God, including the perspective of children, contributions of the youth, as well as insights gleaned from male and female members. These people are sometimes called "ordinary readers" or "real contextual readers" because of their pre-critical contributions to understanding (and interpreting) theology within their local contexts.[108] In addition to listening to what these ordinary readers have to say, I also examine codified statements of belief

---

105. Ibid., 60.
106. Ibid., 17.
107. Ibid., 19.
108. Anum, "Ye Mo Wo Mo!" 8–9.

found in creeds and catechisms, as well as prayers, choruses, sermons, testimonies, and other *implicit theologies*. This *praxis* theology resists tendencies that sometimes situate theological activity solely within the domain of academic professionals. John Mbiti challenges such an assumption and asks, "Will theological education in the West ever get out into the streets without an umbrella, get wet and hear the birds singing? . . . Much theological activity is taking place on the ground and in the streets, in the fields where people are, where the church is."[109] The central task in attending to ordinary readers is to draw these voices out into the open, giving them freedom and safety to disclose their thoughts, needs, and aspirations. The researcher listens to the themes of Scripture most important to the members, attends to any interpretive mechanisms that they utilize, and observes how these are acted upon: all with an aim of understanding *how* theological beliefs relate with real life affairs. This is not to suggest that professional or critical readers are unimportant in the process, but instead offers a more balanced perspective with attention given to the entire people of God. James Cochrane likewise sees a movement where theology turns with greater attention toward the voices and perspectives of the masses. He offers this critique regarding their contribution:

> Their reflection may be, and usually is, that of the theologically untrained mind. It may be naïve and pre-critical; it may be unsystematic and scattered; it may draw incongruently on a range of symbols, rituals, narratives and ideas which express the encounter with the sacred. In these senses, the theology present in communities of ordinary Christians may be seen as incipient rather than overly articulated. But it remains nevertheless theology.[110]

Besides wrestling with the thoughts of God, theology has a tendency to reveal much about the people doing it: *what* they think about God, *how* beliefs are shaped by various contexts, *why* issues are important, and *how* people act upon their theological presuppositions. Since humans create culture (while doing so within cultural frameworks), a theological methodology that focuses upon humanity should not neglect empirical or sociological contributions, but carefully integrate them within traditional theological analysis. Similar to Orabator, "The position adopted in

109. Mbiti, "When the Bull," 170.
110. Cochrane, "Theology and Faith," 34–35.

this study is that theology cannot avoid dialoguing, interacting or correlating with the human sciences, especially because the character of the Christian faith and divine self-revelation upon and about which theology discourses does not exist in a vacuum. Faith is a lived experience."[111]

Orabator presents a methodology that combines empirical research with theoretical constructs, in a process of "observation, description, explanation, and (theological) interpretation."[112] Yet this process is not always linear, since the empirical "data" coming out of the lives of the people carries commensurate theological meanings. For example, *matatu* frequently display slogans that attest to some attribute of God, while colors of furnishings in churches often represent some aspect of divine nature. Thus, when humans represent God, they likewise interpret his nature for their specific contexts. This highlights the importance of theological reflection taking place *within* empirical research, since, while sociological methods provide basic *data* about what people think, how they act, and what they envisage pertaining to God's power, these images often utilize theological resources for making sense of the world. I therefore argue for a more integrated approach between the disciplines, moving back and forth between sociological methods and theological reflection in order to attend to human and divine components that constitute the image of God on earth. This "represents a shift from theology as informed speculation to theology as critical reflection *informed by* empirical investigation."[113]

CONTEXTUAL THEOLOGY

Modern missions and particularly global forms of Christianity have been instrumental in raising awareness for greater collaboration between theology and the social sciences. Evangelical scholarship has slowly followed, developing reflexivity from years of listening (with varying degrees of attentiveness) to Majority World[114] scholars and watching the southward movement of Christianity. Dana Robert, Lamin Sanneh, Philip Jenkins and Andrews Walls, among others, have repeatedly reminded evangelicals of these shifts, and made Kwame Bediako, John Pobee and

---

111. Orabator, *Ecclesiology*, 48.
112. Ibid., 18.
113. Ibid., 20.
114. I will be largely using *Majority World* as an appellation for the non-Western world, since it conveys the numerical significance of these societies who, until recently, have been neglected in terms of their respective contributions.

Themes of Discourse and Methodological Issues

John Mbiti familiar names within Christian scholarship. Movements in these directions have roughly correlated with the rise of *contextual theology* beginning from the early 1970s (with many different appearances).[115] One of the motivations behind the growth of contextual theology was the need to articulate the Gospel *within* the context of cultures around the world. What followed was greater awareness among (some) Western theologians to the blind spots and presuppositions that have inflicted their discipline over the last millennium. This is not to assume that all the wrongs have been righted or that evangelical theology presently reflects the voices of the masses living in the majority world. I am merely pointing out that evangelical theology is gradually becoming more aware of itself, its surroundings, and how it fits (or does not fit) within the global world. In days past, most of the attention given to global theologies was largely confined to departments of history, missions, or intercultural studies, and perceived by theological departments as *exotic* with condescendingly romantic approbations. Presently, a shift is underway where scholars previously committed to operating within the norms and conventions of their systematic or biblical faculties are beginning to move in ways that acknowledge the contributions of other contexts. One example would be Kevin Vanhoozer, formerly of University of Edinburgh, UK and presently at Trinity Evangelical Divinity School, Illinois, USA.

Vanhoozer's journey in this direction comes via his research into hermeneutics and the post-modern condition. A concern for Vanhoozer is how the "situatedness" of humans affects some of the modernistic trappings of theological methodology, where he perceives tendencies to treat the Bible (for example) as the subject of scientific inquiry, and where subject-object distinctions and commitments to logic and reason feed a kind of obsession with method.[116] A central question in one of his writings is "whether, and why, Christian theologians from other parts of the world must play by Western Christianity's rules in order to do theology?"[117] He suggests that global Christianity ushers forward an era of "after method,"[118] where no particular methodology dominates the landscape, and where theologians in various parts of the world are free to

---

115. Related to contextualization is *inculturation*, which developed much of its impetus in the late 1980s from the work of Roman Catholic theologians such as Shorter, *Toward a Theology*.

116. Vanhoozer, "One Rule," 87.

117. Ibid., 88.

118. Ibid., 91.

31

use their languages, resources of culture, and interpretive mechanisms in order to undertake theological scholarship.

In order to move in this direction, Vanhoozer wants to see theology slowly unwind from its traditional reliance upon philosophy and move toward other disciplines (especially the social sciences) in order to create symbiotic relationships for the purpose of exegeting text *and* context.[119] He says, "The key methodological issue is no longer that of right procedure (how?) but location (where?) and position (who?)."[120] This should not indicate that he wants to give less importance to Scripture, or diminished concern for *validity* and *reliability* in the process of methodology. Rather, these issues should no longer be preconditioned upon a positivistic reading of the Bible where complete objectivity defines the domain of the researcher.

Context, he contends, is critical to faithful hermeneutics. Thus, Vanhoozer proposes that theology be approached as "theodrama" where it moves from private meditation to public activity and where it is played out on the world's stage: "the Bible as a script, doctrine as theatrical direction, and the church as part of the ongoing performance of salvation."[121] The Holy Spirit guides the entire process, since the script (Bible) is indwelled by the various actors rather than followed with mechanical precision. A certain amount of imagination (Vanhoozer even speaks of improvisation) may be necessary for understanding how ecclesiastical communities *act out* the revelation of Jesus Christ, and participate in Gospel realities within their particular stages.[122] The central points of doctrine—creation, fall, redemption—provide meaning and direction to the drama, and human actors occupy the roles. They perform the story lines of the Gospel within contemporary realities of life, illustrating examples of faithful imaging.

Though not without its own concerns, this approach guards against the two admitted dangers. Firstly, in the face of tendencies within Western Christian scholarship where theology focuses exclusively upon the meaning of the text, Vanhoozer's methodology highlights the importance of context for authentically representing Christ within the world. The struggles, questions and challenges facing each and every situation

---

119. Ibid., 95.
120. Vanhoozer, "One Rule," 95.
121. Ibid., 109.
122. Ibid., 113–14.

around the world must be answered anew. Contemporary actors occupy roles that must be performed for the benefit of the entire (global) Body of Christ. Furthermore, rather than just trying to find the right answers, this approach recognizes that each contextual act contributes to the *theodrama* by faithfully communicating the story of God within the various vicissitudes of life. Context affects the meaning and appropriation of theology. There are always dangers of some actors taking the spotlight, or relegating others to "stage hands" as if their job was to watch what is taking place, and/or assist where possible. Yet by emphasizing the importance of context, it is possible to guard against some of these hazards. Actors participate through their specific roles. A parishioner raised in New York City, for instance, might naturally find her own scene fun and easy to engage in, but would struggle in other situations. No context has privileged seating. Diversity, furthermore, proves instrumental to faithful imaging of Christ on earth. Paul Hiebert refers to such global interdependence as the "hermeneutical community"[123] where contextualization undertakes a highly critical stance that recognizes the viability of different perspectives regarding the text of Scripture, and where the cumulative affect of these interpretations produces a more balanced reading of the Word of God. Faithful hermeneutics requires rich diversity. Furthermore contextuality extends beyond continents and even countries to include such diverse representations as gender differences, urban communities, socio-economic classes, and particular denominations.

Admittedly, some evangelicals may find this approach unsettling. The historical-critical method and its (sometimes) positivistic underpinnings provide a measure of certainty within rapidly changing contexts. Others may fear that words such as "imagination" or "creativity" when applied to Scripture may preclude faithful interpretation. Yet, I am not suggesting contextual theology should jettison the historical-critical method or other procedures for exegeting Scripture, but look for new methodologies alongside the old (often including the social sciences). Context becomes critical for theological methodology. The other concern is that contextuality, taken alone, can become relativizing to the central tenets of Christian doctrine. This fear is not without warrant. If Christians react against forms of Western theology by turning to the global Church, they should not assume that diversity naturally breeds authenticity (although

---

123. See Hiebert, "Critical Contextualization," 288–96; *Anthropological*, 75–92.

it certainly helps), nor should they romantically imagine that majority world contexts more accurately represent Gospel realities.

There are always risks that certain actors may extemporize too freely, but this has always been the case throughout church history. No theologian is without blind spots and misguided presuppositions. One could certainly argue that Vanhoozer's "theodrama" offers nothing new that has not already been occurring over the course of the last two thousand years. What is more, the insights revealed in this study of Akamba Christianity attest to the authoritative role of Scripture in all three denominations. The churches studied here demonstrate that perhaps more (not less) emphasis may be given to the Bible within global forms of Christianity, albeit manifested in different ways. The various interpretations of Scripture seldom mirror the historical-critical method of biblical interpretation, usually placing greater emphasis upon story telling and imaginative re-constructions of the text to fit particular situations. However, this should not imply a diminished role given to divine revelation (nor a lack of integrity in handling God's truth).[124] Text and context continue to speak with one another in dynamic ways.

FIELD RESEARCH

In order to provide empirical data for this study, I undertook field research into three evangelical churches from May 2006 to June 2009. I focused exclusively upon those denominations most prominent in Ukambani (particularly those within the Machakos District), and specifically three ecclesiastical communities with distinct origins within Ukambani. It is possible that each of the churches would exhibit different characteristics in other parts of the country, but my primary purpose was to understand them from within Ukambani so as to draw broader insights regarding Christianity in this region. There were four phases to the research as described below, but where each was not demarcated with nice and neat boundaries, but characterized by a degree of flexibility where I could move back and forth between them. What follows is a rough approximation of the various contours given to the research, with reasons for undertaking this particular methodological approach.

---

124. And even when certain deficiencies appear, the hermeneutic community guards the Body of Christ from suffering at the hands of certain misguided interpretations.

My involvement in each of the churches lasted the entire three years of field research, although participation with the Redeemed Gospel Church had a more concentrated time period, where the majority of interviews and participatory observation took place from October 2006 until October 2007 (with a few subsequent visits or interviews). The purpose of the field research was not to provide a detailed ethnography, but to attend to the voices, structures, and implicit/explicit theologies within the churches, toward understanding how faith communities utilize power for social construction (what I am roughly calling modernity).

Phase One

The first step was to interview the leaders. This was particularly important for the ABC and RGC as I was relatively unknown to them. I asked broad open-ended questions that endeavored to allow the leaders to present the main characteristics of their churches in ways comfortable to them, and in words that expressed their desires. Leaders in the different churches were generous with their time, and usually provided me with further contacts. Interviews with ecclesiastical authorities were usually conducted in English, with the sole exception being the Deputy Presiding Bishop of the RGC where we used a combination of Swahili, English, and Kikamba, through the assistance of a translator.

I used the interviews with leaders (whether Bishops or pastors) to provide the general parameters for understanding the ecclesiastical structures, their explicit theologies, and how they understood power. Each directed me toward formal documents of the church, and encouraged me to return and share some of my findings with them. This underscores the openness of these churches to outsiders.

One of the questions asked of all leaders was, "How is power evidenced in your church?" with similar follow-up inquiries related to the nature and expression of power. As stated previously, I had expected them to talk mainly about leadership structures but was surprised to hear them describing how power transforms their communities, and especially where they used Enlightenment-associated words such as *development*, *self-reliance*, *autonomy*, *progress*, and *education* to articulate specific ways these are enacted. Furthermore, the basis for using these words usually corresponded to theological points of interest, for example, ABC leaders described the doctrine of creation for understanding their "holistic gospel" and how it leads to development; or, how the AICK utilized an apologetic perspective of the Bible to engage in contemporary realities. Many of these Enlightenment-related words became the basis for understanding their theologies and how the churches employ God's power to image themselves within their communities: highlighting the need for modernity to function as a theological category.

Phase Two

During this second series of visits, I focused upon participating in the different churches and conducting formal and informal interviews with laypeople. I took extensive field notes on how they conducted their services, theological themes, furniture arrangements in church buildings, music, prayers, colors of wall hangings, announcements, sermons, and other observations. In every congregation I was either asked to preach, share my testimony, or give a word of encouragement to the people.

I likewise met with groups of lay leaders and church members. Because of my gender and ethnicity, it was important to meet with these in focus groups of varying sizes to lessen their awkwardness with my presence. I kept all of these informal and used my previous discussions with the leaders to discern how the people perceived the main characteristics of the churches: drawing connections between explicit and implicit theologies. It was common for the *washiriki* to mention only the positive aspects of the churches, with the sole exception being those in the AICK who felt more comfortable with me (due to my more extensive involvement with the church) and thus freer to discuss struggles and discouragements.

In each of the denominations, I attended several (sometimes many) different local congregations to make certain my findings were well representative of the different churches in the region and not biased by any particular fellowship (with an assortment of town and rural churches). Because I was least familiar with the Redeemed Gospel Church, I participated in a greater variety of congregations and interviewed many different informants to ensure the results accurately expressed the characteristics of the denomination. Whenever possible, I also visited other ministry projects of the churches in order to more fully understand how they were involved with their communities. These included Bible Schools, agricultural and/or development programs, missions, and other compassion ministries.

Phase Three

During the third phase of my field research, I returned to the leaders to have them clarify some of the ambiguities (wanting to make certain that I was observing things accurately) and have them assist with certain interpretations. For example, a common word in the RGC was "autonomy," and I was struggling to understand how they were intending it. I met with the Bishop of the Eastern Region and he spent considerable time explaining to me the various ways that people use it within their churches. The leaders were pleased to be able to assist me in the process of interpretation. There were some instances where the people expressed concepts or theologies in ways that made the leaders uncomfortable. I took note of their corrections but maintained the viability of the previous meanings as important to my overall findings. There were other instances when I felt the leaders posited a more conservative theological position because of my involvement with Scott Theological College. For example, leaders in the RGC were often critical of the prosperity gospel and intent upon giving me their explanation for how material blessings related to the power of the Holy Spirit. I further tested these against the wider symbols and voices of the people to see if they accurately reflected the church as a whole.

Phase Four

In the last stage (covering the period of September 2008–June 2009), I enlisted four Akamba research assistants to return to the *washiriki*.[125] I had been concerned that my previous interviews were not yielding the kind of honest "data" that I desired, despite all my efforts to lessen any degree of discomfort they experienced with my presence. The focus of this study as contemporary contextual theology demands that ordinary people be given priority in articulating the various contours of the churches. I therefore directed these four research assistants to attend the churches, observe, and transcribe songs, prayers and sermons; they were also to conduct informal interviews with children, youth ,and women in local congregations. In cases where these were accomplished in Kikamba, they were to translate them into English. I gave them very general guidelines and did not explain my previous research findings with the concern that

---

125. These included Dionysius Malusi, David Mutiso, George Kiasyo, and Stella Munyao; I occasionally use other interviews conducted from my leadership and cultural anthropology courses.

it would predispose them in certain ways. I wanted honest and uninhibited voices of the *washiriki* to occupy center stage in the research findings: *why* people believe certain things; *how* the church relates to society, and/or *what* interpretations people bring to the subject of power. Each of the research assistants took extensive notes and met regularly with me to discuss and/or explain their findings.

METHODS AND SOURCES OF DATA COLLECTION

Qualitative methods were the primary means of collecting data in these churches. The main advantage of proceeding in this direction is that qualitative research is particularly effective in attending to the voices and symbols of everyday life. The precise kind of contextual theology presented in this study presupposes that theology should not operate solely with *professional* theologians but occurs as people think about God, themselves, and their relationship with the world. Hence, qualitative methods approach the world inductively and interpretively: where the researcher seeks to understand how people think about God, and what this means for how they position themselves within the contemporary world. Information is drawn from the people, who occupy prominence in the process of research as they speak for themselves and make their perspectives known. Furthermore, such methods operate well within African contexts due to strong relational predispositions and person-to-person approaches for gathering data.

Alan Bryman explains the primary intention of qualitative research as "seeing through the eyes of the people being studied" and where face-to-face methods for gathering data provide the best means for this to be accomplished.[126] People are valued. The researcher attends to their perspectives by listening and taking their viewpoints seriously. "Qualitative researchers want those who are studied to speak for themselves, to provide their perspectives in words and other actions. Therefore qualitative research is an interactive process in which the persons studied teach the researcher about their lives."[127] Mass questionnaires or surveys may give the impression of impersonalizing the informant and can be particularly challenging in situations of illiteracy or where multiple languages are used. The methods employed in this study focus exclusively upon qualitative practices, and with the greatest care toward accurately representing

---

126. Bryman, *Social Research*, 279.
127. Blaxter et al., *How to Research*, 61.

the people: their thoughts, actions, motivations and interpretations. The following presents some of the ways this was accomplished.

Participatory Observation

My involvement in the churches was primarily as an active observer. Participatory observation usually implies *immersion* in a particular context, and where active observation, asking questions, and listening become the defining characteristics of gathering data. The researcher looks for a comprehensive picture of reality by collecting available information "from people with every possible vantage point and every conceivable perspective."[128] To accomplish this, I took extensive notes on the various churches (including, symbols, particulars related to their compounds, sermons, prayers, and anything else apparent). When something appeared arresting, or themes arose in various contexts, I was able to bring these before the people to have them help interpret the data (examples might be a well-manicured compound with the ABC, colors or symbols occupying prominence in the RGC, or the prominence of prayer or Bible reading in the AICK). People infuse meanings into their worlds. The primary purpose of ethnographic research, therefore, relates to accurate "description."[129]

Participation takes place on many levels. I attended elder meetings, visited various congregations, travelled to different ministry sites, talked with the people, and often preached or shared my testimony in the churches. However, the degree of participation was not always the same for each denomination. My involvement with the AICK for the past ten plus years and related work with Scott Theological College (STC) provided me more freedom and deeper insights into these churches. I have relationships with people at all levels of the ecclesiastical structure and have attended hundreds of church services, most within the vicinity of Machakos. This kind of intimacy naturally leads to heightened awareness of the problems and struggles facing these churches; therefore, it is possible that the chapter on the AICK might appear more highly critical (in positive and negative ways) than those of the other denominations. This should not imply that this church has more challenges, only that I was able to read these with clearer eyes due to more extensive involvement in almost every aspect of the church.

128. Dorsten and Hotchkiss, *Research Methods*, 127.

129. Jenkins, *Religion*, 5ff.

Re-Imaging Modernity

I was relatively unknown to the ABC until 2006 when the Bomani congregation requested STC to send them some student workers. I was assigned as the faculty mentor to oversee this relationship, and have continued in this capacity for almost three years. This has been a strategic time for the denomination. The founding Bishop passed away in March 2007, and thereafter they appointed only the second Bishop in the history of their church.[130] I had become friends with Timothy Ndambuki (the new Bishop) before he was appointed to this post, and had forged other relationships with many of the top leaders. I have regularly attended services in the Bomani church, but also visited Mitaboni, Mbooni, and Kibwezi where they have Bible Colleges and agricultural enterprises. I have likewise developed friendships with members of the Canadian Baptists who partner with the ABC in various development projects, and thus feel confident in my ability to view both sides of the relationship.

My involvement with the RGC was the least participatory in the sense that I never became a member of any local congregation and was most likely viewed as an outsider. Historically, the RGC has been suspicious of non-Pentecostal churches and those with formal theological education, but much of this is changing and their recent openness to dialogue with other denominations and their slow and gradual movement towards ministerial training has allowed greater degrees of receptivity than might have been present ten years ago. In order to compensate for less intimate knowledge, I tried to compensate by visiting more local congregations and interviewing greater numbers of people, including some of who were instrumental in the early years of the church. One of the founders, Bishop Paul Mutua, was generous with his time, and welcomed me to visit any aspect of the ministries of the RGC within Machakos.

A final facet of my participatory observation involved gathering data from contemporary *symbols* within Akamba society. This involved writing down the names of shops (*duka*) and public service vehicles (*matatu*), and analysing these into thematic groupings. I collected hundreds of these from the immediate area surrounding Machakos, providing non-ecclesiastical forms of data that could be analysed to see whether the observations from the churches were indicative of broader societal meanings, and/or if any other kind of relationship existed.

---

130. In fact, he is the third Bishop, but most ABC people are reticent to speak of the first because of a sexual indiscretion. More recently, Bishop Ndambuki has begun making a concerted effort to acknowledge the important contribution made by the first Bishop, Simon Mulandi.

Keeping detailed field notes was often challenging, since the period of research lasted for three years, and it was not always possible to suspend my activities in order to record notations in a notebook. Nor was it always appropriate to do so. Sometimes, it was necessary to make mental notes and later record them in written form. Most of the field notes pertain to actual church services, and/or visits to ministry sites.

Interviews

In all the churches, I sought to listen to the voices of clergy and laity through formal and informal interviews. In the beginning, all questions asked were largely similar, so as to provide a comparison that would serve as the basis for much of the contextual theology appearing in Chapter 6, yet with enough flexibility to move in directions suggested by the respondents. I did not utilize a standard questionnaire but began most interviews by asking a series of open-ended questions related to power: "Who has power in your church?" "What are the purposes of power?" and "What does power look like?" While some of the answers pertained to governing structures within the denomination, others moved in distinctly theological directions. For example, people usually described power with reference to God's nature, the Bible, Holy Spirit, the Great Commission, and Creation. Through follow-up questions, informants proceeded to express their understanding of these elements by using sociological terms. They talked openly about issues such as education, development (especially with holistic components), progress, autonomy, or self-reliance. Many of these concepts were developed and interpreted from within the churches, and the resultant forms are described in Chapters 3–5. The findings show that churches in Ukambani are very concerned with how they relate to contemporary society and especially where divine power provides them with a means for engaging in global themes.

I employed a wide range of formal and informal interviews. The main determining factor was ascertaining the degree in which the various respondents felt threatened or intimidated by my presence. Benny and Hughes describe the ideal interview as one where "both parties behave as though they are of equal status for its duration, whether or not this is actually so."[131] This was often hard to achieve. I always undertook formal interviews with educated leaders. In some instances when I had never previously met the leader, another informant came along with me

---

131. Benney and Hughes, "Of Sociology," 142.

to mediate the relationship. This served an important role of respecting the leaders, while following some of the customary practices within the country. I usually met with women and youth in focus groups, unless I personally knew the informant. Focus group discussions were kept informal, personal, and affirming. Feminist researchers caution against treating the informant as an object and/or the source of data; they advocate personalized and sensitive approaches that affirm the life and meaning of the individual.[132]

All formal interviews were recorded and later transcribed in full detail. This was also true for most of the focus groups. Yet the presence of a tape recorder was clearly intimidating to some people, and so I had to adjust in certain circumstances and take cursory notes on paper that would later be transcribed in greater detail. In other instances, even scribbling notes in front of the interviewees was cause for their concern, and so I tried to remember the details and later transcribe the contents from memory. All of this acknowledges that power dynamics are very palpable in the Kenyan churches (and society), indicating that methods need to serve the context rather than the other way around.

Whenever possible, I allowed the people to supply the data and bring their own interpretations: asking them to respond to my observations or testing the accuracy of details from multiple sources. This moved inquiries from *what* to *why* and *how* questions. The chapters that follow attempt to weave together all the available data to provide expansive description of the churches accompanied by relevant interpretations.

Reflexivity and Insider/Outsider Issues

Research methodology is not a linear process moving from the researcher to the informants, but can proceed in the other direction, where the researcher learns more about him or herself by interacting with the respondents. Elements of this are often referred to as *reflexivity* and reveal an epistemological shift in social science research that acknowledges the illusiveness of *objectified* forms of knowledge with corresponding acknowledgement to certain degrees of subjectivity that enter into the methodological process. Acknowledging the importance of *subjectivity* need not abandon validity and reliability. In fact, the researcher can benefit from being more aware of him/herself by acknowledging that explicit or implicit presuppositions enter into the process of gathering

---

132. Denzin and Lincoln, *Collecting*, 65–66.

Themes of Discourse and Methodological Issues

and interpreting the data. Even the best qualitative methods that seek to induce the data from the people cannot guarantee that the findings are untainted by the researcher. Nor should this imply that all knowledge is ultimately relativistic and that attempts to achieve validity and reliability are therefore illegitimate. Instead researchers need to understand how they influence the process, and be open to adjusting data gathering or analysis depending upon these self-understandings.

Reflexivity pertains to this study in several ways. Firstly, I mentioned previously that my initial thoughts on power were such that they would relate to ecclesiastical leadership. I assumed that most of the respondents would talk exclusively about power in terms of positions, structures, and people who have power; I had not suspected that they would move in such sociological directions, especially with modernity-related terminology. I therefore shifted my research focus away from leadership, turning instead to how divine power relates to modernity. This acknowledges that pre-understandings (such as how we define a term) come with cultural information, and the researcher must subject these often hidden assumptions to the rigors of self-examination and critique. Secondly, I adjusted my research methods to allow for more informal settings where the *washariki* could talk freely about their perspectives without tape recorder or, sometimes, notebook and pen. I further employed four Akamba research assistants in the final phase of the research to attend to the voices of the people, with an aim of comparing them with what I had received so to offset or lessen any biases that might exist.

Finally, reflexivity relates to understanding oneself in terms of the overall research process. Kim Knott presents four categories along a continuum that show the various ways researchers participate in methodological practice. These relate to what are often called "insider" or "outsider" perspectives, and move from the extremes of complete observer (outsider) to complete participant (insider).[133] Each perspective carries its own advantages and disadvantages. Furthermore, the researcher oftentimes occupies more than one of these perspectives at a given moment. I previously mentioned that my research into the three denominations carried different degrees of participation, ranging from the AICK where I am a *complete participant* to the RGC where I was more *observer-as-participant*. Alternatively, other factors influenced the insider-outsider dynamic. As a white American, many people perceived me as an outsider.

---

133. Knott, "Insider/Outsider," 243–57.

43

This had certain benefits, as it allowed me to ask very simple questions and solicit answers to basic components within the churches (or culture) without appearing to insult the respondents with naïve inquiries. Informants were usually very receptive to these kinds of probings, and eager to tell me about their culture or church-related characteristics. In other instances, however, my presence was an inhibitor to the process, especially related to the *washiriki*. I therefore utilized four research assistants in order to collect data from these people, to ensure their contributions were included in the overall perspectives of the churches.

While my ethnicity casts me an outsider, my faith convictions present a different perspective. As an evangelical Christian, many people saw me as *one of them*. This was particularly important for the churches studied. Ukambani embodies a strong conservative milieu due to its historical connections with various mission societies. My evangelical tradition enabled me to participate in the churches without raising concern that I was going to undermine their teachings, and further facilitated the interpretations of theological positions according to a shared (although rarely identical) Christian heritage.

Literature/Documents

For all the churches studied, I was able to collect valuable written materials, which included an assortment of historical (especially for the ABC), constitutional, catechismal, and other doctrinal-related resources. The RGC had the least official documentation, since it is the youngest and still in the process of strengthening its structures; but had significantly more brochures, magazines, and other paraphernalia related to its various ministries. None of the literature was accepted uncritically. Sometimes the churches stated in their constitution that some particular characteristic of theology was important to them, but through my observations and interviews, it appeared that the case was overstated; other times (and more frequently) aspects of the church's ecclesiology or doctrine arose out from the methods of research without any representation in the church's official documentation.

METHODOLOGICAL ANALYSIS

The following provides a brief overview of how I used the data in relation to theological analysis. The primary purpose of sociological methods is to provide rich description into the churches with regard to theological

Themes of Discourse and Methodological Issues

resources, which then can be utilized for extrapolating sociological conceptions of power and modernity. The general framework appears similar to that used by Orobator, where I employed observation/description, interpretation, and reimaging to constitute the primary components of methodological analysis.[134]

Observation/Description

Qualitative methods present a multifaceted and detailed picture of the churches in relation to power. This portrait combines what the churches are doing with how people in the churches are thinking. Thoughts and actions go together in this *praxis theology* to present a fuller picture of the primary contours of the churches, and especially how divine power motivates churches to engage in broader societal concerns. Don Browning explains how "description" fits within theological methodology, where its primary purpose is "to describe the contemporary theory-laden practices that give rise to practical questions that generate all theological reflection."[135] Yet one could also argue the other way around, that *practical questions* give rise to *theory-laden practices* and in this way make a stronger case for theology to function as independent variable. Either way, or in the case of both, description relates to thoughts and practices that coalesce to furnish an accurate view of the churches in relation to power. The first half of Chapters 3–5 will offer these descriptions.

Interpretation

Churches are not unresponsive agents in the midst of global *flows of meaning* but carry their own interpretations (often theological in nature) into social interactions. Bodil Frederiksen describes some of these dynamics in terms of "active answering back," where churches have commensurate powers for inculcating meaning into contemporary situations.[136] Examples may include theological priorities that relate to social constructs or traditional elements reinterpreted within distinctly modern categories. Theological resources help ecclesiastical communities connect God's nature with contemporary contexts. The second half

---

134. Orobator, *Ecclesiology*, 42–44.
135. Browning, *A Fundamental*, 47–48.
136. Frederiksen, "Popular Culture," 210–11.

of Chapters 3–5 provides expression to these interpretations as they fall along modernity-related themes.

Reimaging

The final process in this methodology involves utilizing the various elements from the different churches to create a more comprehensive picture of power and humanity as it relates to theological conceptions of modernity, set within Ukambani. This involves a number of presuppositions. Firstly, theology is a process that involves the entire people of God as they image themselves within the world. David Ford describes something similar for the role that religion contribute to "questions of meaning, truth, beauty, and practice," describing how each of these areas needs to be "constantly re-imagined, rethought and reapplied."[137] All Christians, no matter their level of education or theological sophistication, are involved in the process of reimagination.

Secondly, the process of reimaging attends to linkages within an integrative cosmos, and affirms that humans are constantly trying to utilize their relationship with God to make sense of (and interact with) their surroundings. This is not to reduce theology to mere *human projection* but to say that precisely because humans are the image of God, they image God in profound and meaningful ways: bringing significance and meaning to how they function in the world.

Finally, the diversity of powers within the churches remains critical for providing a more comprehensive theological and sociological image. Taken separately, each of the denominations offers particularities that reveal theological bias. However, as these come together, they form a more comprehensive and balanced *hermeneutical community* where collective representations of God's nature provide richer powers for imaging. This perspective guards against certain propensities within theology (whether conceived in terms of the thoughts of individual professionals or along broader denominational forms) where people image their beliefs for others as decisively authoritative. Chapter 6 of this thesis attempts to bring together the various representations of power for the purposes of a more comprehensive picture of Christianity in Ukambani. It is less a critique and more a generative project.

---

137. Ford, "Theology," 77.

2

Images of Power

My intentions for this chapter involve drawing closer connections between divine power and generative life growth, by building upon a range of social science and theological studies on the continent, and later sketching some of the predominant ecclesiastical and non-ecclesiastical images of power found in contemporary Akamba society. The focus will be upon showing continuity between "traditional" and contemporary worldview affirmations. Subsequent chapters will then utilize this framework to demonstrate how different churches in Ukambani reimage power for the growth of Christianity in the region: concurrently for the development of modernity.

ANTHROPOLOGICAL INSIGHTS INTO POWER AND HUMANITY

I begin with some general reflections gathered from anthropological studies that examine some of the underlying sources and functions of power in Africa. Three edited collections stand out: Arens and Carp (1989),[1] Jackson and Karp (1990),[2] and Lambeck and Strathern (1998).[3] These books provide an assortment of ethnographic research from throughout the continent with regard to issues of personal agency and power. It should be noted that none of these assume privileged insight into an authoritative and traditional past. In some instances, the ethnographies pertain to African reactions to changing social conditions brought about by Western contact, and therefore relate well with the objectives of this

1. Arens and Karp, *Creativity*.
2. Jackson and Karp, *Personhood*.
3. Lambeck and Strathern, *Bodies*.

book by demonstrating how Africans use power to navigate through modern socioreligious contexts.

All of the research found in these studies share common concern for identifying broader perspectives regarding power and human agency on the continent, perhaps correcting some of the stereotypes that have erroneously portrayed African societies as inherently fatalistic or deterministic. Cultural/religious resources are fundamental for how Africans conceptualize themselves within the cosmos. Western societies tend to associate power with "control" or "overcoming resistance,"[4] much in the way of Max Weber, while African cultures view the concept through the lenses of an integrated cosmos. Arens and Karp describe characteristics of African worldview(s) in terms of "centers and epicenters of power in dynamic relationship with one another,"[5] where human agents move in and out of different realms (pictured through interlocking spiritual, natural, and social spheres of influence) in order to "tap" into power for the enhancement of life growth. "Transformation is the key to understanding concepts of power in African societies," they argue; or later: "The stress in Africa is not on the elements of control but on the more dynamic aspects of energy and the capacity to use it."[6] Africans actively draw upon power, Jackson and Karp likewise argue, for the purposes of "constructing and reconstructing a world which adjusts values and goals inherited from the past to problems and exigencies which comprise their social existence in the here and now."[7] Dance, witchcraft, spirit possession, and politics (among others)[8] become places where people actively engage in power for the purposes of cosmic transformation.

Among the Yaka cult in southwest Congo, for example, humans traverse through spiritual, material and social dimensions of power in order to grow. Rene Devisch says, "The more the individual enters into these multi-dimensional spheres, the more he constitutes an identity known to many, the more their gazes and their words refer him back to himself and to reaffirm him in his identity."[9] Jacobson-Widding explains how people negotiate "public" and "private" selves in order to fashion

4. M. Weber, *The Theory*, 152.
5. Arens and Karp, *Creativity of Power*, xvi.
6. Ibid., xx, xxi.
7. Jackson and Karp, *Personhood*, 28.
8. I might add, *Christianity* or *church-related practices*.
9. Devisch, "Treating the Affect," 130.

identity in everyday life. Human agency relates to choices people make about self-disclosure. For example, she alludes to the concept that to step on someone's shadow or take someone's picture is to impinge upon their personal domain, depriving them of power.[10] Alternatively, a person may reveal aspects of their private self to other members of the community for the purposes of developing intimacy, or withholding the same if they are in unequal relationships of power.[11]

Other studies hold more overt focus upon spiritual power. Ivan Karp and Ellen Corin[12] both deal with the "possession cult" in Kenya and Congo, respectively, in order to gain insights into how people appropriate power within seemingly powerless situations. Women take advantage of the spirit-possession cult, they argue, to mediate between spiritual and natural realms. Karp says, "Possessed women have gone to the source and returned unharmed. They are better able to deal with the dangers of power because they became androgynous characters. They know both active mastery and female techniques of growth."[13] Spiritual domains provide women with the means of asserting themselves within situations where they typically feel impotent; women cured of possession feel "more powerful" and thus more in control of themselves.[14]

These examples introduce the need to look at power not as some localized entity, but as a generative potentiality situated along the whole spectrum of African cosmology. Human bodies serve as one of the primary vessels for mediating these activities. This is particularly true for dance. Jackson and Karp explain the "metaphorical" character of dance as "creating links between the vital energy of the individual body, the social body, and the cosmos."[15] Humans enact these kinds of representations, as it were, on a stage, in order to symbolize broader cosmological concerns. Later in this chapter, I will show how some of these beliefs receive new interpretations within Christian categories, providing continuity between traditional and modern modes of thought.

Of course, these studies give the impression that power always maintains a generative predisposition. However, such spheres of power

---

10. Anita Jacobson-Widding, "Shadow," 31ff.
11. Ibid., 33, 47.
12. See Corin, "Refiguring," 87, 100
13. Karp, "Power and Capacity," 89.
14. Ibid., 90.
15. Jackson and Karp, *Personhood*, 22.

(i.e., nature, culture, or spiritual) can likewise diminish human agency. An example might be where the powers of divinity (or nature) impede human freedom and become self-determining: where the spiritual, for instance, acts as preordained destiny; or, where humans feel helpless against the *forces* of nature. Access to these powers can also lead to competition, where people exploit the "centers and epicenters" for personal gain. These concerns notwithstanding, the ideas arising out of these different ethnographies provide a kind of anthropological baseline by which to proceed with further linkages between power and humanity.

THEOLOGICAL INSIGHTS INTO POWER AND HUMANITY: THE "CHRISTIANIZATION" OF POWER

Similar to the themes just mentioned, theological activity in Africa has likewise found rich resource from topics related to power, especially by developing interconnections between God's power and life growth. I am using the term *Christianization* to refer to ways that traditional elements of African cosmology have been expressed and reinterpreted within Christian language, providing scholars with a means of articulating the Gospel in Africa.

In 1945, Placides Tempels published a seminal piece of scholarship, *Bantu Philosophy*.[16] He originally wrote the book in French, and later had it translated into English. While Tempels' work was not directly intended as theological exposition, it had the affect of orienting subsequent Christian theology on the continent. Many African theologians have identified with the basic principles set forth in *Bantu Philosophy*, altering and using these ideas to fashion different Christian interpretations. Sometimes these efforts have led to creative articulations of Gospel realities, and other times amounted only to "baptizing" Christian ideas on top of traditional values. One of the reasons why Tempels' ideas have been so instrumental in shaping African scholarship is that he provides a singular hermeneutic for understanding (and interpreting) the diversity of phenomena within African cosmology.

Initially, Tempels sought "to trace out the elements of this [Bantu] thought, to classify them and to systematise them according to the ordered systems and intellectual disciplines of the Western world."[17] His supposition that African thinking could be set within Thomistic-Aristotelian

---

16. Tempels, *Bantu Philosophy*.
17. Ibid., 21.

interpretations of ontology, and framed within dichotomistic categories, contrasting Westerners (*we*) with Africans (*they*), prompted the greatest amount of criticism levelled against his work. Aside from these concerns, however, his defining contribution comes from the use of power language for cosmological interpretation, especially the idea of "vital force."[18] Tempels saw all of life from within this concept. "In the minds of Bantu, all beings in the universe possess vital force of their own: human, animal, vegetable, or inanimate. Each being has been endowed by God with a certain force, capable of strengthening the vital energy of the strongest being of all creation: man."[19] He explains that power relates directly to ontological matters. Hence, "Force is the nature of being, force is being, being is force."[20] Tempels endeavors to dissociate divine power from any intimation with animism or magic,[21] for in his mind it emanates from the Creator (Force)[22] to give life to all things. The cosmos, therefore, represents a hierarchy of power, where God alone possesses inherent energy. Humans derive their identity from God as they occupy strategic position in the cosmos: the epicenter of all created powers. Such proximity provides them with heightened "powers" by which to engage with other "forces" that exist within the world. Through divine power, humans grow (or, become); or, alternatively, they decrease in being. Human existence is defined, as such, by the moral and ethical values of increasing power to increase life (or being).

Subsequent scholars have built upon Tempels' idea of "vital force." Most of these writers were likewise Christians and wrote from the perspective (whether intentional or inadvertent) of using the concept for the development of Christian theology in Africa. Alexis Kagame took up this project soon after Tempels' French publication, with a more specific aim of explaining "vital force" from within linguistic analysis of Kinyarwanda, a Bantu language. He takes departure from Tempels in wanting to describe "life force" as the fulfilment of being, rather than the basic substance of the cosmos (seeking to avoid the kind of overtly Western, philosophical language used by Tempels).[23] Kagame establishes certain

18. Ibid., 44.
19. Ibid., 46.
20. Ibid., 51.
21. Ibid., 53.
22. Ibid., 71.
23. Kagame, *La Philosphie*, 210–18; Ng'weshemi, *Rediscovering*, 15ff.

"categories of force" in order to show cosmological interdependence.[24] As such, *ntu*, is the source of all power and force, emanating from God, but never seen apart from its manifestation within the world. From this *ntu*, which is the stem of the linguistic analysis, various kinds of powers proceed: *muntu* (humans, but also inclusive of spirits), *kintu* (things), *hantu* (the when and where of these powers), and *kuntu* (recurring patterns of *hantu*).[25] The entire world for Kagame displays inherent interconnectedness through the "vital force" concept.

In the years that followed, many other scholars took up these issues, whether directly or indirectly related to continuing the discourse begun by Tempels and Kagame. Among these were Jahn[26] (1961), Taylor[27] (1963), Moore[28] (1967), Mulago[29] (1969) Parrinder[30] (1969), Okafor[31] (1982), Nyamiti[32] (1990), Anderson[33] (1990), Ng'weshemi[34] (2002), du Toit[35] (2004), and Kapolyo[36] (2005). While not intending to offer an exhaustive list, these citations do show the historic resiliency of the topic in African theology, as well as noting for many of these how interconnections between power and life directly relate to Gospel-realities. I will briefly highlight some of the ways theologians have used "life-force" (or associated concepts) in their quest for theological exposition, acknowledging that their work sometimes suggest idealistic intentions, and/or is formulated within "traditional" categories that fail to show how such ideas are re-interpreted or re-packaged into "modern" frames of thought and practice.

During the 1960s and 1970s, theologians took up the task of articulating the nature of this ultimate *Force*, namely, the essence of God. E. Bolaji Idowu argued in favor of "diffused monotheism" in response to

24. See Lucier, "Dynamics," 30ff.
25. Ibid., 31.
26. Jahn, *Muntu*.
27. J. Taylor, *The Primal Vision*.
28. Moore, "God and Man," 149–60.
29. Mulago, "Vital Participation," 137–58.
30. Parrinder, "God in African."
31. Okafor, "Bantu Philosophy," 83–100.
32. Nyamiti, "The Incarnation," 3–27.
33. Anderson, "Pentecostal Pneumatology," 65–74.
34. Ng'weshemi, *Rediscovering*.
35. du Toit, *The Integrity*.
36. Kapolyo, *The Human Condition*.

charges that African religions were pantheistic.[37] John Mbiti focused attention on continuities he saw existing between the God of the Bible and those found within African Traditional Religions.[38] While E. G. Parrinder expressed insights into God-concepts through similar language used by Tempels, stating that "God in African thought is not just a 'sky deity,' a personified firmament, but the personal essence and power inspiring all life and the universe."[39] However, not all of these scholars were convinced that the notion of *vital force* accurately reflected African realities. Mbiti, for one, criticizes Tempels' work for extrapolating these ideas too broadly across Africa, since, he argues, they came from only one cultural source.[40] While questioning the fuller framework behind vital force, Mbiti seems, at the same time, to implicitly support connections between God's power and human fruitfulness. In one of his articles, he narrates two traditional prayers. In the first, the supplicants ask,

> O God, you are the Creator of all. Today we, your creatures, prostrate ourselves before you in supplication. We have no strength. You, who has created us, have all power. . . .

And in the second,

> O God of our forefathers, all our lives depend on you and without you we are nothing. . . . Without you we can't live because we have no food or water to drink. You are the source of life.[41]

These two prayers express prevailing themes of power (seen the former) and life (expressed in the latter), within traditional supplications, hinting at linkages that might exist between the two. Later in this chapter, I will show how these interconnections continue to form the basis for ecclesiastical expression within contemporary forms of African Christianity.

As indicated in the prayers above, dependency remains a cardinal attribute of human identity. God alone *possesses* power. Humans (for their part) tap into this vital force by means of nearness to the divine, and by appropriating divine power within the range of human experiences. Moore argues that "Man, likewise, is a person, dependent upon God for his share in the vital forces with which he interacts with other

---

37. Idowu, *African Traditional*.
38. Mbiti, *African Religions*.
39. Parrinder, "God in African," 125.
40. Mbiti, *African Religions*, 10–11.
41. Mbiti, "Change of the African Concept," 58–59.

men and the other creatures, thus securing for himself the best possible life."[42] Dependency has both vertical and horizontal dimensions (though ultimately sourced in God). Humans interact with God, other humans, and the natural world in order to increase in life. Since God's power permeates all facets of an integrative cosmos, the entire world (with all its elements) remains "open" to humans: who benefit as they interact with the "powers" inherent within the world. Therefore, dependency on God's power displays a decidedly temporal orientation, where humans relate to God in order to engage in the cosmos.

Mulago expresses similar ideas within the framework of more active terminology, wanting to stress the dynamic nature of these relationships; hence, in lieu of "vital force" he prefers "vital participation." God gives power to humans so that they can participate in his nature (as it were) by turning these energies toward the growth of their communities: "it is life in its simplicity, in its essence. It is life as it has been derived and received from the source of 'power,' as it turns toward power, is seized by it and seizes it."[43] In as much as humans receive power from God, they extend it to others. He says, "The life of the individual is grasped as it is shared."[44] Human communities provide the epicenter of these powers, where people grow in their identity through participating in the comprehensive life of the community. Power thus relates to ontological concerns. Yet, herein dangers exist. If "being" relates to "nearness" to the source of the powers (God), then it is possible to envision hierarchies in which some people (i.e. pastors or politicians) have more power, and thus more being. Mulago never mentions these concerns. He does conclude by relating "vital participation" to some of the sacraments of ecclesiastical liturgy, wanting to show how Christian theology might utilize these cultural resources to enhance church-related practices.[45]

Another perspective comes from Okafor, who praises Tempels for providing an overarching cosmological system for interpreting the whole of Bantu culture.[46] However, he finds the notion of "vital force" too ambiguous and instead prefers "life" as an appropriate replacement for conceptualizing African societies, expressive of tangible points of

---

42. Moore, "God and Man," 156–57.
43. Mulago, "Vital Participation," 138.
44. Ibid., 139.
45. Ibid., 157.
46. Okafor, "Bantu Philosophy," 90.

human interest, and preconditioned upon spiritual power.[47] Charles Nyamiti similarly uses the framework of power and life to fashion an African understanding of Jesus Christ. Hence, he says, "A person is one who is endowed with power or force, precisely because he is endowed with fullness of life. Life is essentially power; the two are inseparable."[48] For Nyamiti and others,[49] Jesus Christ represents the consummate representation (or image) of divine power within humanity, and offers himself for the humanization of African communities. Anderson draws upon similar concepts for interpreting the role of the Holy Spirit. He reacts against propensities within Western societies that make distinctions between personal and impersonal forces; instead, opting for a comprehensive picture that connects power with human growth. "To Africans, our life, or very existence is inextricably tied up with our power. To live is to have power; to be sick or to die is to have less of it."[50] Anderson understands these "traditional" concepts as bearing points of similarity with Christian understandings of the Holy Spirit, and builds upon these ideas to offer theological appraisal for the Spirit's "enabling power" within African societies.[51]

All of these studies harmonize on the general desire to articulate African cosmology within power relations. Humans utilize God's power for the growth of the cosmos. People grow (and, potentially, diminish) in life through divine power. This at once speaks of the availability of power in all facets of life as well as establishing certain domains of poignancy and vitality: especially by framing the process within language associated with Christian theology.

Ecclesiastical communities represent the primary agents for enacting these realities; they utilize divine power for the growth of the cosmos. All of this is possible, these studies argue, due to the ways that humans occupy ontological priority with the divine. God is the source of power, while human communities are the nexus for its appropriation. Ng'weshemi says, "As long as human life originates from God, it is God-given. Life therefore, reveals a divine attribute. Achieving life in its

---

47. Ibid., 92.
48. Nyamiti, "The Incarnation," 8.
49. See Ng'weshemi, *Rediscovering*, 145ff.; see also Bediako, *Christianity*, 101ff.; Dedji, *Reconstruction*, 95ff.
50. Anderson, "Pentecostal Pneumatology," 68–69.
51. Ibid., 73.

fullness is the main aspiration of African people."[52] For many of the aforementioned writers, humans participate in God's nature[53] by employing divine power for temporal concerns. Recent work is underway to connect these ideas with ecological issues on the continent, drawing upon ethical responsibilities associated with divine power for causing the earth to flourish in relationship with human communities.[54]

This overview has sought to accomplish several things. Firstly, it highlights the importance of vital-force or power for Christian theology in Africa. It is unclear, at times, how influential Tempels was in contributing to the development of this theme. His ideas appear to lie implicit behind many of these writings. Whether or not this is the case, these studies do demonstrate that power remains a fertile topic for theological reflection, especially when set within a holistic system of interpretation. Secondly, traditional notions continue to feed theological expression. The perspectives set forth in this section show that African theologians continue to draw upon cosmological imagery in order to connect divine power with their world. These writers are sometimes guilty of idealizing the past, expressing traditional ideas with sacralistic undertones, or failing to re-articulate these concepts within contemporary stages; however, the continued presence of disquisitions set within cosmological language shows that greater effort needs to be given to understanding these things, and particularly through contemporary ecclesiastical practice. Finally, this overview highlights important linkages existing between power and life. God's power provides the basis for viewing humans as *powerful*. Greater theological effort needs to be given to providing ethical parameters to govern the appropriation of divine power within the world; or, in words more conducive to this study, where humans image God in (and for) the world by means of resources related to divine power.

HUMANITY AND POWER IN TRADITIONAL AKAMBA SOCIETIES

For the remainder of this chapter, I will narrow the parameters of the study to the outworking of divine power within Machakos district. I will

---

52. Ng'weshemi, *Rediscovering*, 25–26.

53. Kapolyo, *The Human*, 37.

54. See Conradie, "On the Integrity," 107–51 where he takes as his point of departure the "seamless totality of interacting vital forces; whether human, animal, seasonal, material or spiritual" (109).

Images of Power

begin by describing a more traditional reading of power from within Akamba communities, and then bring the discussion into "modern" stages to show elements of continuity, integration, and reimaging taking place. I am not attempting an ethnographic study of Akamba cosmology, nor do I want to place traditional and modern contexts in polarity with each other (something I actively sought to oppose in the previous chapter). I merely want to attend to continuities between traditional and modern ideas, and further show ways that Akamba Christianity makes use of cosmological ideas through images associated with divine power.

In his treatment of the Akamba people, Kivutu Ndeti describes Akamba cosmology in terms of an integrative system of interactions, inclusive of God, spirits, humans and physical world:

> The cosmological man is the man who seeks the meaning of his existence by redirecting his natural powers to the phenomena of cosmic existence. Unlike the anthropological prophet, i.e. the interpreter of reality as an order of the human soul, cosmological man sees reality only in the unity of the cosmos.[55]

Ndeti's comments highlight an important feature of Akamba societies. People often look for connections between spiritual and material realities; they seek to understand *why* certain things occur within their world. There are always underlying *reasons* for success, failure, or any other occurrence; hence, interpretation of the "phenomena of cosmic existence" remains a central feature of Akamba communities.

Creation provides the framework for understanding these interconnections. The Akamba believe[56] that power originates within the spiritual realm. Initially, *Mulungu*[57] (the Supreme Being) created the spirits (*aimu*) and then humans (*andu*, plural of *mundu*).[58] The order of creation also relates to proximity to the source of power: where the *aimu* have greater

---

55. Ndeti, *Elements*, 184.

56. In this section, I will be using the present tense with acknowledgement that some of these ideas (in the precise forms given here) may not be readily observable in contemporary societies. The present continuous tense serves to communicate notions of continuity that exist even though the forms may receive new interpretations within Christianity (seen later in this chapter).

57. The Akamba alternatively use *Mumbi* (Creator), *Mwatuangi* (Cleaver) and *Ngai* as names for God; the latter comes from the Masai word *En-kai*, meaning God, rain and sky; see Munro, 19. Evangelical churches in Ukambani prefer calling God *Ngai* rather than *Mulungu*, since the latter carries connotations of traditional religious practices.

58. Ndeti, *Elements*, 28–29.

powers by virtue of being the first act of creation. The first humans were "tossed from heaven" onto the earth or brought up from a hole in the ground, and were called, together with their descendants, Clan of the Spirits (*Mbai ya Aimu*), due to their immediacy to the act of creation and proximity to the spirits.[59] Humans, by virtue of their *nearness* to the source of the powers, function as interpretive and integrative agents within the cosmos. Mbiti says of the Akamba,

> This is an intensely anthropocentric ontology. It is unity centered upon Man, in such a way that death cannot destroy him. To destroy Man would, in effect, mean destroying the whole coherence of being, including the destruction of the Creator.[60]

Spiritual power provides the interpretive mechanism for viewing the integration of the cosmos. Everything in the world has power, but with varying degrees due to its *hierarchy* (quite literally, proximity within the order of creation). *Mulungu* is the origin of power; the spirits (and with them, the ancestors) are the secondary sources of power. Ndeti refers to *Mulungu* as an "extremely impersonal force"[61] and therefore not directly experienced. However, this is widely debatable since people refer to *Mulungu* in prayers and other ritual practices. Humans, therefore, relate to *Mulungu* directly, or through the spirits and ancestors, in order to maintain cohesion within the world. Integration relates to the dynamic interplay between "forces" (whether spirits, humans, land, or natural objects). The entire cosmos has power yet with varying degrees. Furthermore, the purpose of these powers relates to the growth of human communities. For such reasons, Ndeti describes *Mulungu* as the "logos underlying the Akamba tradition,"[62] and where interactions with divine power lead to generative or reproductive results.[63]

People access spiritual power primarily through the spirits. Mbiti differentiates two different kinds: (1) the "living dead," who are recently deceased (up to three to four generations) and still remembered by their descendants; and the (2) *aimu*: spirits that died a long time ago and are no longer remembered.[64] He argues for continuity between spirit and human

59. Ibid., 29.
60. Ibid., 132.
61. Ibid., 175.
62. Ibid., 128.
63. Jacobs, *The Cultural Themes*, 73.
64. Mbiti, *New Testament*, 10.

realms, even describing the "living dead" and *aimu* as "real 'people' living in a land very much like their own."[65] These spirits do not dwell with *Mulungu*, but exist on an altogether different plane where they maintain some interaction with humans and the rest of the "natural" world. Correspondence between spirit and human domains provides much of the impetus for applying spiritual power within Ukambani. Akamba cosmology highlights "six integrated domains, namely, *Mulungu* (God), *aimu* (spirits), *andu* (people), *syindu* (things), *kundu* (time/space), and *maundu* (matters)."[66]

All humans contribute to the cosmos according to their own status or powers (often with correlation between the two). Akamba communities, like their neighbors the Agikuyu, display de-centralized forms of authority.[67] For this reason, generalizations should be avoided in terms of delineating Akamba-wide patterns of governance, as these often vary from one region to another. Mbiti says there are thirty or forty clans[68], while Munro mentions twenty-five.[69] Clan names are associated with objects of cosmological significance, such as animals (*Amoini*, young female cow), rain (*Ambua*), the home place of the founder of the clan, or even characteristics of members (beer brewers, beekeepers, etc.). Clan identity continues to be of great importance to the Akamba. Most *Wakamba* pay a yearly fee to the clan administration (*atumia*). Under the clans, further subdivisions exist, with elders guiding the affairs of "gates" (*mivia*), "houses" (*nyumba*), and families (*misyi*).[70]

As people grow older, they move from one age set (*iika*) to the next. Humans increase in power by successfully completing the various initiations that accompany the age sets, as well as by aging, and thus gaining greater proximity to the ancestors (and, therefore, the source of power). Ndeti refers to this as the process of humanization[71] and includes the entire community interacting with spiritual powers within the world. The Kikamba word for humanization is *kuimithya*, and pertains to a ceremony that takes place after a child is born; "the ceremony incorporates the child

---

65. Ibid.
66. Ness, *Cultural Transmission*, 67.
67. Munro, *Colonial Rule*, 22.
68. Mbiti, *New Testament*, 6.
69. Munro, *Colonial Rule*, 11.
70. Mbiti, *New Testament*, 6.
71. Ndeti, *Elements*, 82.

into the community of human beings—it 'humanizes' him, transforming a *thing* or into a *person*."[72] This process continues through a person's life.[73]

Power is therefore located within humanity, and described as the "invisible power"[74] that governs the day-to-day life of the community. Contrary to kingship-based societies, the Akamba believe that no single human (king, prophet, or ruler) adequately represents all of the people.[75] The elders (*atumia*), along with other age-sets, preside over the affairs of human existence. Each of the age-sets (*iika*) has different responsibilities and therefore plays a part in the humanization of the community. Spiritual specialists—such as *priest-doctors* or seers—contribute to the growth of others by discerning the various forces operating within the world, reminding people of the ultimate source of all of life (*Mulungu*).[76] Ritual practices are directed toward the *aimu*, who serve as mediators between humans and God. These ceremonies govern the effective use of spiritual power, either, to guard against evil or promote cosmic fruitfulness.[77] Divine power enables humans to grow in their personhood (individual and corporate) while negotiating through the various vicissitudes of life. Spiritual power thus has a distinctly utilitarian character.[78]

Older people have more power than younger individuals, and therefore in a manner of speaking, more life. They are more fully human. An elder may bless a youth by spitting on his face and pronouncing a blessing, such as, "May God go with you!" or, "May you live to see your children's

---

72. Mbiti, *New Testament*, 94. The Kikamba name for infant is *kiimu*, which literally means "little spirit" (*ki* = diminuitive; *iimu* = spirit), suggesting linkages between spirits and humans; see Ness, "Cultural Transmission," 55.

73. The Akamba have a saying: "As the sapling is bent so the tree grows"; which refers to the malleability of children and young people. See Ness, "Cultural Transmission," 69.

74. Ndeti, *Elements*, 97, 100, 103.

75. Mbiti, *New Testament*, 7; see also Munro, *Colonial Rule*, 15 for a description of the egalitarian nature of Akamba communities. Mbiti further cites the account of C. Dundas "History of Kitui," *The Journal of the Royal Anthropological Institute* 43:16 (1913), 488 where it is said of the Akamba: "They could not submit to a common chief, or join to oppose a common enemy. Above all the Mkamba prizes his independence, to be subject to anyone or bound to anything beyond mere family ties is hateful to him" (Mbiti, *New Testament*, 7).

76. Ndeti, *Elements*, 177.

77. Mbiti, *New Testament*, 95.

78. Ibid., 96.

children!"⁷⁹ This act transfers blessings from one person to another, with the intention of imparting spiritual "powers" (through vital life fluids). Informal education provides another venue for human growth. Elders teach children the values of the culture: around the *thome* (open courtyard) for men and boys or *iko* (hearth) for women and girls. This kind of knowledge comes with commensurate responsibilities (i.e., powers) for humanizing youth into responsible persons within the community. Therefore, blessings are very important to the Akamba; they symbolize one of the most important means of transferring "powers."

Spiritual power, therefore, serves a utilitarian purpose. All of life flows from the divine. Humans interact with divine power in order to grow: harnessing these powers present within the cosmos for the humanization of their community, which corresponds directly to the cultivation of the land, care of animals, and other interactions with the natural world. The sun, in particular, is viewed as a source of power, whereas lightning and thunder represent *Mulungu's* wrath.⁸⁰ "The Akamba believe that every object has its 'force' or 'power' and the entire universe is knit together by the invisible 'force' of Nature."⁸¹ The Akamba participate in certain rituals in order to appropriate spiritual power for the prosperity of the land, or the fertility of livestock. Humans function as interpretive agents of integration and growth, which carries strong correlation between divine power and cosmic fruitfulness.⁸²

HUMANITY AND POWER WITHIN CONTEMPORARY AKAMBA SOCIETIES

Building upon these foundations, I now turn toward identifying images of power within contemporary Akamba Christianity, showing elements of re-interpretation taking place with traditional cosmological beliefs. This will be an integrative project, and, as such, offers no exact correlations. I am merely looking for themes that continue to reinforce linkages between spiritual power and human growth.

Mbiti's research on Akamba cosmology was for the purposes of interpreting Christian eschatology within the worldview of his people's

---

79. Ibid., 92.
80. Ndeti, *Elements*, 183–84.
81. Mbiti, *Akamba Stories*, 17.
82. Mbiti explains that "fertility" is the most accurate Kikamba translation for this kind of physical prosperity; see *New Testament*, 80.

traditions (especially against what he perceived to be the foreign teachings of the missionaries). However, his work reveals tendencies that argue the Gospel around traditions, giving the impression that the former always enters through the gateway of the latter, while offering a commensurate reading of culture bearing static and idealistic undertones. For example, Mbiti reviles the missionaries for how their teachings on the subject of heaven "create a false spirituality" and "encourage an attitude of indifference to the world in which Christians are called to live; they encourage them [humans] to escape from physical reality to a largely fictitious reality."[83] Or, later, where he makes a more striking claim related to his Akamba tribe: "People have little or no notion of how to relate this life to the life in that other world, except insofar as they can psychologically escape to that dreamland."[84] These statements do little to explain why churches such as the ABC, with their strong Akamba origins, combine eschatological teachings they inherited from the missionaries with a focus upon holistic development. Nor do his comments offer sufficient reason why the AICK has moved so vigorously into education, with little detriment to their eschatological emphases.[85] Mbiti is fair in questioning the extent to which elements of evangelical confession (found in hymns or other material) may divert attention away from transformation in Christ and/or associates heaven with an idyllic place.[86] Yet he fails to show how Africans have repackaged these teachings to fit contemporary frames of thought. His work gives the impression of Africans uncritically accepting Western teachings, without regard for how they imaginatively engage in Christianity precisely by re-interpreting these realities to fit ever-changing contexts.

In the remainder of this chapter, I will draw upon a wide variety of images dealing with power taken from Machakos district, including non-ecclesiastical and ecclesiastical stages. This overview will seek to establish a framework for showing how theological communities utilize divine power in order to reimage themselves within the contemporary world.

---

83. Ibid.

84. Ibid., 90.

85. Although, admittedly, at the time Mbiti penned this work, AIM/AICK commitments toward education were tenuous, at best.

86. Ibid., 80–81.

Images of Power

Non-Ecclesiastical Images of Power

During the year 2008, I wrote down signboard names from over two hundred shops (*Duka*) and three hundred public service vehicles (*Matatu*) from within Machakos district. I was interested in what these everyday appellations might convey about what is important to people in modern Akamba society. From these lists, I indexed the data into general groupings.

SHOP (DUKA) NAMES

Signboards were broken into six categories: (1) Names of People, (2) Names of Places, (3) Kikamba/Kiswahili words or values, (4) Christian words or values, (5) Natural Objects, and (6) a final category for those items which appeared non-descript. The grouping that received the highest number of entries was Kikamba/Swahili words or values (almost fifty out of two hundred), and included titles such as *Mshono* (knitting), *Ngomano* (meeting place), *Kathemboni* (small shrine), *kwa Atangoi* (for leaders), *Makolongi* (for people), *Taratibu* Green Grocery (moderate pace), *Wakujaribu* Fashions (to try) and *Thome* (a place where men used to sit). Christian words or values were the next most common category (thirty-three out of two hundred), including names such as Glory Café, *Imani* (faith) Shop, Genesis House, *Huruma* Shop (mercy), Blessed Ebenezar, Grace Butchery, *Ombea Adui yako* (pray for your enemy), Emmanuel, Vatican, and Israel Shop. A recurrent word in the natural object category was *star*, as in Starcom General Merchants, Middle Star Hotel, and Starlight Saloon. I asked various informants if there was any significance for this in Akamba history or traditions, yet most people seemed to think the name had contemporary meaning, where it signified something outstanding, a model of excellence, or with exceptional qualities. Sometimes a shop could carry a designation that associated it with a spirit or *aimu*, especially if the shop owner had recently experienced notable material success. In such a case, people are led to believe that the business enterprise may be associated with the presence of some ambiguous spiritual power. Financial prosperity requires a spiritual reason. Partially for this reason, considerable overlap exists between Kikamba/Swahili titles and Christian categories. Store names such as *Wikwatyo* (hope, Kikamba), *Tumaini* (hope, Kiswahili), *Upendo* (love), Unity Shop, *Amani* Dental Clinic (Peace, Kiswahili), *Muuo* (Peace, Kikamba), and *Baraka* corner (blessings) could fit into either of the groupings, showing continuity

63

between Akamba and Christian values. A handful of shops drew upon associations with Western people or places (Kofi Annan, Manchester, Pentagon Corner, and Florida Shop), but these were not common.

Matatu Names[87]

By way of contrast, when analysing *Matatu*, I needed to create a new heading for *Western/Modern* names, as these were the most common titles among all categories (ninety-three out of three hundred). Examples included well-known sports teams or global businesses; alternatively, they consisted of made-up words with intimations of Western power or success. By way of illustration, Manchester United, Arsenal, Sony, Nike, or Shakira were frequent names occupying public service vehicles in Machakos. Another common sub-category involved descriptors with overtly modern connotations, such as Lap Top, Futuristic Epic, World Changer, Hotline, or Internet. *Matatu* names could express general needs and aspirations for what people desire in contemporary societies (Lover Rhythm, Not By Luck, The Best Ever, Be Cool, The Theatre of Dreams, or 100% Pure Pleasure); or, they could convey representations of power (Still Strong, Banger, Power Deal, Power Coach, or The Fighter). All of these, taken collectively, demonstrate ways in which humans draw upon Western symbols in order to image themselves successful, appealing, or powerful within contemporary societies.

The other predominant theme drawn from *Matatu* names relates to overt representations of Christianity (seventy-five of three hundred). I divided these into various sub-categories, which included general values (Blessed, Harmony, Honesty, Innocent, Wisdom, Promise); human responses to God (Praise, Glory, Peace Maker, Agape, and Clean Heart); names from the Bible (Jubilee, King David, Exodus, Zion Train, Red Sea, Emmaus, and Gilead Express); and, the nature of God. This final category was the most common (thirty-four out of seventy-five), highlighting the importance of confessional affirmations regarding the divine for everyday life. Examples include Jesus is Alive, God's Grace, King of Kings, Lamb of God, God Provides, Jehovah Jireh, God with Us, *Yesu ni Bwana* (Jesus is Lord), Glory be to God, Trumpet of Hope, Amazing Grace, Everlasting God, Try Jesus, God's Power, God is Able, God is our Defender,

---

87. I am using the term *Matatu* to include all public service vehicles, inclusive of Nissans (fifteen passenger vans) and larger mid-sized buses (those normally called *Matatu*).

Images of Power

El Shaddai, The Power of the Cross, Jesus is Love, With God all things are Possible, My Doulos, and *Yesu Tosha* (Jesus is Enough). The above ascriptions reveal the relevancy of God's nature for non-ecclesiastical contexts. In many of these examples, God's power lies implicit behind the title and makes correlation to everyday existence. God's power: defends, gives power, provides for human needs, enables, and/or orients humans to him (as King of Kings, Lord, or Savior).

ANALYSIS

From the above data, it appears that shop names tend to reflect Akamba/Christian values, perhaps providing talisman-type blessings onto the commercial enterprise: in order to associate it with something reputable; or link the business with some kind of spiritual power (whether spirit-related or Christian). Signboards further display similarities with Akamba clan names, showing a predisposition for natural objects, animals, places, and names of people. It was rare for any *Duka* to express an attribute of God, while they did occasionally draw upon global images to reflect some intimation of international success. Businesses bearing a Kikamba name (or, Akamba value) entice consumers with a predilection for the traditional past, as if envisioning a return to those traditions that formerly governed their communities. Similarly, Christian names convey perceptions of integrity and trustworthiness; or a blessing from God. What is more, a name serving both purposes (Akamba and Christian) suggests a blending of traditional values with Christian expression, reinforcing spiritual blessing upon the enterprise.

On the other hand, *Matatu* carry stronger, more overt messages. This may be due to the nature of road transportation in Kenya, where accidents are common and *Matatu* owners (and drivers) live with high degrees of personal risk. It is possible that popular and powerful images (drawn from sacred and secular sources) entice travelers by offering them protection from the innumerable hazards associated with public transportation in the country. *Matatu* are frequently adorned with bright colors and have loud horns that announce the vehicle's arrival, or serve as warnings for anyone that gets in its way. One tout carries the nickname *Manguvu* (literally, *one who is powerful*) to attract people to his *Matatu*;[88] while another explained the reasons for various images on the vehicles (like a cobra, eagle, or cheetah): "each vehicle is associated with a picture it

88. "Manguvu," interview by David Musyoka, Machakos Bus Stand, June 1, 2009.

Re-Imaging Modernity

bears, in terms of speed, strength and comfort."[89] Generational issues influence the choice of vehicle names (as well the particular *Matatu* people choose to ride upon): younger owners and travellers opt for more modern, Western themes, with loud, contemporary music and video screens, while older proprietors/travellers choose vehicles with traditional and/or Christian values.[90] Power is a common theme in all the vehicles. Powerful images represent streams of continuity with African cosmology insofar as they reveal ways in which humans tap into cosmic forces for dealing with uncertain vicissitudes of life. Powers may be overtly Christian, or they may draw upon contemporary forces within global societies. God's nature remains central to many of these with clear points of relevancy for how understanding how humans tap into the divine in order to interact within the world.

Ecclesiastical Images of Power

A cross-sectional look at church-related images reveals similar perspectives but through more overt spiritual language. The following data arises out of the three denominations, but with further extrapolations that could easily encompass broader swaths of Christianity in Kenya. Some differences exist between the churches as it pertains to what songs they sing, and/or how they pray. At this point I will attend to similarities between the churches. This is possible because of shared histories and/or points of contact between ecclesiastical members: firstly, because of mission-based traditions that developed within Ukambani through the influence of the AIM/AICK (and subsequently affecting other churches in the region); and secondly, from Christian Unions (CUs) within Secondary schools, Colleges, and Universities throughout the country.[91] Choruses and charismatic ways of praying are common within these school-based organizations making it possible for students to import them back into their churches. Other points of contact may exist between the denominations, serving to express shared practices or implicit theologies, but the two outlined above are the most compelling. In this section, I will focus upon similarities within the churches with brief mention to any differences that might exist.

---

89. "Mutiso," interview by John M. Kioko, Machakos Bus Stand, June 1, 2009.
90. Paul Mulei, interview by Samuel Mulonzya, Machakos Bus Stand, June 4, 2009.
91. Kalu makes this point; see *Power, Poverty and Prayer*, 113.

Choruses

Most of the choruses arise directly from the CUs. Some of these songs originated within Western evangelicalism, and have been repackaged and reinterpreted to fit contemporary, Kenyan domains; others are entirely original to African forms of Christianity. English and Swahili choruses flow intermixed with one another and are particularly loved by the youth. These songs often have dancing movements, which allow human bodies to act out the meaning of the words with fuller degrees of participation and meaning. In English, the most common choruses are, "He has done so much for me that I cannot tell it all"; "Jesus, you are a winner"; "The Lion of Judah has given us power; he has broken every chain"; "You are the alpha and omega, we worship you O Lord, you are worthy of our praise"; "How excellent is your name, O Lord"; "Father, let your will be done"; "You are so mighty; you are so caring; you are so loving"; "Lord, you reign"; "Remember me, oh mighty Father . . . remember me O Lord"; "You are the spring of my life, the well that never will run dry; you bring healing in my life"; "If Jesus says, 'Yes,' nobody can say, 'No'"; and, "I'm going to conquer, conquer in the Spirit." People draw upon popular ("winner," "excellent") and powerful ("mighty," "Lord," "you reign") images of God to project themselves as popular and powerful agents within the world. These types of songs enable congregants to tap into God's nature for the reconstruction of a new way of living—often in the face of hopelessness and despair. Worship songs are repetitive and emotional; they empower people to existentially relate with God for the purposes of conceptualizing themselves as new people, equipped with the character of God as their fundamental basis for life.

Application is made to human existence. People beseech God, "Remember me," as they recount God's glorious acts of salvation: understood with spiritual and material components. They stand submissive before the throne of God ("let your will be done" or "I surrender all"), but in ways that vitalize human agency ("I'm going to conquer in the Spirit" or "the Lion of Judah has given us power"). Dependency upon God informs human responsibility within the world.

Similar themes appear within Kiswahili or Kikamba choruses, but often associated with more vigorous singing and lively dance movements. Some of these songs are the same as those listed above (with translation into Kiswahili); while others are altogether different, and include

- *Jina la Yesu Jina tulilopewa* (the name of Jesus is the name we have been given; Kiswahili)
- *Unatawala; Amen Alleluya' wewe ni Bwana* (This is a song sung by the late Angela Chilbalonza). The message in the song is one of praise for the reign of the Lord. When the leaders praise God for what he has done, the people respond by saying, "Amen, Alleluya." It is a moving song, especially as people ponder the sovereignty and mighty deeds of God. (Kiswahili)
- *Wanawako wanakuzanyika angalia Baba* (Your children are meeting, see them Father; Kiswahili)
- *Naijulikane Kwamba yuko Mungu wa Eliya* (Let it be known there is the God of Elijah; Kiswahili)
- *Anaweza, anaweza Bwana* (He is able, He is able Lord; Kiswahili)
- *Yesu ni ngwatilo yakwa* (Jesus is my anchor; Kikamba)
- *Yesu niwe ivia Ilumu* (Jesus is the strong stone; Kikamba)
- *Ni mapambano ha shetani* (It is battle with the devil; Kiswahili)
- *Bwana wa mabwana ameshinda vita* (The Lord of Lords has won the battle; Kiswahili)
- *Nita mwimbia Bwana kwa kuwa ameniona* (I will sing to the Lord because he has seen me; Kiswahili)
- *Hakuna mungu kama wewe ... nimetumboa, numetafula, nimezunguka* (There is no God like him. I have walked or travelled in places searching and have gone around, but have never seen one like you; Kiswahili)
- *Mungu, unaweza, mkono wako ni mkuu sana* (God you are able, your arm is very great; Kiswahili)
- *Kimbilio kwa yesu. Kimbilia utapona* (Run to Jesus and you will be healed) The song is sung while congregants run in place. People make haste as they pursue Jesus for healing, whether sickness, material, or for sins they have committed. (Kiswahili)

Choruses focus upon the uniqueness (*hakuna kama wewe*, "there is no God like you") and praiseworthiness of God's nature (*unastahili kuabudiwa*, "You are worthy of worship"), along with power to provide, protect, heal, and guide people within this trouble-filled world. Direct correlations are made between divine and human realms, as evidenced in the Kiswahili chorus: *Wanawako wanakuzanyika angalia Baba* (Your children are meeting, see them Father) or, alternatively, as humans look toward Christ: *Tembea, tembea Yesu tembea tukuone* (Move Jesus so that we may see you). There is a bit of irony in the fact that humans "praise God to a higher place" in order to relate his nature to temporal needs, whether sickness, financial difficulties, or even death. "Lifting God higher" makes God more accessible to humans. This is possible because of ontological connections between divine and human domains (within an integrative cosmology). God is the source of power and should be elevated in order for humans to draw upon his energies.

Another common theme in these songs involves victory over the devil, where daily existence is pictured as a "battle" between good and evil, with Christ as the ultimate champion: "breaking every chain." Spiritual warfare features prominently within all the churches but particularly so for the RGC. These churches utilize dualisms to articulate broader narratives of conflict. Pentecostal churches invoke the Holy Spirit's power, whereas non-Pentecostal churches are more likely to focus upon the saving work of Jesus Christ (singing, "there is power, power, wonder working power in the blood, of the Lamb").

Hymns

Power-related themes remain conspicuous elements within hymns, but tempered by Christological and soteriological language. Similar to Mbiti's argument, many of these songs place emphasis upon the coming Kingdom of God and other images of future glory, yet the churches interpret these eschatological elements in ways that give present meaning to human existence. Most of these hymns are direct translations from the English equivalent, but sometimes with different tunes. I am listing those songs most common in the churches, and with brief comments where relevant:

- "God is here, and that to bless us, with the Spirit's quickening power" (English, Kiswahili or Kikamba). Especially loved by the ABC.
- *Chakutumaini sina* (Kiswahili): "My hope is built on nothing less than Jesus' blood and righteousness" (English equivalent, yet sung to a different tune). This is perhaps the most loved hymn of the AICK. Most people have memorized the song, and frequently sing it as a worship chorus.

- *Bwana Mungu na Shangaa Kabisa* (Kiswahili): "How Great Thou Art." Most people have it memorized, and where it is sung with deep emotion. Especially common among the AICK.
- *Nitabibu wa Tabibu* (Kiswahili) "The Great Physician." Most frequently heard in RGC churches.
- *Metho Makwa Nimamwonie Mutangii Yesu* (no. 3, Kikamba hymnal): "Our God is Marching On." Older people like this song. The message is that "my eyes have seen Christ promising us the way to take us to him." In another stanza the singer says, "I put aside all *my own fashioned gods of the past* (emphasis in Kikamba) since I have known the true one." The chorus says, "we are supposed to praise him, giving him all the glory because of his truth." This song conveys praise for deliverance from the powers of darkness, especially when older people remember "their own fashioned gods of the past" (*ngai syakwa syakwiseuvisya sya tene*).
- *Etikili onthe ni Nimetitwe Yu* (no. 296, Kikamba hymnal): "Send the Light!" This is a common missions hymn in the churches, whether or not people are involved in any evangelistic/missions activity. It projects church members out into the world, equipped with relevant powers.
- *Ve Musyi Wonekaa Iulu wa Mwanda wa Kikw'u* (no. 155, Kikamba hymnal): "There is a home beside the valley of death." The song looks forward to the future dwelling place with God and counts the blessing and benefits of being there. In one of the stanzas, the song says, "When we arrive, then we will reign forever and ever with Christ."
- *Vakuvi Naku Ngai* (no. 42, Kikamba hymnal) "Nearer my God to Thee"
- *Yesu Nimunyanya Wakwa* (no. 188, Kikamba hymnal) "What a friend we have in Jesus"
- *Twaviau kwa Musumbi* (no. 143, Kikamba hymnal): "We Stand Before the King." The message in the song expresses people's desire to be in the kingdom of God where they (together with the angels) shall praise God. Because of their desire to praise God within his kingdom, the singers call for Jesus to guide them until they arrive at that place.

- *Vinyani wa mwiaii Tukakilya* (no. 441, Kikamba hymnal): "Rock of Ages"; people attest to the fact that they are "conquerors through the blood."
- *Musumbi wa Thayu Wakwa*: (no. 109, Kikamba hymnal): "King of my soul"; "Lead Me to Calvary." The song praises God because of the salvation Christ has given humans. People promise to praise him because he is King of their hearts and their Savior.

Hymns are favored by older people, and provide a degree of continuity between the early missionary presence and the contemporary order. In the minds of many *wazee* (older people), hymns directly correlate with the Bible and Akamba values (often taken collectively), while choruses are perceived as something new and modern: repetitive, emotional and not as Biblical. Early missionaries translated hymns into Kikamba or Kiswahili. Over time, the churches selected their favorites and reinterpreted them for their contexts. In 1972, six evangelical denominations collaborated (including the AICK and ABC) to publish a hymnal of Kikamba songs. This edition remains one of the most important faces of Christianity in the region.[92] Hymns represent comfortable and conservative vestiges of a traditional order.

Hymns are particularly prominent in the AICK and ABC, and the center of conflict with youth who favor more lively choruses. The RGC have much less of this tension. Most of their members are young, and CUs heavily influenced older parishioners in the 1970s and 80s where they were exposed to a wide range of choruses. The RGC sing more contemporary, lively choruses, and less hymns; while the AICK and ABC prefer hymns and fewer choruses.

God's power remains the prevailing theme in all these songs, whether expressed Christologically, (based upon Jesus' nature), Soteriologically, (through emphasis upon the cross), Eschatologically, (where the focus is on the eternal Kingship of God), or in cosmic conflict language, where God achieves victory over Satan (with direct benefit to humans). African churches carefully select songs that relate to everyday needs and aspirations. God's power situates humans within the epicenter of the cosmos, where they apply his nature to the various inconstancies of human existence.

---

92. Ukamba Christian Literature Joint Committee.

Re-Imaging Modernity

Choir Songs

The recent popularity of choirs represents the fastest growing element of evangelical expression in the region. Within the last five years, it has become common (and almost expected) for every congregation to have one or two choirs, write songs, perform them in other churches, participate in area-wide competitions, and produce tapes, CDs, and/or videos. One talented choir master from Tanzania leads choirs in AICK and ABC churches. Another receives a stipend for his services greater than those offered to local Pastors. Churches spend considerable money on colorful robes for choir members. Town churches purchase buses to provide transportation to area events. One local congregation sent its choir as far away as Morogoro, Tanzania, to participate in an evangelistic outreach. On a certain Sunday, the pastor of a local congregation implored his elders to keep it quiet that the choir was going to be away on a trip, fearing that if the parishioners knew, no one would attend the service.

These comments underscore the importance of choirs in contemporary, evangelical churches in Ukambani. Songs are often locally written, or borrowed from professional music artists in East Africa. A few examples include

- *Harambee tumshinde shetani, nguvu tunazo kutoka kwa Mungu, chukua Chepeo ya wokovu la ushindi twende tukapambane* (Let us come together to defeat the devil, we have strength from God, take the helmet of victory to go and fight; Kiswahili)

- *Twakulilia Baba utuponye nashida za dunia; magoniwa yasiyo na tiba kama ukimwi* (We cry to you, Father, to save us from the world problems, incurable sickness like AIDS and cancer) *Dawa ni Yesu mwana wa Mungu* (Christ the son of God is the cure; Kiswahili)

- *Jina la Yesu ndilo pekee tulilopewa kuokolewa hapana jina lingine* (It is only the name of Jesus that we have been given) *watu mashuhuri wamekuja na wamepita lakini jina la Yesu linaishi milele* (Famous people have come and gone, but the name of Jesus lives forever; Kiswahili)

- *Atupenda Baba, Yesu uliteswa kwa ajili Yetu. Ukombozi akika leo tunao, tuliteswa tulipokuwa Babeli* (The Father loves us, Jesus was troubled because of us. Today we have deliverance; we were troubled when we were in Babylon; Kiswahili)

Images of Power

These songs are performed with lively, choreographed dance movements. Bodily motions communicate a story filled with meaning. Jackson and Karp describe *dance* as "metaphorical in character, creating links between the vital energy of the individual body, the social body, and the cosmos."[93] Choir members perform cosmic battles as they enact God's power within their songs, participating with the divine as they engage in contemporary realities (expressed in terms of overcoming sickness or deliverance). One small choir in a rural village sang about how they were "going on a journey to defeat Satan."[94] During the performance, choir members clasp hands together to signify the collective victory that they experience. Another choir stands with fists clenched in a posture of defiance as they openly declare God's power for spiritual warfare. Any contemporary reality or problem is open to this medium, as there is little opportunity for ecclesiastical leaders to censure or control what is written, or how it is performed. After the post-election violence of 2008, Christian artists wrote songs that dealt with prevalent themes of conflict experienced by the people, and called upon churches to bring the country together for healing and reconciliation.

Youth express much of their inner angst through music. Churches allow youth the opportunity for participation on Youth Sundays (especially for AICK and ABC congregations), or in regular services (typical for the RGC). Individuals or groups perform songs that they have written, or heard on the radio. Several AICK youth sang, "Freely, take away these pains were feeling . . . from these chains that you and I can see"; "Heal me and take away this pain that I'm feeling."[95] In such ways they express inner struggles, but through appropriate mechanisms that do not openly conflict with elders or pastors. Youth use music to give voice to real human needs, and reach out to God's power to bring meaning in their lives.

Choirs likewise offer strategic forums for fostering social relationships within the churches, especially between unmarried men and ladies. Choirs will practice as often as five times in a week, which enables youth to meet with members of the opposite sex within formal and informal settings and develop relationships that often burgeon into marriages.[96]

93. Jackson and Karp, *Personhood*, 22.
94. AICK Makyau, Jan. 4, 2009.
95. AICK Bomani, Dec. 21, 2008.
96. Interesting correlations exist between moder- day choirs and traditional Akamba dances, in terms of offering a venue for youth to interact with each other through music and dance.

Re-Imaging Modernity

Youth groups tend to be virtually synonymous with Choirs. For example, one small rural church had eighty people in their choir from a total congregation of less than 150.[97]

PRAYERS

Individual and corporate supplications offer one of the most intimate ways of looking at how *washariki* appropriate God's power in their lives. Prayers serve to confessionally articulate human desires before the throne of God. I have recorded dozens of prayers drawn from all the denominations and offer this overview with the aim of showing similarities in how people express God's nature, and further use it to connect with human needs and aspirations.

The most common appellations for God are, "Jehovah;" "Mighty God;" "Mighty Father;" "Mighty Everlasting Father;" "King of Glory;" "Lord of Hosts;" "Mighty Name of Jesus;" and, "Father God." Supplicants will often repeat these words in their prayers, restating such phrases up to twenty times in a single prayer. Vocal patterns of emphasis increase with each repetition, where the supplicant gradually raises his or her voice, seemingly calling down God's power to assist the believer in the face of human desperation. "The names of God are often ascriptive rather than descriptive;"[98] they have the effect of virtually creating a new reality within the world: made possible by tapping into the source of power. Vocal tendencies are especially prominent within the RGC, but are becoming more common in the other churches, especially among the youth.

Similar ascriptions appear in Kikamba prayers, but with greater diversity of expression. The RGC rarely use Kikamba in their services (preferring Swahili or English). Hence, these titles for God's nature are primarily drawn from AICK and ABC congregations. The following are the most frequently heard ascriptions of God's nature in the churches: *Ngai nituukuvoya* (God we pray to you); *Ngai Musumbi* (God our King); *Ngai ututongoesye* (God, you lead us); *Ngai waitu* (our God); *Ngai utuathime* (God bless us); *Twavoya tukiikiia* (we pray trusting and believing); *Ngai twienda ukuthaitha* (God we want to worship you); *Yeova Ngai mwene vinya wonthe* (Almighty God); *Musumbi wa Asumbu* (King of Kings); *Ame Yehova* (oh, Jehovah); *Klisto wa ituni* (Christ of heaven); *Asa Mutheu* (Holy Father); *Asa isyitwani ya klisto yesu* (Father in the name

97. AICK Wetolo, Mukaa, Kenya.
98. Percy, *Words*, 73.

of Christ Jesus); *Ngai wakwa* (My God); *Ngai wa Isilaeli* (God of Israel); *Ngai wa ituni* (God of Heaven); *Ngai wa Avalaamu, Isaka na Yakovo* (God of Abraham, Isaac and Jacob); *Ngai wa ingai* (God of gods); *Ngai mwene tei* (Merciful God); *Ngai mwene vinya* (Almighty God); and *Ithe waitu wa ituni* (Our Father of Heaven). Older people tend to refer to God as "Father," "Almighty God," or other references to his sovereignty and authority, while youth combine God's power with his love and mercy.

AICK and ABC use the title *Ngai* for God, as the early missionaries disapproved of the name *Mulungu* because of its usage in the shrines and during traditional forms of worship. It is rare to hear anyone refer to God as *Mulungu*, or the equally religious *Mwatuangi* (which means, *divider* or *cleaver*). One young man told me that the latter represents the unspoken name for God, similar to the Israelites refusal to utter the name YHWH.

Divine ascriptions often correspond to human needs. Supplicants will relate God's power with financial distress, the need for a job, or healing for the sick. Inasmuch as people express God's nature in supernatural ways (Father of Heaven; Holy Father; Mighty God, etc.), the scope of application bears distinctly earthly undertones. Congregants pray, "Meet us at our various points of need;" "we want to hear from you;" "be with us;" or "your people are struggling." One interesting connection relates to where *washiriki* refer to God as "King of Glory," followed by thanking him "for the gift of life." I have heard this on many different occasions, and in various churches. These types of connections reinforce patterns that associate God's power with human growth.

Prayer in the RGC, unlike the other two denominations, often places the supplicant in direct opposition to ambiguous spiritual forces. Humans appropriate God's power for fighting cosmic battles against noxious powers that inflict damage on human communities. Demons may be associated with any societal problem, whether corruption, tribalism, poverty, or sickness. Congregants pray *Inywi ndaimoni sya yua* (You demons of famine I rebuke you), and where they claim this authority, *Syitwani ya yesu* (In the name of Jesus). Another common phrase is *Satani nienda ukukanya* (Satan, I rebuke you). Direct attacks against unseen forces are possible because of "the mighty power of God" made available to the *washiriki*. Another distinction found primarily within the RGC is that they devote less time to congregational prayers and place greater emphasis upon individual petitions, with the latter sometimes taking up to forty-five minutes during a service.

Re-Imaging Modernity

Power and Loudness

Vocal patterns, noise levels, and other oral characteristics likewise communicate something about God's power. Musical instruments and public amplification systems have become ubiquitous elements in the churches over the past ten years, including electrical guitars, synthesizers, and drums. Youth want the music to be lively and loud, and where the noise level often corresponds with their need to appropriate God's power in their lives. Supplicants cry out to God for help. Preachers shout into microphones in churches, marketplaces, or in *Matatu*. Vocal characteristics express divine power. If a pastor assumes a quiet or unassuming preaching manner, the parishioners often believe the sermon (and/or the pastor's spiritual credibility) to be *powerless*." Likewise, when pastors feel insecure about their position or spiritual authority, they shout louder, physically projecting a sense of intrinsic power. When someone preaches in this kind of manner, people say they are "hammering the Gospel."

Blessings

Another prevalent theme in all the ecclesiastical communities relates to "blessings" (in prayers, sermons or songs), connecting God's power with life growth. In such ways, Christianity in Africa builds upon traditional concepts in order to express the relevancy of spiritual power for everyday human needs. All of the churches make use of these kinds of associations, yet framed in different ways. Blessings come from God to those who are faithful, and relate to observable realities. The ABC defines the object of blessings most broadly, covering spiritual, physical, mental, bodily, material, and social modes of life. The RGC tends to apply spiritual blessings with affect to material benefits, where one might hear them pray, "God, bless our pockets." The AICK struggles with these dichotomies, where God's blessings relate to spiritual things, or material realities, but often with tension or uncertainty between the two.

There are many Kikamba sayings related to blessings. These cover a wide range of prosperity-related images; including a person's relationship with elders (*Muveeka usue ndaa mathungii*: "He who relates well with his/her grandmother does not lack blessings"); fertility of livestock (*Kituuni kyaku vaikaae tusau*: "Let there be calves always in your cow pen"); food and abundance (*Ikumbi yaku vaikaai Ngulu*: "Let there be no weevils in your store room"); biological fertility (*Wisyaa Mavatha*: "Be a

Images of Power

producer of twins"); and good relationships in the community (*Wiikwa oou wambika*: "May you find favour in people's eyes").

Within Akamba Christianity, blessings continue to reinforce patterns of prosperity, but couched in language where God, Jesus, or the Holy Sprit provide the instrumental agency for extending divine favor to the individual. People sing "Showers of blessing;" "count your blessings;" *Yesu wa Baraka* (Jesus of blessings); or "God is here and that to bless us." A particularly striking chorus found in all the churches, says, *Bwana Naomba Kubarikiwa nawe sitoki hapa usiponibariki* (God, I pray that you may bless me. I will not leave here until you bless me). Congregants pray: "bring your blessings to us;" "bless us so that we can feel blessed;" "bless us so that we can have fellowship with you;" "Bless our families: meet our needs, our material needs;" "bless us and meet our needs;" or where a pastor in one of the local churches prayed, "Lord, bless these people; you who gives not just material blessings, but life." Blessings represent a way of connecting God's power with life growth. People generally believe that pastors have extra power for transmitting divine power (often interpreted in terms of "blessings") to individuals. They are seen as "nearer" to the source of power. Touch, oil or other fluids may strengthen these kinds of associations (especially within the RGC). As previously mentioned, dangers sometimes exist when the pastor or other spiritual authority is viewed as residing closer to God, and thus equipped with a monopoly of spiritual resources; however, this is not always the case. The following chapters will focus upon constructive uses of divine power for enhancing life growth (without being blind to any potentially "oppressive coordinates" as they exist).

CONCLUSION

All of these portraits, drawn from anthropological, theological, sociological, and ecclesiastical sources confirm similar connections between divine power and human agency. Nearness to God's power promotes human growth, and ecclesiastical communities repackage these concepts within the framework of Christian teachings (implicit and explicit) in order to engage with social and material realities; where parishioners image themselves as powerful precisely because of God's *mighty* nature.

In the following chapters, I will give individual focus to the denominations in order to show *how* spiritual power enables the churches to promote these generative characteristics, and where modernity-related language often serves to orient ecclesiastical expression. Theological resources (of the divine) are fundamental for these kinds of sociological constructions. Each of the following chapters will begin with a broad overview of the predominant images of power within the denomination, and then proceeds to look at *how* divine power enables the church to deal with specific themes of Western modernity, re-expressed within theological communities of faith.

3

Africa Inland Church: Secularization and Rationalization

THIS CHAPTER FOCUSES ON power and humanity through a study of one of the largest evangelical churches in Kenya, the Africa Inland Church (AICK). I give attention to how faith convictions furnish members with critical resources for engaging in modernity-related themes. The chapter begins with a few comments related to the AICK's missionary heritage and then proceeds to show how the church has utilized (and adapted) the teachings/ideology of the AIM to posture itself favorably within the contemporary world.

MODERNITY AND THE AFRICA INLAND MISSION (AIM)

A study of the AIM provides an interesting context for dealing with topics related to modernity. These missionaries have been pejoratively described as "fundamentalistic,"[1] and "anti-modern;"[2] with racial or oppressive tendencies;[3] or in other cases as socially backward or theologically rigid. Some of these stereotypes arise from historic struggles with educational development, reticence in handing authority to the

---

1. Bengt Sundkler and Christopher Steed, *A History*, 1000. The term *fundamentalism* came later in the twentieth century to describe a return to the basic principles of the Christian faith, much in reaction to perceived *secularizing* or *liberalizing* threats from within Christianity. As stated above, the term as used by some of these authors carries pejorative connotations.

2. Ibid., 886.

3. See Sandgren, "Kamba Christianity," 80–81 where he talks about various church disciplinary procedures; or Isichei, *A History*, 90 where she describes the missionaries as having separate worship services for themselves and others for the Africans, implying separatistic or even racial practices.

national church, and/or elevation of evangelism over other activities. The accuracy of these caricatures appears wanting, though, especially in light of how the AICK has utilized its missionary-heritage to grow in size and scope as one of the most instrumental agents of Christianity in the region. This introductory section will merely highlight some of the ideological currents taking place within late nineteenth (and early twentieth) century evangelicalism. I do not intend to offer exhaustive historical detail for these points,[4] but merely want to call attention to elements within the mission-based heritage of the AICK that would supply the church with important theological resources in which to grow into the contemporary era.

The AIM began in 1895 as one of several faith-based organizations inspired by Hudson Taylor and the China Inland Mission (CIM) to bring the Gospel to the interior of Africa. Peter Cameron Scott, its founder, was motivated by the vision of Johann Ludwig Krapf and others before him to plant a series of mission stations from Mombasa to Lake Chad in which to evangelize the peoples of Africa and provide a spiritual barrier to fend off Muslim advance from the North. The AIM began their work amongst the Akamba, who were viewed strategic due to their extensive involvement in trade networks throughout the region.[5] Subsequent years found the missionaries moving deeper inland: to central and western Kenya, further to Tanzania and Congo, and eventually to over fourteen different African countries. Always their goal has been the same: preaching the Gospel among those who had never heard (the *unreached*).

The first AIM missionaries arriving in Ukambani were recipients of a conservative and revivalistic strain of Christianity that arose in the mid- to-late nineteenth century. The Keswick Piety movement, originating in the Lake District of Northern England, with further development(s) in other parts of the world, promoted world missions through emphasis upon divine *calling*. Steve Morad explains Keswick's American-based appearances in terms of a "broad movement rather than a theological system" that included "Calvinistic adaptation to Wesleyan perfectionism" and the fundamental conviction that Christians would "undergo a second, decisive crisis experience after conversion that would result in inner peace, 'victory' over known sin, and 'power' in Christian service,

---

4. For more information on this subject, see Gration, *The Relationship*; Morad, *The Founding*.

5. Cummings, "The Early," 85–110. Krapf had earlier abandoned the prospect of using the Akamba in such a way.

Africa Inland Church: Secularization and Rationalization

especially in evangelism."[6] Partly in response to revivalistic teachings (such as those found in Keswick conventions), and partly in reaction to liberal elements of Western Christianity, the AIM found valuable resource in the supernatural to provide impetus and rationale for their missionary endeavors.

Similar to other American-based mission organizations, spirituality and a distinct awareness of a divine calling were viewed essential requirements for service in Africa. Non-ordained personalities such as Charles G. Finney and Dwight L. Moody (and later John R. Mott and Robert E. Speer) characterized the prevailing mood of the day, which emphasized the mobilization of lay leaders for Christian service. From its inception, the AIM was particularly mindful that lay leaders should augment professional clergy for the work of overseas evangelism.[7] Their mission magazine, *Hearing and Doing*, reads,

> If the world is to be evangelized in this generation there must be a vast increase in the army of messengers, but there cannot be any vast increase save by the enlistment of thousands of lay workers. It is from such that the Africa Inland Mission expects its material to come.[8]

None of AIM's early missionaries were ordained clergy. Peter Cameron Scott worked as a clerk in a printer's office, while John Stauffacher was a dairy farmer from Wisconsin. In this they may be contrasted in education (as well as socioeconomic status) from the Cambridge Seven who pioneered the early work with the China Inland Mission. However, such comments should not imply that these missionaries opposed formal education,[9] but instead viewed spirituality and zeal as more critical for the work of missions. Peter Cameron Scott and his associates saw themselves as ordinary people called by God to evangelize the heathen; they were "consecrated, ardent workers, each one conscious of a distinct call to Africa."[10]

---

6. Morad, *The Founding*, 29.

7. In 1886, D. L. Moody made the famous announcement that he was targeting "gap men" who would stand in between laity and clergy, and fulfil much of the work that needed to be accomplished in the world to make Christ known to the "neglected masses."

8. AIM Archives, *Hearing and Doing*, Jan. 1896, 4–5.

9. Marsden makes this point in *Fundamentalism and American Culture*, 14–17.

10. AIM Archives, *Hearing and Doing*, Jan. 1896, 4.

Initially, the early missionaries viewed the needs on the continent as requiring spirituality and commitment, not theological education. Africa was, according to Scott, "no Ephesus with its learning; but only sin, darkness, ignorance, barbarism. To meet these, men do not need so much specific scholastic and theological knowledge."[11] The needs on the continent, in the minds of the early missionaries, required those called by God and equipped with requisite "wisdom, energy, zeal, devotion, and close walk with God."[12] However, after spending a few years struggling with the challenges of daily life in Ukambani, Peter Cameron Scott and his fellow workers began to change some of their attitudes towards what was needed for missionary service, acknowledging that certain agricultural and linguistic specialists would be helpful or even suggesting the AIM look for people with business skills.[13] Morad describes the AIM as a dynamic entity, constantly adjusting to the needs on the continent.[14] As early as 1902, a statement in *Hearing and Doing* makes dramatic departure from earlier sentiment, declaring that Africa "needs the brightest of our college trained men and women."[15] Static caricatures of the AIM should be dispensed of in favor of more fluid understandings of the mission as an evolving organization.

Africans watched, sometimes painfully, as missionaries wrestled (ideologically and practically) with changing socioreligious conditions: both within the country and also in the broader, global context. The mission was constantly adjusting to itself, its heterogeneous context(s), and the Africans themselves: sometimes these modifications happened reluctantly, and other times with determination. Theological commitments (whether implicitly or explicitly held) provide one important means for interpreting *how* the missionaries engaged with the Africans, while also contributing to resultant forms of Christianity arising within Ukambani.

Evangelicalism provided much of the problem and solution for the struggles facing missionaries within twentieth century Kenya. The dynamics of this are multifaceted and beyond the purview of this chapter, yet it is important to note that Western evangelicalism blossomed within the soil of Enlightenment thought. Thus, it came equipped with its own

11. Ibid.
12. Ibid.
13. Morad, *The Founding*, 64–65.
14. Ibid., 425ff.
15. AIM Archives, *Hearing and Doing*, Apr.–May 1902, 2. Yet with the caveat that these should be, "those who have been called of God to be the disciples of Jesus."

internal machinery for critiquing (and adjusting to) broader currents taking place in the West.[16] Christian distinctions between sacred and secular were particularly effective in enabling evangelicalism to respond to similar enlightenment dichotomies, yet with greater mobility between the two than might be found within Western societies. Supernatural commitments propelled missionaries into Africa, and around the globe, with corresponding powers for engaging in material affairs. The *world* became the scene of conflict between Christ and Satan; supernatural commitments (such as the Bible and evangelism) emerged as the primary weapons for waging battle.[17]

One example would be the *faith-based* approach for financial giving, made popular by George Müller and, thereafter, Hudson Taylor. The late nineteenth and early twentieth century represents a period when missionary activity was rapidly expanding around the world. Those societies adopting the faith-based approach held that missionaries should not promote their financial concerns, but entrust such things to God.[18] To make an argument for this, it became necessary to see spiritual priorities juxtaposed from material pursuits. The AIM never really detached the sacred from the secular, but gave heightened meaning to supernatural commitments: providing them with certain powers for affecting material domains. Disagreements over education afford one of the best forums for observing these kinds of struggles. Most AIM missionaries were not theologically opposed to education (medical work and/or other forms of development) but gave increased priority to evangelism, Bible translation, and preaching. In reaction to perceived secularizing trends found in liberal forms of Christianity, the AIM overemphasized what they saw to be spiritual matters. Kevin Ward describes some of the nuances of the AIM's conflict with primary and secondary school education, showing that it was never simply the case of pitting evangelism against education, but where other motivations were involved, including faith-based ideologies

---

16. Much in the same way that Walls says that "evangelical religion" came with the ability to "adapt itself to any national or local cultural ethos"; or where the kind of "evangelicalism that emerged from the revival in Britain and North America provided a highly successful form of Christian adaptation to the European Enlightenment." See Walls, "Eighteenth-Century Protestant Missionary Awakening," 40, 29.

17. See Marsden, *Fundamentalism*, 62–63.

18. Peter Cameron Scott says, "No man is expected to go into the field except as clearly led by God, and when such leading has become clear, the worker is to look to God alone to supply the means. . . . Where God leads, there God feeds." AIM Archives, *Hearing and Doing*, Jan. 1896, 5.

embodied (with varying degrees) within the mission.[19] One result of the faith-based approach was that it accentuated subtle differentiation(s) between spiritual and material values, making the former of heightened importance, and necessary as a gateway to the latter.[20]

The sacred and secular, therefore, provided the early missionaries with important theological resources in which to engage in African issues, while simultaneously reacting against what they observed taking place in the West. AIM saw Africa as both escape and promise. In coming to Africa, they were at once (1) retreating from "modernistic" influences they saw afflicting American society; (2) actively drawing upon Enlightenment rational (for example, by offering naturalistic solutions like medicine and agricultural development to Africa's spiritually nuanced problems); (3) advancing elements of supernaturalism; and, (4) inculcating an apologetic posture into their preaching. Therefore, in retreating from the West, they exhibit decidedly anti-modern characteristics; through development and medicine, they show an ability to conform to modernity-related ways of thinking; by emphasizing supernaturalism, they were addressing African worldview affirmations; and through their use of apologetics, they combine supernatural faith commitments with Enlightenment reasoning. Therefore, the AIM imparted each of these characteristics to the AICK, which subsequently repackaged the sacred and secular for the growth of the church within the contemporary world.

POWER AND THE AFRICA INLAND CHURCH (AICK)

In turning to the African Church, I wish to build upon this evangelical heritage and show how the AICK utilized these traditions in order to situate itself most favorably within the post-colonial world. Power remains central to this analysis: whether in terms of leadership, spirituality, doctrines, related to material interests, or regarding the formation of human identity. Throughout this discussion, theological and sociological data provides the means for sketching the primary contours of the church.

The history of the AICK reveals a long and hesitant process of formation. Early missionaries little conceived of beginning an indigenous church. Their focus was upon evangelism and might have assumed that

---

19. Ward, "Evangelism or Education?" 243–60.

20. Interestingly, some of these dynamics would later be repackaged into the Prosperity Gospel, underscoring important connections between the spiritual and material for the development of Christianity on the continent.

Africa Inland Church: Secularization and Rationalization

believers from the different missionary societies would naturally form one unified church. Furthermore, as a nondenominational mission and one primarily composed of laypersons, they did not endorse a single church tradition nor hold strong ecclesiastical convictions. Morad explains how the missionaries were likely unaware of Henry Venn's three-self movement until 1908 when Dr. Henry Scott of the Church of Scotland Mission spoke at their yearly conference.[21] The following year revealed a change in the constitution that for the first time mentioned a "native church." From this point to the full *Africanization* of the church in 1971, the process was gradual and wrought with cycles of advance and retreat depending often upon the leaders of the Mission, prevailing ideological concerns, as well as regional interests of the Africans. Members began financially supporting their own activities in 1933, the name *Africa Inland Church* was introduced in 1943, and the formal constitution completed in 1952. Finally, on October 21, 1971 at Mumbuni station (in Ukambani), most missionary properties were transferred into church ownership and AIM Kenya officially became a department of the AICK.

From its beginnings in Nzaui, Kangundo, and Mumbuni, the church spread throughout the country, but always maintaining significant influence in Ukambani. Two of the first five Bishops were Akamba and even the presence of other denominations such as the Africa Brotherhood Church (ABC) or African Christian Church and Schools (ACCS) reveal distinct origins from the AICK. The strength of the church in this part of the country is somewhat surprising given that the AIM transitioned its field headquarters and primary missionary presence from Kangundo to Kijabe as early as 1901. This solicited numerous complaints by C. F. Johnston and others that the AIM was neglecting the work in Ukambani.[22] However, by 1933 at least a few missionaries were stating that no new personnel were needed for their region.[23] What took place in this span of time to change their attitudes? Early evangelistic efforts yielded negligible results. Few Akamba would publicly risk being ostracized by the community to join the religion and practices of these foreigners. However, great strides were being made by the missionaries to learn the vernacular and from 1909 church services were being conducted in Kikamba. The experience of early missionaries with health-related problems created

---

21. Morad, *The Founding*, 398–99.
22. Ibid., 112, 152.
23. AIM Archives, *BGC*, 2.

points of identification with the Africans that may have contributed more to their evangelistic success than other methods. The first Bible College began in Mumbuni in 1928 and Africans assumed oversight of mission stations such as Kangundo as early as 1911, when missionaries relocated or returned to the states for short furloughs. The self-sufficiency of the church thus stems from a combination of factors: vernacular language and sacrificial living developed bonds between missionary and African; while training centers, scarcity of missionaries, and their sporadic departure created space for the Africans to move and grow as deemed advantageous.

Early missionaries like Johnston had a reputation for conservatism in theology and Christian conduct, yet was among the first in the mission to advocate for a native church and the ordination of African clergy. Meanwhile, the AIM's evangelistic vision moved the missionaries farther away from Ukambani and deeper into the interior of Africa. When J. G. Stephenson suggested that the Mbooni station did not need any other personnel, "for the sake of allowing the believers to develop their spiritual qualities and gifts, some of which can only be developed by being left alone"; or where, in reference to all stations East of Athi River, he stated that the Akamba "are in position to carry on the work the moment we leave, it being so organized as to allow them the privilege of doing so,"[24] the Kenya Field Director responded,

> I cannot conceive of any other policy for the future here in Ukamba. . . . It is unthinkable that we should go on supplying the workers from overseas when they can be had right here, and that in ever increasing numbers, and of better and better quality.[25]

This should not imply the complete indigenization of the church in Ukambani, or the absence of subsequent struggles between missionaries and Africans. Conflicts were frequent, especially over education and the payment of salaries. Yet, from these gradual and cautious deliberations, the AICK emerged as one of the largest in Kenya, with a current membership of approximately five million members corresponding to 5,200 churches throughout the country.

What factors explain this kind of expansion? How have they continued to increase (numerically, if not in other ways) despite the loss of

24. Ibid.
25. Ibid.

members to the ABC and ACCS during the rise of ecclesiastical independency, and the later ascent of charismatic Christianity? Initially, the stereotype of the early missionaries as conservative, backward renegades needs reworking in order to account for the various ways they promoted vernacular languages, enhanced local identities, and created opportunities and space for members to engage in the modern world. Likewise, by emphasizing supernatural commitments to the faith, they communicated the Gospel (to some degree) expressive of African spiritual worldview affirmations. While some Africans reacted against certain aspects of missionary ideology, others like those within the AICK utilized the theological traditions for their own advantage.

Powers: Modern and Traditional

Initially, the church's historic struggles with education yielded heightened emphasis upon learning, and especially the acquisition of degrees as means for upward mobility. The AIM saw education as necessary for biblical literacy; however, the Africans viewed it as a pathway for advancement within a colonial-dominated world.[26] Even as missionaries focused on the vernacular for the purposes of evangelism, the Africans were equally desirous of learning English (and together with it other disciplines) in order to interact with the missionaries as equals. Many influential figures emerged from their schools, including the former President, Daniel arap Moi. A survey of current membership within the AICK reveals a catalogue of key political figures, including the current Vice President, Kalonzo Musyoka, Cabinet ministers such as Mutula Kilonzo, as well as Permanent Secretaries and a large number of MPs. The Chairman for the Kenya National Commission for Human Rights is an active member of the AICK. Similar figures can be shown for business and civil sectors of society. Perhaps because of this, the highly anticipated backlash against the AICK following the 2002 Presidential elections never materialized. The church still possesses significant influence within the country.

Alongside this progressive spirit, however, is a corresponding traditional identity. People think of the AICK as an Akamba and Kalenjin church because of its strength in these rural areas. During the colonial years, the AIM was one of few Protestant missions involved in Ukambani; hence, it is hardly possible to travel anywhere within this region and

---

26. Harries, "Missionaries," 405–27 captures many of the dynamics involved in this process, from a Mozambican perspective.

not find their churches, significantly more than any other denomination. Early missionary activity contributed to strengthening tribal identities, while allowing certain "space" for Africans to grow. AIM missionaries like Lester Severn (one of Scott's original recruits) worked on creating a book of Kikamba grammar that subsequently formed the basis for translation activity. The New Testament was completed in 1920 and the Old Testament in 1956. Most evangelical churches in Ukambani still use this version of the Bible.

Another aspect of their traditional identity appears through extensive networks of filial relationships. In rural villages, the AICK often acts as a territorial church with overlapping roles between the denomination and society-related functions. One elder explained this in terms of the contribution that the church makes in replacing traditional Akamba councils: regulating affairs and providing essential values for society.[27] Parents impart these ecclesiastical traditions to their children, and the church becomes a place where members receive their sense of belonging in the community. It is common for people to congregate several hours after services, participate in community meals, and undertake formal and/or informal affairs. The church building serves as a kind of community center for religious/social interactions, where Battalion (boys meetings), Cadets[28] (girls meetings) and adult fellowships (*ushariki*) take place. Weddings, funerals, and other events occur in and around church property, drawing people together from throughout the community. Meanwhile, membership becomes a critical means for social and economic advancement, as congregants frequently hosts fundraisers (*harambee*) for school fees, wedding preparations, or sending a family member overseas. In such ways, spiritual belonging generates material benefit.

Traditional and biblical values coalesce as the denomination asserts its relevance within the contemporary context, especially considering Kenya's conservative milieu. In asking other denominations what they value most about the AICK, they inevitably mention the strong biblical teaching and commitment to Christian values. A student at Scott Theological College (the highest AICK-sponsored University) was attending Pastor Lai's, Jesus Celebration Centre, which is associated with one of the leading Pentecostal denominations in Kenya. When church leaders

27. Joel Mbai, interview by author, AIC Katelembu, Kenya, Feb. 4, 2007.

28. These names are taken from American para-church organizations. However, the AICK no longer has any direct contact with these Western entities.

discovered he was an AICK member, they immediately asked if he would lead a Bible study. Later, the senior pastor requested the same student to consider teaching within their church-based ministerial training school. Similar stories abound. The AICK has been vocal against the use of condoms to combat HIV-AIDS, as well as attacking abuses related to alcohol, tobacco and drugs. Biblical commitments (especially when framed within traditional values) provide the church significant esteem within most facets of Kenyan society.

The AICK combines modern and traditional identities, enabling members to enjoy freedom of mobility within a wide variety of social contexts. Lay leaders hold notable power within the church. Education remains highly valued, with elders or lay leaders often possessing advanced degrees in secular disciplines, practicing law, or working in various business-related fields. Elders often live in Machakos or Nairobi during the week, but return to their rural homes on weekends where they serve on local church councils and/or are active members of development committees. Rural congregations benefit from their presence and often possess significant material and social influence in their communities, exhibited by sizeable building projects and sociopolitical credibility. This makes the AICK attractive to community members looking for upward mobility. An example would be a local congregation in Kateve, which is located in a small village between Machakos and Kangundo. In 2001, members worshipped in a building constructed out of mud and locally made bricks. Presently, they have a large stone structure capable of seating more than six hundred people. Another congregation meets at Kasinga, less than two kilometres from Kateve, boasting a two-story building capable of seating over one thousand parishioners. These buildings appear incongruous with their surroundings but serve as the confluence of modern and traditional identities. In such ways, the AICK appeals to those who have a foot in both worlds.

Powers: Biblicism

The Bible serves as the central means for communicating modern and traditional values, and the primary authority for guiding ecclesiastical belief and practice. This was the heritage handed down by the missionaries and subsequently reframed by the Africans. The Bible supports many Akamba traditional values, while also supplying believers with "supernatural" powers for confronting contemporary realities. The AICK Constitution begins with a statement regarding the central role of Scripture in the lives of members, declaring: "God's Word is the authority." It then proceeds to describe one of the central responsibilities of the Church as the "defence and confirmation of the Faith."[29] Apologetic reasoning enables the AICK to engage actively in global realities within the framework of traditional loyalties. This point will be further developed later in the chapter.

Every meeting, no matter how small or seemingly insignificant begins with a biblical admonition and prayer. Church services have a first and second reading, where they cover passages from the Old and New Testament respectively, and effectively read through the entire Bible over the course of one (or two) year(s). Before these readings, someone will usually announce, "Let us give attention to the reading of God's Word," and at the conclusion of the passage, "These are the Words of the Lord."

The Bible functions as the primary instrument for growth within the AICK. Children memorize Scripture in Sunday school, Battalion, and Cadets, and sing choruses such as, "Read your Bible, pray everyday, if you want to grow." A lay leader prayed that God would allow "your Word [to] find a way in our hearts, and grow in our hearts."[30] Local youth hosted their yearly camp meetings with the theme, "Growing in the Word; showing others the Word." A pastor began his sermon by asking congregants "Do you have your Bible, do you love it?" and later added, "What does the Lord want us to know from our Bibles?"[31] The constitution cites the main responsibility of the pastor as to "nourish the local church with the Word of God."[32] Thus, the Bible provides central mechanism for applying God's power into contemporary contexts.

The clergy manual prescribes specific Scripture readings for each ordinance (or event) within a calendar year, whether infant dedication, consecration of a building, or comforting the bereaved. Catechismal teaching provides youth with structured biblical training, usually beginning at the age of twelve and lasting one or two years depending on the dictates of the particular District. During catechism, youth learn to respond to basic theological questions with simple biblical propositions of faith and belief, such as, "How may the believer experience joy and abiding peace in his daily life?" and the answer includes, "He should develop

---

29. Africa Inland Church, *Constitution*, 1981, 1.
30. AICK Bomani, Machakos, Kenya, Dec. 21, 2008.
31. Ibid.
32. *Majibizano*, 26.

habits of Bible study," and, "He should memorize Scripture verses."[33] Adults, meanwhile, develop their biblical knowledge through Biblical Education by Extension (BEE) courses where they formally study God's Word and receive certificates necessary for formal positions of leadership in local congregations.

The Bible remains central to testing and/or validating any element of church practice. Because of this, biblical literacy remains a prerequisite for fulfilling any leadership role within the church. Most respondents refer to the Bible as the "ultimate power."[34] All aspects of the church maintain this, whether in preaching or teaching, less often through Bible study. From its rural heritage, the oral presentation of the Gospel (especially in the form of preaching) possesses heightened importance within Ukambani. *Pastor* tends to be synonymous with preacher. When a member of clergy visits a member's home, he or she is expected to expound some element of God's truth. This means that between home visits and regular church fellowships, a pastor may preach more than ten times in a given week. On Sundays, clergy often remain outside the church service only to enter when it is time for the sermon: reinforcing implicit linkages between pastor and preacher.

Governmental authorities further utilize Bible literacy as a way of appealing to their conservative and evangelical constituency. A cabinet minister was visiting an AICK Bible College in Ukambani, and stated, "there is no bigger vocation than the Bible" and later, "the Word of God overrides everything."[35] Churches such as the AICK have contributed to the formation of a significant Biblicism within the country. The Bible combines divine authority with traditional values, in order to confront social, economic or religious problems facing modern societies.

Powers: Pastors and Ecclesiastical Hierarchy

Certain powers are necessary for ministers to fulfil the central role of proclaiming God's Word. Unlike some denominations where pastoral authority extends through sacred and secular spheres of influence, the AICK tends to limit their work to overtly spiritual domains within the church. As will be seen, this narrow sphere of pastoral influence often correlates with certain secularizing tendencies. Pastors are highly respected

33. Ibid., 6.
34. See, Richard Kithome, interview by author, Machakos, Kenya, June 1, 2006.
35. Nduluku Bible Institute, Kiteta, Kenya, Mar. 15, 2008.

for their knowledge of the Bible, yet people associate church ministry as a career for those who could not qualify for university-level education. A student studying at a theological institution shared how many of his friends continually ask why he could not think of a better career than being a pastor. This tension corresponds to power conflicts within the church. Pastors promote the importance of biblical literacy from the pulpit, while elders and other church officials relegate them to a life of poverty due to unusually low salaries (usually only 3000 ksh per month[36] in rural areas) and where funding is dependent upon the approval of the elders (especially for money beyond the basic salary). This may be one of the inadvertent effects of the AIM's faith-based policy, where church members do not want clergy to focus upon financial matters: sometimes envisioning that any association with finance might compromise the pastor's spiritual commitments. Biblical knowledge and (perceived) nearness to God are the pastor's primary powers, and these arise from theological education.

The AICK requires all pastors to attend a sanctioned four-year Diploma or Bachelor in Theology program. There are currently over twenty AICK Bible Colleges throughout the country with more than half in Ukambani. These schools are invariably poor, with scanty libraries and limited facilities, most often in isolated villages such as Mbooni, Nduluku, Nzaui, and Kangundo (on the sites of the early AIM mission stations). Most institutions do not require applicants to have completed secondary education and will admit students with primary school certificates. Support for these institutions by regional church administration remains sporadic. Mbooni Bible Institute provides one example. The school consists of one primary building divided into three separate rooms, existing on the site of one of the earliest mission stations. The facilities are in disrepair and faculty complain of inadequate salaries. Students pay 16,000 ksh per academic year and local churches often struggle to provide this meagre amount. Over fifty students (men and women) attend the Institute,[37] with some coming from distant areas such as Kisumu and West Pokot. Graduates of these institutions typically become pastors or "pastor ladies" in rural churches. Women usually have little or no pastoral authority within the churches; they receive reduced salaries and often oversee hospitality and lead women's fellowships. Yet surprisingly, many

---

36. Approximately $40.
37. Figures reflect the 2007–8 academic year.

of these institutions have an abundance of students (with women rivalling men in numbers). Ukamba Bible College has over 150 students in their unaccredited diploma program; sixty-five of these being women.[38] These figures suggest that while pastoral authority may be perceived as suffering a narrowing scope of influence in church and society (especially related to AICK circles), the thirst for theological education remains as great as ever.

The ecclesiastical structure within the AICK combines various denominational elements, owing to the different traditions of the missionaries. The church's hierarchy borrows from Presbyterian traditions, while the prevalence of elections and much of their theology corresponds with what one might find in a British or American Baptist church. Yet, integration has not always been easy. The church elects a Presiding Bishop, but he maintains little influence in the overall organization, performing duties more in keeping with a Chairman of a council. Even in the years immediately after independence, the church struggled to express its ecclesiology in ways the government could understand. For example, when early AICK leaders attended the inauguration of the first President, Jomo Kenyatta, they arrived dressed in coat and tie, but were turned away because they had no formal ecclesiastical attire to show their respective rankings. Afterwards, they went to the Catholic headquarters to enquire where they might purchase robes. Ever since this time, Bishop, Reverends, and pastors have worn different colored regalia, displayed most conspicuously at formal events such as weddings and ordinations.

On paper, it would appear that the church operates on a top-down structure, beginning with the central church council (CCC) and proceeding to areas (ACC),[39] regions (RCC), districts (DCC), and finally the local church council (LCC). Area Bishops, along with elected lay leaders, comprise the central church council (*Baraza Kuu*) where they make important policy-related decisions for the entire church. However, since congregations give their offerings directly to DCCs (who take their percentage and give the rest to the regional councils, area councils, and finally the central church council), the greatest amount of "power" usually resides at the district level.[40] DCCs oftentimes withhold money from

---

38. Ibid.

39. In 2008, the AICK changed its constitution to allow for the introduction of fourteen "Areas" (similar to dioceses) throughout the country, with a Bishop in charge of each.

40. Another key facet relating to the AIM heritage pertains to the location of

the region and develop sizeable bank balances. Recently, the Presiding Bishop told me of a DCC Chairman who boasted that his district had more than two million Kenya shillings in their bank account (as a result of not giving the required monies to the Region). The *Baraza Kuu* has little authority to regulate these kinds of abuses. District councils consist of a Chairman (ordained pastor), Vice-Chairman (usually, an ordained pastor), Treasurer (lay leader) and Administrative Secretary (usually a lay leader). These people make important decisions for the churches, such as recommendations for licensing and ordination of pastors, allocation of funds, budgets, and pastoral placements. Elections take place every five years, and there are age-related restrictions for these positions where ministers can hold ranking posts if they are over the age of 35 and under 70 years.

Titles for ecclesiastical leaders range from "evangelist," which signifies a low level that can be used indiscriminately for almost anyone with limited biblical training, "pastor," which comes prior to ordination, and "reverend," signifying someone with maturity in pastoral oversight. The title "pastor" is most common, and with fairly loose parameters. When a student begins attending a theological college people typically call him (or her) "pastor." Elders may also assume this title when they occupy a teaching position within a church in the absence of a trained pastor. One local MP has people call him "pastor" because he sometimes preaches within his local congregation. The pathway to ordination is strict and takes a long time. After someone has graduated from Bible College, he must serve for one year before licensing (reserved only for men). This allows the pastor to conduct baptism, dedication of children, and the Lord's Supper. Women may serve as "pastor ladies," be chaplains in hospitals, prisons, or secondary schools, or teach in one of the many Bible Schools, but are exempted from formal positions of licensed or ordained ministry. After licensing, the pastor must be married and serve three additional years (after marriage) before he can proceed with ordination. Then, he needs to wait until the DCC, RCC, and ACC recommends his ordination before the Central Church Office. It is common for this process to

---

missionary governance. Many of the faith-based missions (following the pioneering work of Hudson Taylor and the CIM) believed that it was essential for missionary decisions to be made locally, by the missionary, and not from distant American or European headquarters. This conviction would be an enduring legacy of the AIM, and one imparted to the church: suggested through the prominent role that Districts contribute in terms of ecclesiastical governance.

take ten years (or more) due to church politics. Bishops and Chairmen of regional councils must be ordained ministers. The greater number of eligible "reverends," the more competition for limited seats of power. Furthermore, since only ordained ministers can officiate marriages (and there are additional financial compensations for these services) district or regional leaders often delay recommending applicants for ordination so as to not restrict their access to these funds.

Deacons are appointed by the LCC to care for the temporal needs of *washariki*. Local congregations further elect elders, who serve five-year terms. These people are chosen from amongst the list of official members who attend communion (the Lord's Supper), and have completed at least five BEE courses, or other approved Bible training programs. Together with the pastor(s), elders are supposed to "develop the spiritual life of the local church through evangelism, preaching the Word of God, nurturing and admonition of the members, and visitation."[41] Yet in reality, elders often assume responsibility for "secular" affairs, leaving spiritual matters for pastors.

The AICK structure, with actualized (or, real) power residing at the district level does afford the church considerable flexibility in adjusting to local concerns (with tendencies that mirror AIM field-based governance practices). The *Baraza Kuu* prescribes the policies and practices for all churches (in accordance with the Constitution); yet, great variance exists amongst districts pertaining to the implementation of policy and how they hold theological beliefs. One district requires women to wear head coverings when teaching at Nduluku Bible Institute and preach at a lower pulpit than the men, while another offers women full pastoral authority, salary, and respect in their churches. Some districts actively engage in community development practices while others exhibit certain *charismatic* elements within their local churches, with vigorous singing and greater focus on recognizable gifts and miracles. Even the use of finances reveals disparity. One district may amass considerable financial resources for construction projects, while another allows local churches to increase the pay of their pastors and/or invest discretionary funds into local community projects. The prevalence of power at the district level provides important currents for the growth of the church, challenging the common stereotype of mission-founded churches as hierarchical and lacking *grassroots* relevance. While the AICK may be deficient in displaying some

---

41. *AICK Constitution*, 1981, 5.

of the centralized authority of mainline churches (suggested by less active involved in political and/or socioeconomic endeavors) the real power of the AICK resides in districts. These comments need to inform any analysis regarding the relevancy and growth of the denomination, especially within Ukambani.

Power within the AICK is thus an attribute of mobility between traditional and modern values, the application of the sacred into secular domains, and the product of the church's proximity to local communities. Educated lay leaders mediate between urban and rural communities. Their presence, and especially the prevalence of sizeable building projects, attracts people to the church who are looking for upward mobility. Early AIM missionaries stressed local identities through translation work and living in rural communities. The AICK perpetuates these characteristics through the use of Kikamba and how the denomination often functions as a territorial church, fulfilling some of the roles of former Akamba councils. The Bible provides instrumental mechanism for growth: connecting God's power with local communities. Pastors use apologetic reasoning to inject supernatural faith commitments into rapidly changing social contexts (explained in more detail below). As such, theological education shows no signs of diminished importance. The AIM believed that field-based governance was essential for their leadership to manage the needs facing the missionaries. In similar ways, the AICK maintain power at the DCC level (in close proximity to local congregations), showing elements of continuity with its missionary-based heritage. The AIM began as a movement mobilizing lay leaders. The AICK continues to maintain emphasis upon lay leaders, but with tensions existing between clergy and laity. The remainder of this chapter will explore various aspects of the denomination in terms of larger, sociological concepts: most notably, secularization and rationalization, and specifically, how divine power provides valuable resources for the church to engage in broader, social currents.

SECULARIZATION

The process of probing deeper into the dynamics of power within the AICK reveals a narrowing influence given to the "sacred" that bears similarity with Western forms of secularization. Initially, what I am proposing appears in contradistinction to what scholars like as Monga[42] and

---

42. Monga, *The Anthropology*, 127–37.

Africa Inland Church: Secularization and Rationalization

Venter[43] describe about African societies, where they argue that the topic of secularization cannot apply to this context due to the ubiquitous nature of religiosity on the continent. Others like Jules-Rosette, caution against using Western definitions of secularization for interpreting African contexts.[44] While these points are important for the overall development of this section, it is important to recall the earlier discussion related to the AIM missionaries and how, in reaction to Western modernizing influences, and spirited by their blend of revivalistic, evangelical thought, the missionaries provided distinctions and separations between the sacred and secular, albeit with some mobility between the two. Therefore, any resultant secularization has already been interpreted/modified no less than two times: first by the missionaries, and thereafter by the Africans. This needs to inform the following discussion.

Sacred and Secular Tensions

Pastors have responsibility for preaching God's word. This often stands in contrast to other activities within the church, such as development (often viewed solely in terms of building projects) or business-related affairs (i.e. financial management). These activities tend to be the sole domain of lay leaders. It is important to recall that the AIM itself grew out of the lay leader movement within late nineteenth century evangelicalism, and has likewise imparted a prominent role for laity within its daughter church.

Elders and pastor(s) are supposed to jointly oversee the "spiritual life of the local church," but in reality, they tend to assume different responsibilities that often conflict with each other. A typical order of service highlights some of these contrasts. Pastors sit on one side of the podium and elders on the other. The worship begins with singing and prayers. The elders may or may not be involved with this part of the service, and are often huddled together discussing business-related affairs. In rural churches, the singing can last for two hours, with various groups performing songs, followed by the Scripture reading. At the conclusion of this time, the service moves in the direction of secular or material matters, such as announcements (led by an elder, and often taking upwards to an hour), auction of vegetables or other "first fruits," followed by the offering (usually more than one). This part of the service tends to be quite lengthy and highlights the central function of the elders

---

43. Venter, *Engaging Modernity*, 4.
44. Jules-Rosette, "Sacred in African New Religions," 152–53.

related to business matters. Finally, as the time prolongs, one of the elders announces, "Now, it is time for us to hear from the man of God as he speaks God's Word to us." Available time for preaching suffers from the protracted announcements/business, and the abrupt transition gives the impression of something new and different occurring. Parishioners are dismissed at the conclusion of the sermon; or the elders may return to some important point(s) of business before asking the pastor to give the final benediction.

Lay leaders, by virtue of their "secular" education (and/or business/civil service experience), possess heightened powers within local congregations. I usually begin interviews with the question, "Who has the greatest power(s) in the church?" Invariably, respondents reply that it is the elders or educated laity. One pastor explained the significance of these powers: "The people that are led, as well as some leaders, think that power is supposed to be this way or that way [as experienced in society]; if they follow politics, or companies, or schools; so they have tasted it and want it to experience it in the church."[45] People refer to this as "professionalism" and actively seek to transfer it from secular to sacred domains. For example, educated elders increasingly assert their role in choosing pastors for local congregations (something typically ascribed to the District or Regional officers) and decide how to use local funds. Even though the Constitution clearly states that the Pastor should be the Chairman of the LCC (and development committee), in practice, elders often marginalize them and/or prevent them from serving in these roles. In one local church, an elder with a doctorate insisted on being the Chairman, relegating the pastor to serve as his assistant since he had only a first degree in theology.

Development often indicates church building construction (alternatively, the purchase of musical instruments, or a vehicle). Sometimes the development committee of a local congregation has more power than the LCC, since they handle larger amounts of money and may comprise influential business leaders. Tensions exist between spiritual and material priorities. One lay leader explained his frustration that his church focuses upon spiritual matters but does not think about development and the material needs of the people. He said, "Occasionally you find meetings on evangelism, when we are denying our local people the rights to

---

45. Richard Kithome, interview by author, Machakos, Kenya, June 1, 2006.

accessibilities and necessities, like . . . health care and the environment."[46] Elders may oppose the Constitution (like in the case of an elder serving as the LCC Chairmen) because their "secular" experience tells them that things should happen in other ways. Alternatively, pastors will decry elders, accusing them of neglecting the spiritual values found in the Bible. They fear that a church led by elders will not be "theologically sound."[47]

However, the discontinuity between pastor (preaching) and elder (business) should not indicate a complete bifurcation of powers. Elders respect spiritual authority and pastors seek greater secular status. The main task of an elder is to care for "the spiritual life of the Church," which requires formal biblical training. Frequent requests come to Scott Theological College for various training programs. One man enquired about such a course of study. I shared different options with him and asked why he wanted to study; he simply answered, "I want to preach." Theological education provides one important gateway for elders to access spiritual powers and expand their influence within local congregations.

While secular leaders often pursue biblical knowledge as a means of increasing their influence, pastors are equally desirous of attaining certain secular powers. These may come through the acquisition of higher degrees, wearing expensive clothes, or through other material purchases. One minister explained that he holds the respect of his LCC because he has a Masters degree (in Theology) and owns a vehicle. These secular symbols secure him greater status among the educated elite within his urban congregation. However, it is very hard for rural pastors to achieve this kind of esteem. One of few options available for them is to pursue higher degrees in theology. It is common for a four-year diploma-holder from Ukamba Bible College to enroll at Scott Theological College for a three-year degree course. After completion, these graduates proceed to institutions offering Masters of Theology (such as Nairobi Evangelical Graduate School of Theology (NEGST), or Nairobi International School of Theology). The pursuit of education reflects elements of insecurity among spiritual leaders in local congregations. Alumni of STC are continually urging institutional leaders to begin programs in community development, human resource management, financial management and organizational leadership. They want to be able to interact with elders on their own terms and demonstrate that their theological education has

---

46. Timothy Makau, interview by author, Katelembu, Kenya, Feb. 4, 2007.
47. Dionysius Malusi, interview by author, Machakos, Kenya, Nov. 2008.

secular credibility. Yet, despite these propensities, the number of students attending Bible Colleges continues to grow, showing that spiritual power occupies a prominent role within AICK congregations. These points need to inform any secularizing trends within the denomination.

Another facet related to the discussion of secularization comes through looking at elements of discontinuity between pastoral ministry and politics (or any other type of secular activity). The church constitution states,

> A Pastor who enters politics shall relinquish his pastoral responsibilities. His Diocesan Church Council shall revoke his licence or ordination and inform the Government Registrar. His license or ordination certificate shall be turned into the Diocesan Church Council. Such a person, who subsequently leaves politics, shall not be reinstated to a pastoral position. He shall not be eligible to hold a leadership position in the church for a period of at least five years.[48]

When I probed deeper the reasons for this stance, respondents usually quoted Jesus' words in Matthew 6, that one cannot serve two masters (meaning God and money). Political positions invariably involve association with large amounts of money; while the pastor's "calling" cannot (in the minds of many) be compromised by secular affairs. In another instance, a pastor enjoyed the practice of jogging in the community until members of his church politely informed him that this type of activity was not appropriate for his "calling." This kind of separation reflects the earlier missionary heritage coming out of the spiritual revivals of the nineteenth century, where evangelicals demarcated clear lines of discontinuity between God and the world. The pastor's "calling" is sacred and his or her duties should only relate to the ministry of the Word; this therefore means that he or she should abstain from anything perceived to be worldly.

Payment of clergy remains another source of tension. Members generally believe that pastors should not be concerned with issues related to finances, since their allegiance is solely to God. The AIM's *faith-based* policy for raising funds required that missionaries devote themselves to the ministry of the Gospel and trust God for material needs. Africans observed these practices and adopted similar notions for their treatment

---

48. Africa Inland Church, *Constitution*, 2005, 35. The *Baraza Kuu* is in the process of formalising the new Constitution. It is unclear if this section is among those already ratified.

of pastors, resulting in unusually low salaries. Students entering Scott Theological College report questioning resistance from family members and friends why they do not pursue a secular degree in medicine or accounting, rather than making them beggars. Low remuneration often lead clergy into taking second or third jobs (as chaplains in secondary schools or teaching in Bible colleges) in order to increase their earnings and prove their material legitimacy to elders in local congregations; while others leave the AICK to serve in other churches. People joke that the AICK is a nursery for training pastors in other denominations. Area churches respect AICK's system of theological education and entice pastors away with attractive salary packages, or other benefits.[49] The conflict is inevitably with the elders. Many of these intentionally or inadvertently keep the clergy poor, whether to accent the minister's spiritual calling or increase dependence upon the elders. One student talked openly about these struggles, and how financial dependency often correlates with decreased confidence in confronting corruption or spiritual laxity within the congregation; he surmised: "a pastor who is financially stable will not be afraid to give the whole counsel of God and no one will undermine him with money."[50] As pastors receive more education they purchase greater material powers in church and society.

Theological Characteristics

The prevalence of these tensions within the church may arise from distinctive features within their theological heritage. One of the most notable relates to the dislocation of divine and human elements; seen, for example, in how the church interprets the person of Jesus Christ. The early twentieth century saw the search for the historical Jesus and other movements questioning (or reinterpreting) Christ's divinity. During the same period, the social gospel rose to prominence and stressed the humanity of Christ as a means of enabling the Church with necessary theological resources for addressing mounting societal needs. Conservative aspects of evangelicalism (of which the AIM was a part) interpreted any reference to Christ's humanity as an attack against Jesus' divinity, and responded by overemphasizing Christ's supernatural nature (often, at the expense of his humanity); eventually imparting such a heritage to their churches. The AICK catechism asks the question, "If Jesus Christ is the

---

49. Such as expedited pathways to ordination, or greater honor.
50. Dionysius Malusi, interview by author, Machakos, Kenya, Nov. 2008.

Son of God, how did He become man?" and the answer states, "Jesus Christ the Son of God became man by receiving a truly human body, being born of the Virgin Mary by the power of the Holy Spirit."[51] While affirming the humanity of Christ, this statement suggests that Jesus' humanity applies only to his body (essentially espousing a form of Apollinarianism). I frequently asked my students at STC when they have ever heard (or preached) a sermon in one of their churches touching upon Jesus' humanity and rarely has a student responded in the affirmative. Many times, however, Jesus' divinity has been the subject of ecclesiastical discourse, usually as a means of defending the faith and/or positing supernatural authority to the Gospel. Yet, lessened emphasis on Jesus' humanity hints that church members may have less theological resources in which to *apply* the power of salvation to the everyday vicissitudes of human existence, since the divine and human have no central locus in the Body of Christ. The doctrines most frequently addressed from AICK pulpits are: Christ's deity, salvation, the cross, sin, and Scripture; while those receiving less attention are: creation, humanity and the Holy Spirit. The primary means that the AICK have for *applying* divine power into human life is the doctrine of the Bible, which tends to receive heightened emphasis in order to compensate for lesser prominence given to other beliefs.

While the AICK displays currents of secularization through dichotomies and tensions existing between the sacred and secular, their strong belief in the Bible and its prominence in ordering all affairs (related to the church and even extending into society) represent countermeasures against Western notions of secularization. In like manner, Jules-Rosette suggests that any religious analysis within Africa should consider that secularization and re-sacralization "may constitute two complimentary poles of a single phenomenon."[52] Her comments were in the context of new African religious movements, but similar arguments might apply to mission-founded churches and especially how the AICK reasserts itself into secular contexts through theological education (and the Bible). This will be the focus of the next section.

51. *Majibizano*, 28–29.
52. Jules-Rosette, "The Sacred," 154.

RATIONALIZATION

John Gration's study into the relationship between the AIM and AICK highlights the strategic role that education played in the history and growth of the denomination, noting, "The Church of the Africa Inland Mission not only came into existence largely through the instrumentality of education but continued to increase through this agency."[53] While Gration's intent was to relate these comments to the AICK's involvement in primary and secondary education, the same can be said for theological training and how this forum has provided the church with important resources for growing within the post-colonial world.

As stated earlier, evangelicalism furnished the initial apparatus for engaging with modernity: enabling the AIM to adopt certain Enlightenment resources and resist others (particularly those coming under the pejorative use of the term *modernism*). By espousing a *literal* understanding of the Bible, the missionaries utilized various Enlightenment tools, including scientific reasoning and/or positivistic logic for the defense of God's Word. At the same time, however, they rejected liberal forms of Christianity operating in America and Europe in the late nineteenth and early twentieth centuries. These, the AIM believed, undermined the authority and supernatural origin of Scriptures by subjecting them to rationalistic forms of criticism. Evangelicalism thus became an instrument for Enlightenment thinking, as well as a force in resisting it. An example of how these seemingly antithetical elements merged appears in a document written by an AIM missionary, explaining the concept of modernism to African leaders: "This is the belief that the Bible is not wholly true and must be tested by our reason so that it seems impossible or wrong, the modernist will refuse to believe it and will say it is a mistake." Yet the document proceeds to give the response, "Our reason tells us that if God gave us a perfect Saviour, the living Word, to die for us, He has also gave us a perfect Book, the written Word, to teach us. This is common sense. A perfect Saviour and an imperfect Book, from an omnipotent God—this does not make sense."[54] In the first half of the statement, the missionary opposes any tendency to validate truth claims made in the Bible through the use of "reason," while in the second half, the author explains that "reason" and "common sense" informs the divinely inspired Word. This apologetic stance defines the AICK's engagement with the world around

---

53. Gration, *The Relationship*, 346.
54. "A Short Memo."

them and signifies a unique kind of rationalism coming into Africa: one committed to the supernatural origins of Scripture while supportive of the use of human reason for the defense of God's Word. This heritage would be valuable for the AICK.

If the quest for reading and writing represents certain currents in the process of Africans interacting with modernity, theological education provides another; most notably, by allowing mobility and engagement with global forces and a commensurate identity to confidently handle the Word of God. This rationalism (as I am calling it) corresponds to the use of reason associated with biblical knowledge, but also deviates from the kind coming out of the Enlightenment by its supernatural commitments and the particular way(s) it relates to ontological concerns. I will explain some of the internal logic of this rationalism, especially as it pertains to an apologetic posture within the world, and hence highlight how theological education provides the AICK with significant powers for the development of spiritual forms of rationalism.

Apologetic Rationalism

The AIM formally entered theological education in 1928 with the founding of Ukamba Bible Institute.[55] Since that time, the missionaries (and subsequently, AICK) have established similar institutions all throughout Kenya. More than twenty diploma-level institutions exist in the country, with at least half residing in Ukambani (in places such as Machakos, Nzaui, Mbooni, Kangundo, Kitui, Nduluku, and Wote). Even institutions in other provinces are likely to have large numbers of Akamba students. For example, Moffat Bible College in Kijabe has eighteen of its sixty-five students coming from Ukambani,[56] even though it is a regionally operated school in the Central Province. Similar demographics appear for non-AICK institutions such as Nairobi Evangelical Graduate School of Theology (NEGST) and Nairobi International School of Theology (NIST). What is more, these institutions sometimes struggle to find Kenyan faculty from non-AICK backgrounds, and have a prevalence of Akamba lecturers. These points are self-evident to those working in theological colleges in Kenya. In probing the reasons for this, people refer to the early efforts of the missionaries in this region. Yet this can only serve as part of the total answer, since it was earlier shown that the missionaries

---

55. Later changing their name to Ukamba Bible College.
56. Figures reflect enrollment numbers during the academic year 2007–2008.

were not content to remain in Ukambani but moved to other parts of the country, and even other nations, soon after the turn-of-the-century. A fuller explanation outlining the importance of theological education for the Akamba requires looking into the *content* of theological education and how this relates to epistemological and ontological concerns.

Due to the AICK's lessened emphasis on the Holy Spirit, humanity and creation, the Bible assumes extra responsibility in *applying* salvation and/or connecting humans with divine power. The doctrines of inspiration and inerrancy lend requisite supernatural foundations to the origins of God's Word, while teachings related to illumination provides pastors (less often laity) with power for interpreting Scriptures within contemporary contexts. Bible colleges teach these beliefs to their students (often during the first or second year of studies), followed by separate courses that cover each book within the corpus of Scriptures. Biblical knowledge furnishes Pastors with everything necessary for navigating through the many troubles and travails associated with contemporary society; since, "All Scripture is God-breathes and is useful for teaching, rebuking, correcting and training in righteousness, so that the man of God may be thoroughly equipped for every good work" (2 Tim. 3:16–17).[57] The AICK understands the "man of God" as the pastor; and takes seriously the relevance of Scripture "for every good work" (inclusive of all aspects of life).

Students at Scott Theological College (STC) take courses in Biblical Criticism where they defend Scripture against liberal approaches to God's Word; or, write comprehensive examinations on the doctrines of bibliology and soteriology. These theological beliefs under gird the overall education with sacred power. In such ways, students gain experience in defending God's truth against global systems of belief. They become agents of spiritual power within the contemporary world.

This occurs in many different ways throughout their overall education. One of the most significant is by learning the "original languages" (more often Greek than Hebrew). Ukamba Bible College offers six terms of Greek in their diploma-level program (equivalent to two years of study). These courses are required for graduation. Students in STC's diploma program recently requested the administration to allow them to study Greek "like the other Bible Colleges," feeling that they were being unjustly disadvantaged in their ministerial training. The ability to preach and/or teach from Greek texts provides valuable powers for deciphering

---

57. All Bible references will be quoted in the New International Version (NIV) unless otherwise stated.

the meaning of Scripture and instructing parishioners with authority. Pastors alone have this knowledge. A sermon at AICK Mumbuni shows some of these realities. While exegeting a particular passage of Scripture, a Bible college student (who had not studied Greek or Hebrew) proceeded to talk about "the right meaning from the original languages."[58] The use of the word *right* indicates something irrefutable and known only to those equipped with this special knowledge. This represents a form of positivistic rationalism, albeit one laced with sacred power. Parishioners respond favorably when their pastor commands this kind of expertise. In one sense, biblical positivism affords certainty in a world where few things are actually certain. People expect "right" answers to hard theological quandaries. The pastor (many people believe) resides closer to God, nearer to spiritual powers, more *like God* in terms of spirituality, and therefore functions as a kind of mediator between divine and human realms.

Another way this rationalism appears is through the study of apologetics. These types of courses are common to all AICK theological institutions yet with different varieties. In one course, students learn about global forces (such as secularism, modernism, rationalism and other philosophical systems of analysis) and practice ways of defending the Bible against their claims, effectively motivating students to engage in global discourse.[59] Sacred powers contest rival ideologies within the world. The same applies to African and worldwide cults. Time is devoted to examining the various belief systems of these religious movements, particularly with a view toward defending Scriptures against their respective beliefs and/or evangelizing their adherents. Apologetic courses extend, as well, to the study of worldwide religions, and particularly Islam. Authority claims between the Bible and Qur'an are compared and contrasted; students use human reason and the inerrancy of Scripture to evaluate between the two. Through such courses, students interact (hypothetically, through assessment exercises; or experientially, through field education assignments) in ways that build personal confidence in the employment of God's Word.

Besides the obvious appeal of standing on the side of divine authority, apologetics is attractive because it employs human reason for the

---

58. AICK Mumbuni, Machakos, Kenya, June 29, 2008.

59. In a similar manner, Stambach argues for a reverse in the "classical-modernist" paradigm, where she highlights Kenyans' "attention to rationality" and American missionaries' animistic approach to African Christianity; see "Spiritual Warfare," 140.

Africa Inland Church: Secularization and Rationalization

purposes of enabling pastors to function as agents in the face of nebulous global forces: combining rationality with supernatural affirmations. Around Christmastime, a pastor preached on the "historical fact" of the virgin birth, emphasizing its reasonableness against rival claims.[60] Another spoke during an Easter service on the historic reality of the resurrection, arguing for its validity based upon the testimony of an angel.[61] A recent book co-written by an AIM missionary and eleven students at NEGST (five of whom are AICK) demonstrate the appeal of this kind of reasoning. The title, *Popular Objections, Powerful Answers: The ABCs of Defending the Christian Faith in Africa*,[62] suggests direct connections between apologetics and power. Throughout the book, Christians confront objections to the Gospel through reasoned and persuasive dialogue. The conversational tone adopted by the writers appeals to relational predispositions found within African communities and highlights the need for sensitivity and compassion in dealing with those of other beliefs. Fictitious characters dialogue with one another in the text, and represent a particular kind of "power encounter." For example, a University student named Ahmed (implying a Muslim adherent) talks with Wangari (a Christian) about certain presumed inaccuracies in the Bible. Wangari responds to Ahmed's objections by appealing to her own faith commitments, while combining these with certain anthropological, historical, and scientific evidences.[63] She engages Ahmed in sensitive, reasoned, and personal appeal. Apologetics thus provides a mechanism for combining rationalism with supernatural authority.

Similar to how Pentecostal Christianity envisions a cosmos of conflictual forces, the AICK imagine similar hostilities, but where biblical knowledge positions pastors (less often parishioners) with power to confront any number of religious or secular beliefs within the contemporary world. In the case of Pentecostalism, the Holy Spirit equips humans with spiritual power in order to oppose evil spirits; while for the AICK, pastors utilize supernatural commitments associated with God's Word (combined with human reason) to confront any number of religious/secular/moral ideologies present within the world. The AICK's Constitution supports these perspectives as it defines the Church's main priority in terms of "the

---

60. AICK Makyao, Dec. 23, 2007.
61. AICK Bomani, Mar. 23, 2008.
62. *Popular Objections*.
63. Ibid. 23–30.

defense and confirmation of the Faith (Jude 3)."⁶⁴ Pastors represent the central agents in this process, as they are the ones equipped with spiritual powers related to the transmission and interpretation of God's Word. Preaching within the AICK carries a strong apologetic tone, where pastors are constantly confronting something (gossip, lack of commitment, poor giving, or wrong beliefs) and/or reacting against prevailing beliefs (corruption, tribalism, secularism, or materialism). People respect the AICK's biblical foundations, especially related to its apologetic postures. For example, in Machakos town, it is not uncommon for youth to attend the Redeemed Gospel Church, Eastleigh for their worship (singing) and then walk the short distance to AICK Bomani in time for the sermon. In such ways, youth show how AICK preaching appeals to their desire to connect supernatural commitments (found in the Bible) with contemporary realities, especially through reasoned entreaty (highly esteemed within modern Kenyan society).

Theological education offers other benefits, as well, especially related to ontological concerns. Mastery of biblical languages provides pastors with informal membership within global evangelicalism. Through these skills (such as biblical exegesis) pastors read commentaries written by international scholars, attend conferences, collect libraries, and develop their status as theological experts. Biblical knowledge likewise provides access to global seminaries (most often in America). The Presiding Bishop recently travelled to Dallas, Texas, (USA) to speak with two hundred AICK pastors living around the city. Many of these initially came to America in order to study at Dallas Theological Seminary. AICK pastors may also be found living around Trinity Evangelical Divinity School in Illinois and Fuller Theological Seminary in California. The attraction to these types of institutions may stem from AIM's origin as an American-based mission. The historic perception of America as a Christian nation further accentuates this cultural appeal: adorning sacred powers to "externality."⁶⁵ Airline tags linger on briefcases years after international travel; Western goods are symbols that one has purchasing power outside of Kenya; modified accents show that someone has lived "abroad." One pastor casually told me, "Everyone knows that the best theological education comes from America."

---

64. *Katibu*, 1.
65. Gifford, *African Christianity*, 318.

Africa Inland Church: Secularization and Rationalization

At the same time, these associations with the West correlate with recent trends within global evangelicalism that privilege non-Western perspectives on biblical studies. The recent *Africa Bible Commentary*[66] contains hundreds of essays from African evangelicals dealing with texts of Scripture (often finding a more favorable readership in America than Africa). Most of the contributors received advanced theological training in American or British universities, and may reflect some of these cultural influences through their writings. Despite these possible predilections, however, biblical knowledge (particularly when combined with "original languages") places theological graduates within global flows of knowledge and increasingly lends them credence and recognition on international stages.

Bible colleges in Kenya often function like former mission stations where they serve as "centres of social reintegration in very fluid and changing circumstances."[67] A pastor and lecturer explained that many graduates of STC fail to return to their home areas (especially those coming from rural communities) because "they become changed."[68] He was not just referring to typical growth patterns associated with learning institutions, but a profound reorientation of being that comes from learning and living within a diverse theological community. On one level, degrees or diplomas indicate new status within society. However, the *kind* of education also contributes to shaping the particular characteristics of that social standing. When graduates leave such institutions, they often struggle to find personal satisfaction in rural communities. Greek or Hebrew requires access to commentaries, which may or may not be accessible within their former villages. Diplomas or degrees lead to greater earning potential than are typically reflected by rural pastoral salaries, placing them at odds with elders in local congregations. Rational discourse may not be readily esteemed in rural communities. Membership within the broader evangelical communities requires access to books, forums, and resources to enable graduates to interact with like-minded persons. The personal confidence gained in apologetics leads pastors to covet the kind of diverse interactions found in urban pastorates, chaplaincy, or graduate institutions. These factors translate into high percentages of Akamba pastors serving in Nairobi churches, or studying in theological schools.

---

66. Adeyemo (ed.), *Africa Bible*.
67. Strayer, *Making of Mission Communities*, 59.
68. Shadrack Mukoma, interview by author, 23 Mar. 2008, Machakos, Kenya.

A distinctive feature of pastoral identity corresponds to orientation(s) the student receives with God's Word. Biblical knowledge (and its application vis-à-vis the world) leads to heightened social confidence. Activities such as preaching, teaching, and evangelism, enable students to address local and global concerns; sacred authority (combined with the Great Commission) propels them into active engagement with the world. Internship and field education assignments build upon this to provide actual experience in sharing the Gospel with members of other religious beliefs. One student explained to me that prior coming to STC he never had the confidence to evangelize a university-trained person; but now, he actively seeks such kinds of interactions. Theological education opens these students to seemingly unlimited possibilities. Biblical knowledge (combined with human reason) positions graduates of theological institutions where they can function as powerful agents within contemporary societies.

Apologetics combines reason with revelation. However, these do not always receive equal considerations within the various theological institutions. Some schools privilege supernatural powers of God's Word, and teach their students to memorize verses and preach, "Thus says the Lord." This is particularly the case for rural Bible Colleges where spiritual power holds greater influence within local communities. Other schools place more value on critical thinking skills: encouraging students to wrestle with their understanding of God's Word as pertains to contemporary issues (such as STC). Regardless of the particular emphasis, all of the institutions focus upon applying biblical truth to everyday realities: "contending for the faith" (Jude 3); "guard(ing) the good deposit" (2 Tim. 1:14); "holding fast the Word of life" (Phil. 2:16); or being "always prepared to give an answer to everyone who asks you to give the reason for the hope that you have" (1 Pet. 3:15). These powers do not merely apply to isolated spheres of spiritual realities, but relate to larger, contemporary issues.

Conservatism and Higher Education

The *rationalism* encountered and cultivated at theological institutions is particularly attractive against two broader currents within Kenyan society: conservatism and Higher Education. Biblical knowledge maintains high respect in the country due to the strong missionary foundations. Newspaper editorials, political speeches and even *matatu* (public transportation vehicles) broadcast overt biblical messages. The number of theological colleges surrounding the capital is staggering compared with global cities of comparable size. A modest estimate (not considering many of the smaller schools) reveals no less than fifteen theological institutions within one hundred kilometres of the city[69]

Kenya's conservatism thus stems from a combination of its earlier missionary heritage, a blending of biblical teachings with traditional values, and the role that churches have contributed to higher education. Many current governmental and educational leaders passed through mission-founded secondary schools, and almost all private Universities have Christian origins, including: Catholic University, Kenyan Methodist University, Scott Theological College, University of Eastern Africa Baraton, Africa Nazarene University, St. Paul's University, and Pan Africa Christian University. Nondenominational organizations such as the Fellowship of Christian Unions (FOCUS), which are prevalent in secondary schools and Universities throughout the country, have likewise contributed to the religious conservatism apparent in church and society. Pentecostalism, especially from the 1970s, took advantage of the Christian Unions to nurture charismatic elements of faith and practice. More recently, Pentecostalism has entered into Higher Education with the charter of Pan Africa Christian University (PACU), showing staying power (and institutionalization) within contemporary Kenyan society. Meetings with governmental leaders typically begin with prayer. At a recent forum with the CHE, a ranking member concluded the day by thanking "God for his Son, Jesus Christ and his blood shed for the sins of the world." Such references to the Christian faith are common at almost every different level of government and civil society, though not always with such overt theological language. The proliferation of evangelical missions (in short-term teams and missions societies) continues to carve deep contours into the religious and moral landscape of Kenya, encouraged and sustained by the prevalence of Christian NGOs.[70] The Kenya Anti-Corruption Commission recently initiated a campaign appealing to those holding Christian convictions, it involves a slogan "Corruption is

---

69. This list includes Scott Theological College, East Africa Integrated University (formerly Mitaboni Divinity School), Ukamba Bible College, Daystar University, NEGST, NIST, Pan African Christian University, St. Paul's University, Moffat Bible College, East African School of Theology, Africa Nazarene University, Catholic University, Pan Africa School of Theology, Carlile College, and Presbyterian Seminary.

70. See Hearn, "The 'Invisible,'" 32–60.

Evil" accompanied by a Bible Study course entitled, "Integrity: a weapon against corruption."[71] Therefore, the AICK is not exceptional in regard to its conservatism, but representative of larger currents of thought: where biblical affirmations combine with traditional values to inculcate religious power into social settings.[72]

Concurrent to this Christian conservatism, higher education continues to assume an enlarged role within Kenyan society, especially with increased emphasis given to "secular" faculties such as science and technology. Under the current Presidential administration, there is pressure for all institutions to diversify their programs. Scott Theological College remains the only chartered University in Kenya with sole focus given to theological education.[73] Other Universities traditionally committed to ministerial training have adjusted to these larger, societal pressures; including St Paul's University, which has recently added programs in Business Administration to their traditional program in Divinity. Nairobi Evangelical Graduate School of Theology (NEGST) is changing its name to Africa International University and adding new faculties in Professional Studies to posture itself before the CHE in the hopes of receiving a charter. Scott Theological College has likewise mounted a Master of Education program, attempting to navigate between its mission of training church leaders while responding to the need for diversification (and integration) with other secular disciplines.

While some of these changes have had adverse impact upon student enrolment in departments of Theology, Scott Theological College and the AICK continues to be an exception. STC received its charter from the CHE in 1997, despite having only one faculty (Theology). While this would be difficult (if not impossible) under the current political administration, the College has since received its certificate of reaccreditation and maintains strong relationships with the CHE. STC currently has more than two hundred students enrolled in its programs of theological studies. Compare this with Kenya Methodist University, which has

---

71. See www.kacc.go.ke.

72. However, it may be exceptional in the prominence it gives to biblical admonition.

73. At a recent meeting of the *Baraza Kuu*, the church approved the change of name to Scott Christian University, with the introduction of new campuses throughout the country with faculties such as medicine, communications, chaplaincy, education, and missions. The proposed change needs approval by the CHE and to be gazetted by the Parliament.

forty students in their department of Theology with more than six thousand students enrolled in other faculties.[74] Diversification of programs sometimes leads to marginalizing influences upon ministerial training; however, the AICK resists these tendencies through the strength that it places upon the Bible and how the apologetic nature of Scriptures equips students to act as agents of power within contemporary societies. Therefore, it may be argued that the AIM's earlier emphasis upon spiritual matters (especially in regard to its educational policies) may have been more effective than previously thought. The AICK utilizes supernatural powers associated with biblical knowledge to position themselves as notable contributors within Kenyan higher education.

There are many possible reasons why theological education has proven so attractive to the Akamba. Early AIM work began in this region and created space for Africans to negotiate agency using spiritual motifs: whether training programs at Ukamba Bible Institute, Bible translation, or through Kikamba hymns. "Supernatural" priorities given to the Bible often found points of correspondence with the religious worldviews of the Akamba. Furthermore, the rise of diploma-level institutions often parallels the regionalization of Akamba society. The Akamba have historically operated under regional authority structures rather than central administration: clans versus kingship. The AICK's propensity to place power at the district level often mirrors the governance-patterns of the Akamba. Each district (or region) typically favors its own training institutions, thus contributing to the relative ubiquity of Bible Colleges in Ukambani. Another reason may stem from the historical associations of the Akamba with trade, and how theological education provides commensurate networks of mobility and engagement with broader (global) communities. Finally, the conservatism found in Kenyan society receives much of its impetus from regions such as Ukambani, where churches function as instrumental agents in fostering moral (traditional) values. Some of the smaller theological institutions, such as Nduluku Bible Institute, stand as bastions of conservatism, resisting broader liberal trends within church and society.[75]

Hence, while the AICK struggles with certain dichotomies related to the sacred and secular, there is no notion of the church retreating into isolated spiritual realms (nor secularizing its educational institutions).

74. June 2008 figures.
75. A similar point was made by Christopher Rutto in his study of the Nandi and the ACK; see Rutto, *Nandi Identity*, 142.

Theological education provides specific powers for engaging with global forces. Pastors utilize the Bible to lead their congregations through *power encounters* that exist within the contemporary world. They accomplish this by combining supernatural elements (indicative of traditional societies) with rationalism (privileged by modern societies). Institutions such as Scott Theological College give expression to the ways that supernaturalism and rationalism combine within the confines of a private Kenyan University. Theological education thus provides pathways and powers for traversing throughout contemporary societies.

CONCLUSION

In his study of the Kikuyu churches, John Lonsdale likens biblical literacy during colonial times to what he calls a "new epistemology of power," where it imparts a "ritually encoded skill with which to pursue status and power by other means."[76] The above discussion has attempted to convey similar ideas, by exploring how theological education provides the AICK with significant powers for navigating throughout the modern world.

I have sought to cast new light on the role of mission-founded churches by positing their enduring relevance in terms of resources gained from their missionary heritage. Orientations between the sacred and secular, for example, furnish supernatural commitments for epistemological concerns; or, where ontological issues associated with theological education position pastors to function as biblical agents in the face of nebulous global forces. Therefore, any reference to secularizing currents, within church or society, should also acknowledge "re-sacralization" that is taking place through theological education.

---

76. John Lonsdale, "Kikuyu Christianities," 171.

4

Africa Brotherhood Church: Self-Reliance and Development

THIS CHAPTER FOCUSES UPON the relationship between African Initiated Churches (AICs) and modernity through a study of the Africa Brotherhood Church (ABC). The ABC began from the vision of its founder, Simon Mulandi,[1] to see a church in Ukambani led by Africans and existing for Africans, bringing Christian *brotherhood* and development to a region seemingly torn apart by colonial governance and ecclesiastical division. The church formally started on April 8, 1945 after Mulandi had previously promoted a non-denominational Christian organization modelled after other self-help societies existing in Ukambani at the time. Together with his deputy, Nathan Ngala (who would eventually lead the church for fifty-six years), the founders drew upon Akamba and evangelical traditions to develop what Harold Turner has described as the "best organised church in Kenya."[2]

AFRICA BROTHERHOOD CHURCH: MODERNITY AND TRADITION

Like many *independent* churches arising in Kenya during the period of colonialism, the ABC borrows heavily from African traditions while fashioning a form of Christianity relevant to its context and peoples. Numerous aspects of the church relate to indigenous traditions, including a

---

1. ABC officials have been reluctant to credit Simon Mulandi for the pioneering work of beginning the church; however, some of this is changing. The current Bishop, Rt. Rev. Timothy Ndambuki is making efforts to re-assert Mulandi's role in the history of the church.

2. Turner, *Religious Innovation*, 185.

hierarchical leadership structure modelled after councils within Akamba society, and life tenure in certain positions. Other values such as respect for elders, hard work, cleanliness, hospitality, music, the importance of local resources, and communal harmony contribute to the formation of the church: linking it with Akamba culture in the eyes of many. These values remain conspicuous characteristics of the denomination. When a high-ranking leader walks into a room, all people rise from their seats until the leader sits; or, as church officials enter a service, the entire congregation stands to accord them honor. The bishop explained that this respect extends even to those who do not occupy *positions* of power, but who, by virtue of their age, deserve esteem. He based this upon the view that, "elders were seen as people associated with closeness to God."[3] To this day, the ABC offers a monthly stipend and special recognition to those lay leaders who were instrumental in working with Mulandi and Ngala to found the church. Bishops and Canons have special seats of honor; in front (and separate) from the rest of the people. This respect was further manifested in how they handled the ageing Bishop Ngala. Rather than push him out of office, church officials waited patiently until he died in 2007.[4]

Hard work is another valued component of the church, highlighted in their catechism, youth training manual, and functioning as one of the main criteria for ordination and/or promotion of clergy.[5] When children are young, they are taught to give themselves wholeheartedly to the Lord: through their bodies, minds and as pertains to the use of money. These teachings continue during catechism, leading to the point of baptism where they publicly devote: "all their bodily energies for building the Lord's work."[6] By the time youth reach adulthood, they are prepared for any service in the church, whether as lay leaders or professional clergy (without looking for extra remuneration or other entitlements). The denomination likewise places great emphasis on cleanliness, including how they care for church compounds and/or pertaining to how people are

---

3. Rt. Rev. Bishop Timothy Ndambuki, interview with author, Machakos, Kenya, Feb. 14, 2007.

4. Several lawsuits were filed against the Bishop, with the desire of forcing him to step down; however, these failed in their intent.

5. All church officials are subject to periodic review and assessment regarding their performance.

6. *Order of Services.*

Africa Brotherhood Church: Self-Reliance and Development

dressed. The acting principal of East Africa Integrated University,[7] Edward Nzinga, was asked to inspect one of ABC's institutions where there had been a complaint of students showing "disrespect." When he arrived, the issue at hand was men not wearing ties and jackets as required by the school manual. Upon a recent trip to Mbooni Divinity School, Nzinga remarked to me about the students' "cleanliness" compared with those attending non-ABC institutions.[8] His comments not only related to the absence of dirt, but more so the smartness of the students' attire. Cleanliness, in this case, is a sign of respect, an indication of people's attitude toward church authorities, and even God.

Many other traditions have prominence within the church. Occasionally, the leaders are uncertain to the origins of these customary practices, such as the case with cleanliness. When I asked the reasons for keeping a tradition when they were unclear about its genesis, they took me back to the founding of the church and explained that if these values had been effective from the beginning, there should be no reason to discontinue them now.[9] The ABC's history is therefore of great importance. Every year on April 8, all local congregations celebrate the anniversary of the church, where they narrate its history to children and a moderator reads an official report from the headquarters. These "ritualistic" practices pay tribute to the church's enduring values while bringing all congregations together for the work established by the headquarters for the following year. By annually commemorating the church's inception, they likewise reinforce cohesion (i.e., brotherhood) and find ways to contemporize traditions within rapidly changing societies. Examples include how they have adjusted to music styles and choice of instruments within each generation;[10] or earlier, how church officials accepted polygamous Christians (conditioned upon them not taking any more wives) and created positions for these people where their knowledge and experience of finances could directly benefit local congregations. One of the passages of Scripture recited during this anniversary service is Acts 10:34–35 where

---

7. Formerly Mitaboni Divinity School. The ABC has plans to begin different faculties of education, business, leadership, and management alongside their traditional focus on divinity.

8. Mbooni Divinity School, Jan. 31, 2008.

9. Canon Katiku, interview with author, Mbooni, Jan. 31, 2008.

10. However, they are very cautious in parting from traditional practices; the bishop told me that they introduced choruses into their liturgy, but only "one or two." Rev. Bishop Ndambuki, interview with author, Machakos, June 28, 2009.

Peter talks about how "God does not show favoritism but accepts men from every nation who fear him and do what is right."[11] This verse was especially significant in light of the earlier context out from which the ABC arose.

During the 1930s and 40s, various mission societies were struggling for prominence in the region (oftentimes competing against each other).[12] Into this context, Mulandi began the Akamba Christian Union "to bring together or unite all Christians from different denominations;"[13] eventually, changing the name to African Christian Brotherhood to differentiate it from the politically motivated Akamba Union. His goal in forming this "self-help" society was to unite Christians so that they could provide mutually beneficial development to the region. Later, when the church officially started, the earlier themes of brotherhood and self-help continued to undergird the ecclesiastical identity of the ABC. The church grew rapidly in the years leading to independence, mostly from people leaving other mission-founded denominations to join this new African church.[14] Yet numerical growth had other implications, as well. Colonial authorities perceived the ABC to be associated with the Mau Mau uprising and other resistance movements, which led to heightened suspicion against their activities and eventually to the forfeiture of their schools by the government during the emergency period of 1952–54. Backlash also came from mission-founded churches, and especially the AIM/AICK who resented ABC's involvement in Ukambani, and accused them of "sheep stealing" and distorting the purity of the Gospel with "syncretistic" practices. Thus, ABC's association with African "traditions" had different trajectories; sometimes self-imposed by church officials as a means of upholding their values of respect and hard work; other times misunderstood by government authorities with subversive intent; and still in other instances, where historic churches accused them of being syncretistic as a result of strong emphases upon traditional values.

However, any mention of the ABC's traditional ethos should also include inherited values of evangelicalism that came from years of contact with Western missions. Mulandi received training from the Salvation

11. *Order of Service*, 8.

12. Among those involved in the region were the AIM, CMS, RC, Salvation Army (SA), and Gospel Furthering Fellowship (SFF). Most respondents cite the AIM as the main cause of disunity in the region.

13. *African Brotherhood Church*, 3.

14. Ibid., 8.

Africa Brotherhood Church: Self-Reliance and Development

Army and later the Gospel Furthering Fellowship (GFF), which had earlier broken away from the AIM over leadership disputes; meanwhile, Ngala attended AIM's first theological college, Ukamba Bible Institute. These influences provided the church with spirited evangelical beliefs, including: strong biblical foundations for all their convictions, priority given to evangelism for accomplishing the Great Commission, and energetic social action related to communicating Christ's love to the world in tangible ways. These evangelical traditions proved useful when ABC officials were interacting with historic churches. For example, in 1957, Bishop Ngala attended a joint meeting of the AIM, GFF, CMS and the National Council of Churches in Kenya (NCCK). The issue at hand was whether to allow the ABC formal membership in the NCCK. The Africa Inland Mission, led by Erik Barnett, accused the ABC of political involvement, syncretistic beliefs, and allowing leaders caught in sin to remain in the church. Bishop Ngala adamantly denied any political involvement and stated that Simon Mulandi, who had earlier confessed to sexual immorality, was no longer involved in any leadership position. He likewise went on to affirm that the church only wanted to advance the work of Christ: preaching the Gospel and bringing people to salvation.[15] The ABC were denied admission at this event, but these evangelical traditions served useful for interacting with different mission societies, eventually leading to their admittance in the NCCK under the advocacy of the Presbyterian Church in 1964.

Akamba and evangelical values factor prominently in the history and growth of the church. Traditions are never static, but constantly adjust to various conditions and circumstances. For example, when government and/or mission societies interpreted ABC's traditions in suspicious ways, the church overemphasized its evangelical teachings to better facilitate relationships across the broader Christian community; or, in other cases, church officials have appealed to long-standing African traditions when modern trends appear to threaten the respect or hard work required of church members. Thus, traditions are always reinterpreted within every generation, modifying to the ebbs and flows of rapidly changing societies. In the words of a study commissioned by the World Council of Churches (WCC), "The ABC is very little interested in African traditional practices, like invoking the spirits of the dead, sacrifice and libation. . . . Its main concerns have been with more modern African problems, rather than a

---

15. AIM Archives, "Joint Meeting."

dream of restoring the past."[16] The process of contemporizing traditions should not imply capitulation to modern, Western values or syncretistic forms of Christian belief; rather, reinterpretation brings new meanings (powers) for the present age.

POWER AND THE AFRICA BROTHERHOOD CHURCH (ABC)

On January 27, 2008, I attended a communion service at ABC Bomani, in Machakos town:

> *The podium and chairs are decorated with special white cloths and a banner reading, "Fanyeni hivi kwa kunikumbuka," 1 Corinthians 11:24, hangs in front of the altar, recalling Jesus' words spoken at the Last Supper, and accented by two doves (symbolizing the Holy Spirit). A large crucifix occupies a prominent position in the front of the church, rising over the podium and accenting the pre-eminence of Christ over all things. People are kneeling or praying quietly in their seats before the service. As the leaders emerge from behind a curtain, all the people stand to their feet and then kneel again in prayer before the service begins.*
>
> *The three men up front are all lay leaders and have different colored robes according to their respective rankings. At no point does the pastor appear; I meet him later in his office preparing for the second service. The liturgy is tightly structured. We sing, "God of Mercy," followed by the Lord's Prayer.*[17] *The choir sing a couple lively songs. There is a scripture reading; announcements; prayer; another song, followed by the recitation of the Apostles' Creed; one more song, and then the preacher comes to the pulpit. The passage is taken from Isaiah 6:1–8 and Deacon Sam Mutisya urges parishioners to live holy lives in light of the pressures and temptations facing Christians today. He asks, "Do we live any differently than other people; farm any differently; or lead our businesses any differently?" He addresses the current chaos within the country, with ethnic fighting and dissension resulting from the disputed presidential elections. Most people in the service are Wakamba, but he challenges them, "Do we boast that we are from such-and-such tribe, and that we are peaceful? We need to repent. The only good tribe is the one that fears the Lord." He concludes his sermon*

---

16. "African Brotherhood Church," 157.

17. The liturgy is the same for the second service, but where the various components are translated into Kiswahili (in rural areas, mixed with Kikamba).

by compelling people to go into the world to make a difference for Jesus.

The sermon ends with three questions, always asked at the completion of the preaching, where people can (1) receive Christ as their Lord and Saviour, (2) repent of their sins, or (3) choose formally to join the ABC. Those who raise their hands to one of these questions are asked to stand and the preacher/leader prays for them. The congregants sing, "There is a fountain filled with blood drawn from Immanuel's vein" as parishioners come forward for the offering (one regular, and another special basket for children's ministries). The leaders prepare for the Lord's Supper. After the two officiates partake of the bread and the wine (juice), the washariki are invited to come to the front and kneel, where they are served by the leaders. We sing another song and then there is a third offering where people provide for the special needs of the paid ministers: the pastor and sisters. Finally, visitors are recognized and enthusiastically encouraged to "make this your church." The service concludes by singing, "Lord, dismiss us with thy blessing."

This brief narrative describes many of the characteristics of the Africa Brotherhood Church, including: a strong emphasis on the evangelical doctrines of Christ's atonement and the power of the Holy Spirit. The service incorporates high and low church elements, with a crucifix, robes, and kneeling alongside the singing of lively choruses, dancing, and lay leader participation. In the words of the WCC article, "It is an African Church, but it has borrowed from any source whatever. What it has borrowed it has freely adapted."[18] Spiritual power contributes to the organization and growth of the ABC; some of the main facets are highlighted below and include (typical with indigenous African churches) material and spiritual points of reference.

Powers: Holistic Gospel

The logo of the Church occupies all letterhead, publications and even stamped on church property (such as hymnals); it resembles a badge with a cross etched in prominence and a specific phrase from Mark 16:15–16 written underneath: "Jesus said, 'Go ye into all the world.'" From the beginning, the ABC gave heightened attention to the proclamation of the Gospel with their labors yielding the most success within Ukambani. However, the founders had a vision that was much larger and included

---

18. "African Brotherhood Church," 150.

people from all tribes and nations. The first objective of the original Constitution explains their priority as: "preaching the Gospel of Jesus Christ to all Nations of the world, *throughout the world if possible* [italics mine]".[19] Most of the church's activities display this outward-orientation. In 1947 there was a special contribution called, "Offering for the Good News," where members gave money for new ministries focused upon Western Kenya. Every August (up to the present) the denomination focuses on evangelistic activities, which in the early years involved church members walking across most of Ukambani: preaching the Gospel and planting churches. Later they purchased motorcycles and vehicles for the same purpose. The year 1955 marked the first publication of their in-house magazine, *The Completion of the Great Commission of Jesus Christ* (Matt 28:19–20), which was originally written in Kikamba, and later translated into Kiswahili, chronicling many of these activities. Kiswahili functions as one of the predominant languages for the ABC, which allows them to cross ethnic boundaries in East Africa while remaining true to their "African" identity.[20] Over ten percent of all tithes and offerings go into the *outreach* budget, mostly directed to their work in Rwanda and the Democratic Republic of Congo (DRC). Recently it was announced that the ABC Bomani choir was preparing for a friendly musical competition with other ABC churches. The moderator of the service told the congregants, "If the choir goes to Taveta and returns without saving anyone who is lost, it will be a total loss."[21] This statement seems to imply an over-privileging of the spiritual mandate of the church; but in fact, their view is more balanced than this would appear. Bishop Ndambuki explained how the founders of the ABC differed from the early missionaries in their understanding the Great Commission:

> The AIM was concentrating on the Gospel alone, but here they said, we want to go a step beyond the Gospel and outreach the whole personality, that is why they looked at the holistic gospel. Wherever we have a church, we shall be planting a school, or a dispensary. . . . As they preached the Gospel to convert people, then they go another step and deal with the whole personality.[22]

19. "Constitution and Rules."

20. However, in rural parts of Ukambani, Kikamba remains the central language for ecclesiastical discourse.

21. ABC Bomani, Apr. 7, 2008.

22. Rt. Rev. Bishop Timothy Ndambuki, interview with author, Machakos, Kenya, Feb. 14, 2007.

Africa Brotherhood Church: Self-Reliance and Development

The ABC therefore interprets the Great Commission to include physical development, where spiritual and material elements flow together in organic unity. This point is critical for understanding the origins and subsequent growth of the church.

From the very beginning, the leaders of the church witnessed their people divided over denominational lines and caught in situations where the Gospel appeared ineffectual for improving the basic needs of people living in rural Ukambani. By emphasizing a holistic reading of the Great Commission, they envisioned a broad and diverse community united together in Christian love (brotherhood), with the Gospel producing spiritual and material growth: elevating the quality of education, equipping African leaders, and improving people's access to quality health care, and agricultural development. The original objectives of the church testify to this multifaceted (holistic) approach. The document states that the main purpose of the ABC will be

1. The preaching of the Gospel of Jesus Christ to all Nations of the world, throughout the world if possible;
2. To teach all new Christians so that they may be able to teach and preach the Gospel to others;
3. To aducate [sic] children and adults by the way of opening schools to them wherever there is a need.
4. To train some Christians to become leaders within the church who can, after completing training, may become leaders of Christians in the A.B.C. branches or pastorates;
5. To help people by way of Medical Treatments, and to teach them the modern way of living;
6. African Brotherhood Church is a non-political body;
7. A.B.C. is intended to open branches.[23]
8. The Great Commission, therefore, serves not just as the first among several objectives, but the very basis for extending into broader human communities with spiritual and material aims; hence, evangelism naturally encompasses all aspects of human life.

---

23. "Constitution and Rules."

Re-Imaging Modernity

Powers: The Holy Spirit

The Holy Spirit provides the instrumental agency for understanding their holistic gospel. Mission churches are sometimes perceived to neglect or overlook the doctrine of the Holy Spirit, focusing instead upon the power of the Word, or the cross; meanwhile, *Spirit* or Pentecostal churches have been accused of placing inordinate emphasis upon the Holy Spirit, especially to bring personal power into chaotic contexts riddled with unseen forces. The ABC avoids both extremes. They understand the Holy Spirit as the power behind the Gospel, and thus the locus for guiding human communities (inclusive of material and spiritual points of reference). Confidence in the Holy Spirit enabled the founders to envision themselves (especially as marginalized Africans living within a colonial and mission-dominated society) capable of beginning a church that would move from Ukambani, throughout Kenya, and as the first objective above reads, "throughout the world if possible." Their world-oriented vision was particularly remarkable in light of the absence of sponsorship from any Western organization. Such a goal would not have been possible without the confidence in the Spirit's power: especially focusing upon how the Spirit *guides* human communities.

The dove (symbolising the Holy Spirit) hovers over the words of the Great Commission to form the ABC's logo. Early converts wrote Kiswahili hymns, and the first song composed for the denomination communicates a prayer to the persons of the Godhead, seeking spiritual guidance. It is always the first hymn sung at the beginning of their liturgy, and states in one of the stanzas: "God the Father, Son and the Holy Spirit, Let us see your power in this service." While the Spirit has prominence within their worship, their interpretation of the Spirit's activity is couched within a fuller understanding of the evangelical doctrine of the Trinity. Emphasis upon the Spirit's work remains congruous with traditional African cosmology where power proceeds from God (and/or the spirit world) to benefit human communities. The ABC's history document frequently mentions the Holy Spirit's role in relation to achieving the Great Commission;[24] or, in the absence of any external organization for funding, how the church depends upon the "guidance of the Holy Spirit"[25] for development and growth. In interviews, I asked youth how they understand power within the church; they immediately answered,

24. *African Brotherhood Church*, 11.
25. Ibid., 94.

"In our church, power is with the Holy Spirit. He speaks through the people."[26] Many people illustrated these points to me through the story of the former Bishop, Nathan Ngala, who led the church from 1951 until 2007. For years, he experienced pressure to step down from leadership and/or appoint a successor; in at least two instances, members filed lawsuits against the church to challenge the legality of his tenure. In 2006, prior his death, he made a rare public appearance. He asked Timothy Ndambuki to sit on a chair before him, and with silent expectancy before a crowded congregation, Bishop Ngala held his hands over Ndambuki's head for a period of twenty to thirty minutes, waiting for the Holy Spirit's confirmation that this was the man to lead the church. At the completion of this time, he finally lowered his hands, resting them upon his head, and thus announced the Spirit's blessing upon the decision. A few months later Ngala died and the Governing Council held an emergency meeting to appoint the next Bishop. It was unanimous among all members that Timothy Ndambuki would assume that post: with no dissenting opinions or prolonged leadership wrangles.

The Holy Spirit not only empowers spiritual leadership, but also undergirds the activities of believers. Because of this, the ABC heavily relies upon the involvement of lay leaders for all ministries within the church. From the beginning, this was crucial for the denomination's growth. Churches began through the efforts of elders; buildings were constructed through the patronage of wealthy individuals. Trained pastors were few, and hence the majority of early evangelistic activity came through the labors and finances of lay leaders: walking throughout most of Mbooni, Kangundo, or Kitui and using their own money to support the early work. To this day, as my earlier narrative suggests, lay leaders play conspicuous roles. Youth participate in singing, cleaning, evangelism, and other duties around the church compound; women raise funds for development projects, counsel younger girls, and plan for women's fellowships and Bible Studies; men serve as trustees, elders, or deacons: with notable responsibility pertaining to spiritual and material matters.

Powers: Pastors and Ecclesiastical Hierarchy

Each local congregation elects seven men and seven women to form the primary leadership team within the church, assisting wherever possible with the pastor and/or sisters. Women supervise all their own affairs.

---

26. Stephen Kisilu, interview with author, Machakos, Kenya, Mar. 18, 2007.

They may undertake development projects, do house to house visitation, organize fellowship meetings and/or participate in various financial campaigns. Women can also plan for events in the church and wider community. Men assist the pastor with collecting and counting the offerings and are usually the ones leading the worship service (although women may also be involved). Once a man is elected as a lay leader, the pastor is responsible to see him trained, which may include a three-month or one-year ministerial program at Mitaboni or Mbooni Divinity College (now called East Africa Integrated University). This kind of education enables lay leaders to preside over Holy Communion, dedicate children, assist with baptism, or perform other ministerial duties with the exception of officiating a wedding ceremony. After showing competency and faithfulness as lay leaders, they may be promoted to elder, and after elder, ordained as deacon if they show by their life, work and commitments they are worthy of this calling. Deacons serve in many of the same ways as pastors. Each of the three (lay leader, elder, and deacon) has a different uniform to show their respective ranking, and the positions are usually for life tenure.

All pastors and sisters attend one of the East Africa Integrated University's theological colleges. For acceptance into one of these institutions, the applicant's local church must write a letter of recommendation, followed by a rigorous oral interview (the bishop participates in all interviews related to admittance for ministerial training). Prospective students are required to have had secular training and preferably another profession prior to enrollment. The reasons for this are twofold: Firstly, the church is concerned for the individual in case of *backsliding* or falling into moral sin that he or she may not be left destitute, and secondly, they want to see evidence of personal sacrifice prior to acceptance. If the candidate held another job, with a higher salary, and then decided to leave this career to become a pastor/sister, church officials perceive the prerequisite sacrifice and posit the student's calling to be true.

Sisters are permitted to do anything the pastor can, with the exception of serving the Lord's supper, officiating a wedding, or leading other rites within the church; however, they may preach, teach, and are specially trained in the area of finances and administration. Several sisters joked with me that they had "more power" in the church because they handle money matters.[27] They are permitted to marry, but usually

---

27. Mary Katiku, Esther Mwaka, and Elizabeth Musau, interview with author, Mitaboni, Kenya, Nov. 1, 2007.

Africa Brotherhood Church: Self-Reliance and Development

the church recommends they wait five years after the completion of their studies. Men and women work together in all ministries of the church. If a pastor has a wife, the headquarters will usually assign him one sister with which to serve; if he is not married, two sisters will join him. In one local congregation, a sister served for a period of a year while they looked for a suitable pastor. When the pastor came, the other leaders quipped that previously they had a spiritual mother; now, they have a mother and father. This kind of language reveals a certain comfort with female roles of leadership: acknowledging the essentialness of women for community affairs. One young lady conceived a child out of wedlock. Bishop Ndambuki pointed her out to me as someone who had experienced hard times but now had become instrumental in leading the youth. Pastors and sisters are intended to complement one another: men in management and pastoral functions, while women in areas of finance and administration. Different roles enhance the collective good of the overall community.

Unlike traditional theological institutions, these men and women study disciplines such as cross-cultural studies, chaplaincy, community development, primary health care, and agricultural studies. At one point in their training, they attend the agricultural project in Kibwezi for four months where they learn about intercropping, drip-irrigation and other techniques to improve the overall quality of life among their people. One pastor explained that the ABC demands so much more of them than simply spending their days "having the Bible in your hands";[28] they serve throughout all areas of church and society. People often talk about the pastor as the "role model" for the entire community, visibly demonstrating God's power throughout all facets of life. Clergy show the Gospel through their work (one of the fundamental values of the church). The responsibilities of a pastor and sister are tremendous. They usually live on the church compound, away from their spouses and children (if married). The reason being the prodigious amount of service required for all paid ministers, as well as wanting members to be accessible to them all hours of the day or night. Pastors usually oversee four to five churches (called a branch) and function as the focal point and/or catalyst for all activities: whether finances, development, evangelism, preaching, counselling, teaching, missions or anything else the church undertakes (working with sisters and lay leaders).

---

28. Pastor Simeon Kitoo, interview with author, Machakos, Kenya, Jan. 17, 2008.

Re-Imaging Modernity

When they enter divinity school, men are called "evangelists" and ladies, "miss." After completion of their studies they become ordained for the work of the Lord and may rise to the level of pastor, reverend, and canon (for the men), and sister and deaconess (for the women). The last of these categories (canon and deaconess) require exceptional commitment/work in the church, and thus are rare. At present, the church has a membership of approximately 1.5 million people with 670 congregations. In order to lead something of this size and scope (extending through Ukambani, but with churches on the Coast, Nairobi, Central, Rift Valley, and Western provinces; as well as Uganda, DRC, Tanzania, and Rwanda) they utilize 2,200 laywomen leaders and 2,700 laymen leaders, while only one hundred sisters/deaconesses, sixty-two pastors, and sixteen canons.[29] These numbers reveal a disproportionate reliance on lay leaders while hinting at tremendous expectations required of clergy.

Lay leaders are likewise conspicuous members on all committees within the church, from local congregations to the Governing Council. A pastor usually has oversight over four to five churches, called a branch. Lay leaders assist with organizing the wider affairs of the branch, whether planning fellowships or collecting money. Sub-pastorates are a collection of ten to twenty churches in the same area. From all local church committees, members elect twelve men and twelve women to work with pastors (and one elected pastor-in-charge) on the sub-pastorate council, providing oversight to the entire area. Sub-pastorates combine to form the sub-headquarters, which includes approximately sixty to eighty different churches. The sub-headquarter council includes twelve elected men and twelve women working alongside the different pastors, and led by a pastor-in-charge.[30] All the pastors-in-charge of the sub-headquarters, along with one elected lay leader from each, comprise the *Baraza Kuu*, or Governing Council (working under the leadership of the bishop). In all the councils, there is equal distribution of ordained ministers and lay leaders. However, there are two other committees attached to the headquarters: the planning committee (seven elected lay leaders and five clergy) and the finance committee (three lay leaders and the bishop). This leadership structure combines centralized authority with strong lay participation

---

29. Figures reflect the 2008 calendar year.

30. Canons usually lead the sub-headquarters; however, the bishop explained to me that if a Canon shows that he is not able to undertake this responsibility, the leadership can be given to a pastor. Performance appraisals form the basis upon which these discernments are made.

Africa Brotherhood Church: Self-Reliance and Development

through all levels of the hierarchy, resembling how traditional Akamba councils used to operate. All decisions are based upon two central criteria: if the proposal (1) biblical and (2) constitutional. Any member of a council can challenge a decision using one of these two criteria, even should it go against a pastor-in-charge or the bishop. Biblicism and the church's historical foundations combine to form the basis for church governance: underscoring the importance of evangelicalism and African traditions for interpreting ABC's ecclesiastical identity.

None of this would be possible without the Holy Spirit's power: taking the vision of the Great Commission and making it realized through an interconnected community of believers, built upon Akamba values of brotherhood, hard work, and shared material resources. Power within the ABC is therefore an expression of human communities, who by preaching the Gospel to all nations broaden their conception of brotherhood to include a diverse, self-sufficient church where people contribute according to their gifts and abilities, and in the process fashion their own place within the modern world. These ideas will be explored with greater depth in the following sections as I deal with two concepts commonly associated with Western modernity: self-reliance and development. The ABC provides their own interpretation to these concepts through association with spiritual power.

SELF-RELIANCE

Recently the ABC launched a micro-credit scheme targeting six hundred churches throughout Kenya. Any member of the church can participate in the project by contributing shares in the enterprise (giving 200 ksh initially, and then at least 100 ksh every month thereafter).[31] Funds are pooled together where they gain interest in collaboration with a local banking agency. Members can then apply for loans where there is a minimal interest fee of 1.9 percent. I attended one of their meetings in Machakos. Men and women sit around a room in a semi-circle and take turns giving their monthly contributions. A secretary or treasurer provides detailed accounts of all transactions and publicly reports those who have given and for what purpose(s). Meanwhile, the leader talks with members about various income-generating projects to boost the collective funds further, such as purchasing a tent or chairs for rental

---

31. In August 2012 the currency exchange was $1 US dollar = 84 Kenya shillings (ksh).

to other groups. Occasionally visitors are invited to provide finance and management training for those wanting to begin small businesses. There are currently six micro-credit projects in operation throughout the country and the atmosphere is generally optimistic and progressive. At the inauguration, a member of the Canadian Baptist Ministries (CBM) challenged church leaders to use this project to assist widows and other needy people. ABC officials have likewise applied for a grant from the CBM to enlarge the funds available in this account. At the end of the ceremony, Bishop Ndambuki stood before the people and announced, "This launch is a realization of the dream of our visionary founder and leader, Bishop Nathan Ngala. He wanted church members to be self-reliant."[32]

The concept of self-reliance factors prominently in the history, discourse, and daily affairs of the church. Initially, the word conjures an image of autonomous selfhood, where, coming out of the Enlightenment, increased emphasis was placed upon individual powers to self-create identity without interference from religious, social or kinship-based authorities. A more community-based reading of self-reliance would imply a separatistic group rebelling against certain norms or conventions of society. Neither of these are accurate depictions of the ABC. Their view focuses on the wider populace rather than individuals; furthermore, rather than isolating themselves from others, they utilize the concept to move into other human communities: bringing the Gospel, hard work and shared material resources to unify diverse peoples. At the inauguration of the micro-credit scheme Bishop Ndambuki spoke about the church's historic emphasis upon self-reliance while members of the Canadian Baptist gave various speeches. On the surface, the presence of a foreign mission organization working alongside an autochthonous church appears to undermine any notion of autonomy, compromising the essential integrity of self-reliance; however, closer investigation reveals that some of these associations may have been envisioned by the founders long before they were realized, bringing new interpretations to the concept of self-reliance than among those typically understood within Western frameworks.

Brotherhood

Unity was a key concept in Ukambani during the years before and after the founding of the church. Various "self help" groups sprang up across the region trying to bring people together for the purpose of addressing

32. Mutuku, "African Brotherhood," 5.

material needs. At the same time, however, colonial suspicion had been increasingly directed against the Akamba, perhaps because of certain ethnic similarities with the Kikuyu (or proximity to central Kenya), and possibly resulting from these very unification efforts. Mulandi initially began an association called, Akamba Christian Union (ACU), which had its primary goal "to bring together or unite all Christians from different denominations."[33] The rapid growth of the fellowship attracted the attention of the politically motivated, Akamba Union, which tried without success to merge with Mulandi's fellowship. On August 14, 1943, the ACU decided to change their name to the African Christian Brotherhood (ACB), partially to avoid any perception of being involved with the more controversial Akamba Union, as well as envisioning a larger scope of influence for themselves, with specific Christian purposes. Less than two years later, the fellowship officially became the African Brotherhood Church, mostly to support those Akamba who had been expelled from their historic, mission churches.[34]

Akamba unity was a strong motivation for all groups, whether those involved in political activities or the religiously minded African Christian Brotherhood (and later ABC). Their understanding of unity carried with it commensurate emphasis upon material benefit: whether providing political voice to the needs of the Akamba and/or assisting people in rural Ukambani to improve their lives. Nathan Ngala, in an interview before he died, explained some of the early rationale for the church: "My urge and desire was to encourage people to employ their own initiatives in managing their affairs, leading to self-reliance, hence improve their standards of living."[35] In his mind, this required the collective efforts and pooled resources of all people; showing how unity of diverse peoples and self-reliance could be interrelated. Therefore, the founders of the ABC reveal certain characteristics of Akamba unity by emphasising material development alongside religious unification. God's power, mostly seen through the Holy Spirit, guides people for the betterment of local communities. "Brotherhood" serves as a central concept to connect these notions together.

33. *African Brotherhood Church*, 3.
34. Ibid., 7.
35. "Kenya: Trumpet Blows for Champion of Christian Unity." Kenya *Daily Nation*, Apr. 4, 2007, http://allafrica.com/stories/200704030924.html?page=2 [accessed November 14, 2007].

Re-Imaging Modernity

Inclusivism

Contrary to stereotypes sometimes given to tribes in colonial Kenya, Akamba visions for brotherhood reveal a more inclusivistic vision for ethnic unity. Historically, the Akamba had been traders, moving between the coast and Ukambani, and extending their travels throughout most of central Kenya. Their mobility may have been a contributing factor to the development of this broader notion of brotherhood, especially pertaining to material goods and the unification of diverse communities. Certainly these tendencies were aided by evangelical convictions of the Great Commission. Western missions came to Africa in order to transform communities with the Gospel of Jesus Christ: a message of salvation to "all peoples." However, early ABC leaders perceived that the missionaries were using the Gospel to segregate tribes and denominations, while neglecting many of the material interests of the people. Hence, the founders of the ABC started an African church to finish "hatred among the churches in Ukambani,"[36] address material needs, and proclaim the Gospel of Jesus Christ "throughout the world if possible." The early leaders saw these as mutually inclusive, and fundamental to what it means to be self-reliant.

The perception of the ABC as a local, tribal church, therefore, must take into consideration how, from the beginning, church officials saw brotherhood through the lenses of the Great Commission, propelling themselves as the body of Jesus Christ into other regions of Kenya, and later different countries. They began their work in Nyanza (Western Kenya) as early as 1946, a year after formally beginning the denomination, and presently have churches in Tanzania, DRC, and Rwanda. The change of name from Akamba Christian Union to African Christian Brotherhood further reflects that prior to the founding of the church (in 1945) early leaders were already looking beyond Ukambani, and even conceptualizing "brotherhood" across national borders. The church's history document gives the reason for changing the name: "The presence of other ethnic communities [required a more expansive approach] and therefore the organization ceased to be a Kamba affair; it incorporated all Africans."[37] Later, during the inception of the church, they similarly adopted the broader "African Brotherhood Church" to reflect the vision

---

36. Rt. Rev. Bishop Timothy Ndambuki, interview with author, Machakos, Kenya, Feb. 14, 2007.

37. *African Brotherhood Church*, 7.

of incorporating all Africans together. From 1945 until 1991, the name remained unchanged until partnership with the Canadian Baptists precipitated a very subtle movement away from the possessive *African* to the more inclusive *Africa* (revealing the current Africa Brotherhood Church). This reflects an additional reinterpretation of the concept, so that self-reliance could include collaboration with international partners, and where the church might equally involve African, Canadian, or American membership. All of my respondents saw this as compatible with the original intentions of the founders; where their view of self-reliance did not exclude any person from participation, but counted upon interdependence for its fundamental expression: whether in Ukambani, or extending throughout the entire world.

The relationship with the Canadian Baptists began at a time when the church needed encouragement to develop some of their holistic and inclusivistic visions, but lacked some of the resources to do so. The initial conversations between the parties took place in 1975, seeing in each other similar priorities for self-sustainable development and holistic ministry. Three years later the relationship became structured, built upon a series of five-year, renewable Memoranda of Understanding (MOU), with missionaries teaching in the Mitaboni Divinity School and/or others assisting with educational or development projects. In 2008, the partnership progressed to a new level with an indefinite *covenant* signed between the CBM and ABC where they essentially merged as far as the ministry in Africa is concerned. This covenant tries to avoid dependency scenarios by placing the greatest responsibility upon the ABC for identifying potential projects, raising funds, and managing the day-to-day affairs: reconceptualizing self-reliance within a framework where the Canadian Baptists (and potentially others) equally represent brotherhood in Africa.

Church leaders are sensitive to the charge that the fundamental characteristics of self-reliance have changed. Recently, four administrators from Canadian Universities came to Machakos to consider how they might assist the newly formed East Africa Integrated University. During these discussions, Bishop Ndambuki pledged that the church would annually contribute five million shillings to the University project: demonstrating local ownership and self-reliance without discounting the important contribution these Western Universities might provide in terms of textbooks, faculty exchange, or accreditation of programs. Hence, the ABC's view of self-reliance initially places the main impetus upon Africans to care for their own needs. Ndambuki explained what this meant for the early leaders: "The *wazungu* (white person) has left this country . . . and now the church should learn to be self-reliant; we taught stewardship and how to support the church; our projects that we plan for are *our* projects."[38] During a recent trip to Canada, Bishop Ndambuki continued a long-standing tradition (previously established by Bishop Ngala) of bringing ABC money to help with Canadian Baptist needs. He gave the money to assist some projects the CBM were undertaking in Central America. None of these points, however, should indicate that Western partners (like the CBM) are devalued (or that there is not financial benefit to the partnership); only that the ABC is mindful that it must retain primary responsibility for its affairs. Self-reliance, therefore, relates to a diverse, interdependent community of people from many different contexts contributing for the growth of local (and global) communities.

This brings the discussion back to the connection between humans and power. The ABC attests to the value of all people by virtue of God's creation. God, they affirm, has established his goodness within the world. However, salvation, in the words of Bishop Ndambuki, provides "added value"[39] to humans through the Holy Spirit's presence, enabling Christians to contribute more to the development of communities through spiritual and material components. As youth go through the ABC's catechism, they learn the following: (1) It is mandatory for all believers to give themselves wholeheartedly to the Lord, whether through their time, work, money, minds, or any other part of their person; (2) if they fail to do this, Satan will take these things away from them, since he came to steal, kill and destroy; and, finally, (3) the ABC does not have a sponsor, and therefore it is for the people themselves to advance the work of the Lord. Through such teachings (and via the modelling of older members) they readily accept their responsibility within the church, whether through giving, working, or any other service required by the leaders. Failure to do so opens them to the destructive forces of Satan, resulting in the loss of fundamental human powers. Thus, they have little patience for anyone claiming to be poor, and hence unable to contribute to church or society. Bishop Ndambuki proposed such a hypothetical scenario with me and replied, "So, if you don't have money, bring two pieces of firewood; you

---

38. Rt. Rev. Bishop Timothy Ndambuki, interview with author, Machakos, Kenya, Feb. 14, 2007.

39. ABC Bomani, May 27, 2007.

don't have this, but you have mangoes."[40] Humans have value and thus possess power (regardless of their socio-economic status). Furthermore, Christians have added value and thus additional powers available to them for the good of society.

All members contribute regularly to the church by means of tithes and offerings, of which there may be upwards to five in a given service. People give toward missionary projects in Rwanda, the East Africa Integrated University, youth evangelism, recording projects for the choir, various development undertakings, or even monthly water and electricity bills. All members likewise pay a yearly membership fee that supports the Bishop and Governing Council: men give 70 ksh, women 50, youth 20, and children 10. All funds go to the headquarters, where they are distributed according to the needs of the greater whole. Furthermore, lay leaders on the various councils do not ask for a "sitting allowance" or any other financial reimbursements (except for modest travel expenses). They understand their responsibility as to assist the church with their time, money, and expertise, even if it means great personal sacrifice.

Self-reliance, therefore, is an expression of diverse human communities who come together in Christian brotherhood and transform societies through their collective powers. These powers may be material, spiritual, social, or cognitive and appear most advantageous when combined with the *other*. To this day, the ABC participates in projects in Rwanda and the DRC, works with Roman Catholics and/or other Christian denominations on various ecumenical projects, and combines male and female leadership within their hierarchy. Furthermore, they continue a longstanding policy of placing pastors in different areas from where they were raised: hence, churches in Western Kenya are staffed by Akamba or Agikuyu ministers; while Luo pastors serve in Ukambani or along the coast. Heterogeneity brings greater powers for the fuller representation of humanity.

The ABC, therefore, demonstrates that Akamba views of brotherhood and evangelical teachings on the diverse, Body of Christ are mutually compatible in so far as they allow for the incorporation of the *other* for the growth of humanity, inclusive of spiritual and material concerns. This enables the church to work freely with the Canadian Baptists, accept converted polygamists, or undertake ecumenical projects. Yet in the minds of ABC members, they still retain the primary responsibility to

---

40. Rt. Rev. Bishop Timothy Ndambuki, interview with author, Machakos, Kenya, Feb. 14, 2007.

work, give, and contribute in whatever ways; otherwise, Satan will come and steal away their fundamental powers. God's power resides within human lives. Individual responsibility rests comfortably within a communal orientation to provide the principal meaning and values of self-reliance: a concept which initially buoyed the hearts of marginalized Africans living in a colonial society but now indicates a multi-national church that actively uses divine power (located within humanity) to engage in all facets of the world. This will be seen more clearly in the next section.

DEVELOPMENT

Development is not a new concept to societies, nor something confined to Western cultures; however, it does display unique elements coming out of the Enlightenment, illustrated particularly by the notion of *progress* and a dichotomized understanding of the world where secular realities increasingly define human aspiration and identity. These influences tend to make the physical world (including modern facets like technology) assume heightened importance, leading to the common supposition of Western societies as developed (and African societies as developing). However, such a demarcation overlooks the integrative nature of African traditional cosmology, and undermines different notions of progress that may arise from within these societies. African churches factor significantly in contributing to different understandings of development by combining traditional elements with evangelical teachings to situate themselves most advantageously within the world. The ABC illustrates one notable example of this through their holistic gospel. Their view utilizes theological rationale (especially giving attention to the doctrines of humanity and creation) for talking about the integrative and transformative role that humans play within modern societies.

I accompanied Edward Nzinga to the ABC farm in Kibwezi about three hours drive south east of Machakos. We passed mile after mile of arid scrubland before finally arriving at the property where Millicent Manesa, the Program Officer, greeted us. She introduced us to the project as we toured their fifty-two acres, which included citrus trees intercropped with vegetables for export, agro-forestry plantation (emphasizing reinstatement of medicinal, indigenous trees), livestock breeding, community training center, experimental plot where they demonstrate the latest hybrid seeds or drip-irrigation methods, water conservation, health center and church. Manesa explained that the original purpose of the project was to "change the place religiously,"[41] which for the ABC means that all aspects of life within Kibwezi should be transformed according to the Gospel, accounting for the presence of a church, health clinic, agricultural center, livestock project, water storage and community training center. Previously the land was destitute and subject to extreme drought; now, it has become a model for the entire community and a prime example of what they signify when referring to the *holistic gospel.*

Holistic Gospel

The original vision of the ABC leaders featured communal, material, and spiritual characteristics all flowing from the Akamba worldview, where humans serve as the epicenter and integrative agents within the entire cosmos. Akamba views of unity naturally accounted for material development. The mission-church tradition of the founders further reinforced this perspective, with both the Salvation Army and the AIM actively involved in spiritual and material projects, even if Mulandi and Ngala perceived that the missionaries did not go far enough towards meeting these ends. Thus, from the beginning, church leaders began primary and secondary schools and sought to assist people with reliable access to water and basic health services, while incorporating these aspects into their overall ecclesiology. Through the years, the ABC continued to emphasize this holistic Gospel, yet struggled at times with how to organize and promote their vision beyond Ukambani. The incipient ideas were there, even if they lacked maturation. However, the relationship with the Canadian Baptists began to change things. When the two parties began dialoguing in the mid-70s, they saw in each other a desire to affect holistic growth. The CBM perceived a potential overseas partner, and the ABC recognized the value of these people to help them articulate and develop this vision for wider representation. Gradually, the holistic gospel began to take new shapes and utilize more Western "development" terminology. Pastors and sisters began their training in community development while studying for four months at the Kibwezi farm. Various ministries opened in Rwanda, Tanzania, and DRC, which promoted such a holistic emphasis. The earlier commitments to educational development continued with greater zeal, yet broadened to include programs for assisting people with special needs. To this date the ABC surpasses many other missionary societies and churches in these endeavors, operating: 338 primary and

---

41. Mllicent Manesa, interview with author, Kibwezi, Kenya, Nov. 15, 2007.

secondary-level institutions (most of these in rural communities), six Bible colleges; 175 pre-primary schools, thirty polytechnics (especially focused upon providing tangible skills such as sewing and cooking for girls lacking secondary school education), and four special needs institutions where they assist blind, deaf, and disabled students. The bishop recently launched a University, where, besides theology, students study in such disciplines as agriculture, community development, nursing, management and/or education (hence the new name East Africa Integrated University).

Since the 1970s, the ABC has taken great strides in developing its primary health services, providing support for HIV/AIDs patients, as well as beginning micro-credit schemes, food relief, water conservation/management, and *capacity building* through various educational and training operations. The community development arm of the church officially opened in 1998 with the goal to "contribute improved standards of living of the target community through continuous capacity building using social and economic interventions for integral sustainable development." This mission statement appears little different then that of other NGO's operating in the country, but the prevalence of Western development language should not detract from the church's desire to effect holistic change in African communities, inclusive of strong spiritual influence. Elements of this have been present from the beginning, even if the newer language seems to convey a more recent genesis. Traditions are always reinterpreted into modern contexts, and the ABC show how Akamba views of holism can combine with evangelical teachings, and subsequently find new expression within secular NGO language.

The key to understanding their view of development lies in their "spiritual" reading of humans in relation to the physical world. Bishop Ndambuki and others repeatedly explained the fundamental concepts of the church by referring to Genesis, where creation and the original purposes of God provide essential theological underpinnings for the principle values of the church, including community, work, blessings, and/or cleanliness. Unlike Western societies where physical realities tend to largely define development, the ABC begins with spiritually motivated communities, buttressed through the Holy Spirit's power. This foundation enables them to move confidently into all aspects of the material world. The bishop explained, "When you talk about development, you will look at the whole person. . . . There is no development in a sick society."[42] Healthy persons (viewed holistically) remain fundamental to the proper functioning of creation. Furthermore, by combining this with their diverse reading of brotherhood (with *added value* that comes from salvation), believers have "more powers" to bring to the task of development. One development officer told me that in order for communities to grow, it is essential that there be a "common pool of resources" and that these be utilized for each other.[43] Thus, the relationship between humans and the physical world is highly dynamic. By emphasizing brotherhood, the ABC directly impacts the physical world by means of diverse otherness, yet a healthy world also brings human growth.

Creational Values

In order to accomplish these ends, the church emphasizes basic values inherent within the creation account, including: work, commitment, responsibility, cleanliness, giving, and blessing. Each of these originates (implicitly or explicitly) from God's stewardship mandate in Genesis 1–2, and is reinforced from within Akamba traditional values: providing essential ethics and meanings to govern human interactions with the physical world. One example would be their theology of labor. From the beginning of the church, the founders borrowed their motto, "Hearing and Doing," from the name of the AIM's earliest publication. For the missionaries these words connoted obedience to the Great Commission, characterized primarily through evangelism and preaching of the Gospel in the remotest areas. The ABC accepted this meaning, but with a wider scope of application: motivating church members to influence entire communities with the Gospel of Jesus Christ (inclusive of health care, food, and other basic human needs). From the time children are young, they are taught the value of hard work and the importance of utilizing all material resources for the good of the community, culminating at the time of baptism when they publicly declare their allegiance (inclusive of bodies, finances, and efforts) for the Lord's work. Pastors and sisters *role model* the importance of manual labor in their communities and show its significance for their calling as ministers of Jesus Christ. The Bishop

---

42. Rev. Bishop Timothy Ndambuki, interview with author, Machakos, Kenya, Feb. 14, 2007.

43. Peter Mutua, interview with author, Machakos, Kenya, July 2, 2007.

explained that "theology involves labour,"[44] which he related to the work of pastors and their responsibilities pertaining to agriculture, evangelism, or other needs within modern societies. The church demands much of the people, constantly reminding them, "your labour in the Lord is not in vain."

Hard work relates to responsibly caring for the physical world. When a person enters an ABC compound, the natural beauty is immediately recognizable: fruit trees, well-manicured grass, flowers, and plants occupy prominence around the various church buildings. I asked the Bishop about this and he related it to the Garden of Eden, where God placed humans into a world of natural beauty and endowed them with responsibility (and power) to care for creation. He said, "If you visited . . . Eden you will find it very beautiful, you will find fresh water, flowers, vegetation; all these things were given to man so that he can emulate God. In the areas where we plant churches, where people meet with God, it needs to be beautiful, like God himself had shown to Adam and Eve."[45] Christians are to replicate Eden all throughout the world so that they can "emulate God." Power proceeds from God into human communities for the purposes of caring for the physical world. This means that in addition to attractive compounds, the church actively works to achieve healthy water supplies in arid places throughout Kenya, Tanzania, and DRC, and explores medicinal qualities inherent within God's creation: seeking to utilize God's intrinsic goodness for human benefit. This is no small vision, but takes the church boldly into all areas of God's creation.

Blessings provide another instance where Akamba and evangelical values meet. Their theology of creation furnishes humans with a practical venue in which to apply the benefits of the Gospel. A recent sermon provides an example of this. One of the sisters preached on the Abrahamic blessing in Genesis 12. She explained to the congregants that God's original intention was to bless humans and provide everything needed for their goodness and growth. She said, "When someone says to you 'be blessed' they are asking God to give you all that is good: food, wealth, happy life, even eternal life." She proceeded to explain that Christians, with the salvation received from Jesus Christ, should be the main instruments of blessing to all people, even to the extent that they "should be

---

44. Rev. Bishop Timothy Ndambuki, interview with author, Machakos, Kenya, Feb. 14, 2007.

45. Ibid.

the first people to contribute to nation building."[46] God's intentions for humanity include all aspects of his goodness, located, and applied within the physical world. Christians are the fundamental agents of God's power to others. This is in keeping with beliefs within many traditional societies, where blessings flow from God, through humans, and with benefit to the physical world: with the understanding that as the natural world prospers, human communities would likewise flourish. The ABC see this as compatible with evangelical teachings from the book of Genesis. Yet they avoid/resist contemporary conceptions of the prosperity gospel through the way they focus on basic human needs (health care, safe water sources, fair prices for harvest, etc.) rather than extravagances associated with modern interpretations of *wealth* (e.g., expensive Toyota Prados, large houses, and imported clothes). If a person has extra money, God intends that surplus for the benefit of others. Thus, their doctrine of creation provides not only the linkages between humans and creation, but also essential values and/or ethics to govern its representation.

Holy Spirit

The Holy Spirit provides the essential power needed to enable humans to emulate God in the world. This is consistent with African traditional beliefs where spiritual inter-mediators often act between God and humans, as well as linking humans with the natural world. It is also consonant with the biblical role of the Spirit to reveal God to humans and guide them through all facets of the world. Spiritual power from the Holy Spirit equips humans to confidently engage in all facets of society: allowing the ABC to work on ecumenical projects, assist governmental agencies regarding *nation building* exercises, undertake agricultural projects, and promote evangelistic enterprises throughout East and Southern Africa. They do this, however, without charismatic interpretations of the *baptism of the Holy Spirit*. In fact, they actively oppose these kinds of teachings, standing more on the theological side of mainline churches in their understanding of the doctrine of the Holy Spirit while sensitive to see the practical manifestation of the Spirit's power visible in the natural world. One of the main ways they apply the doctrine of the Holy Spirit is through development. The physical world becomes the primary medium by which the ABC administers their powers, showing that God entrusted

---

46. ABC Bomani, Mar. 18, 2007.

Re-Imaging Modernity

humans with authority and placed them strategically as agents of blessing in the world.

Hence, the strength of their development comes from the prominence they give to the doctrine of creation (especially through the mediation of human communities) and buttressed by ethical values (like hard work, responsibility, blessing, and honor) that govern this relationship. Other evangelical churches tend to place lesser emphasis on Genesis, favoring the doctrines of sin and salvation. The ABC retains a very strong Christology, but by emphasizing the doctrines of humanity and creation, possesses a wider scope of application for salvation to affect.

Pastors and sisters serve as *role models* for the entire process. Besides their training in community development and primary health care, these people cultivate their own *shambas* (agricultural land) in order to demonstrate the newest techniques or hybrid varieties. They travel throughout their branch, sub-pastorate, or sub-headquarters, and constantly advise people upon spiritual and material matters (taken collectively). A pastor may go to a member's house in order to pray for someone who is sick and end up giving suggestions about their health, recommending medicinal trees they could grow, or new crops that might bring financial benefit. Likewise, their view of evangelism may include meeting with village elders to talk about sustainable development, or ways in which the church might be able to assist with community needs. One lay leader underscored the importance of the pastor's role in all of this by saying, "All development occurs through the church; therefore the pastor is central to development."[47] He chairs all meetings, and therefore must be conversant with the needs of the community as well as broader concepts related to holistic growth.

The church rejects a dichotomized understanding of development, where the spiritual and material act in polarity with each other; for example, where progress serves as a "carrot on a stick" for spiritual activities. The Kibwezi farm, for example, works with people regardless of their denominational background and/or ethnicity. They refuse to place requirements upon participants to join their church, nor do they give evangelistic entreaties at their development meetings. They accept people for what they can contribute to the whole. (Perhaps inferring that this kind of service will naturally lead people to join the ABC.) As stated previously, greater diversity means increased resources for the benefit of

---

47. Titus Kiilu, interview with author, Machakos, Kenya, July 2, 2007.

the entire community. They begin by sitting with community leaders and identifying the primary needs facing people (in the case of Kibwezi, it was water, roads, and reasonable prices for produce); then, the church mobilizes the people to accomplish these objectives. They provide skills training and incentives for community-related work and assist with funding larger-scale projects such as water storage and/or irrigation facilities. This should not suggest that physical development projects are devoid of spiritual rationale. The bishop explained how the ABC understands all aspects of humankind as fundamentally spiritual, and therefore valuable. He also shared how holistic growth directly benefits the church: "We are building the person," he told me, "who will bless the church in turn."[48] This may result in increased offerings, or more healthy members functioning within modern societies.

On the surface, their developmental efforts appear little different than those of other NGOs operating in the country: working on *capacity building*, agricultural projects, and micro-credit schemes and intent upon providing sustainable growth for grassroots communities. However, closer examination reveals that their doctrine of creation (especially focusing upon the powers of humanity) enables them with important theological rationale and resources to apply salvation on a broader scale, comprehensive of material realities and societal concerns. Spiritual power moves the church confidently into all areas of humanity because of the intrinsic goodness of creation, distorted though it might be because of sin. The Holy Spirit's presence allows church members to apply the benefits of salvation (inclusive of the original intentions of God for the world) so that humans can emulate God and bless others in whatever they undertake. Theological resources, therefore, provide important linkages that connect spiritual and material realities: allowing the ABC to see continuity between development and the Great Commission. Power within human communities therefore relates fundamentally to agency and stewardship with the physical world.

CONCLUSION

This chapter presents a study of how one AIC contributes to reconceptualizing modernity in Africa. Words such as self-reliance, development, or capacity building are reconfigured around Akamba traditions and

---

48. Rev. Bishop Timothy Ndambuki, interview with author, Machakos, Kenya, Feb. 14, 2007.

evangelical beliefs to provide members agency within an integrative cosmos (and subsequently re-interpreted within NGO language). The ABC believe that humans occupy privileged positions of power within the world; while diverse, interrelated communities apply the Gospel to the physical world. In this way, the founders of the church reveal an inclusive picture of Akamba unity, where brotherhood (including ethnic diversity, gender complementariness, denominational ecumenicalism, and international partnership) combines with the Great Commission to compel believers outside of themselves, while focusing upon material and spiritual points of interest.

Modernity, thus, relates to integration: God with humans; humans with each other, and the spiritual community in relation to the material realm. Power remains central to understanding how evangelical doctrines and Akamba beliefs combine to formulate a hermeneutical framework that provides motivation, resources, and values for humans to actively engage with the world around them. Work, stewardship, interdependency, responsibility, and blessings set in place valuable ethical parameters to govern the outworking of spiritual power. Traditional values are thus contemporized and evangelicalized within ABC teachings. Hence, this study reveals new insights into how African churches contribute to global themes; or in the words of Kwark, how "Africanness and modernity relate to one another in a complex solidarity."[49]

---

49. Kwark, "The Reinvention," 127.

5

Redeemed Gospel Church: Individualism and Materialism

THE THEME OF MODERNITY and power continues through a study of Pentecostalism, focusing on the Redeemed Gospel Church (RGC) in Ukambani. There can be no contesting the remarkable explosion of Pentecostalism on the continent as even the most cursory survey of the religious landscape reveals large churches in urban areas, amplified preachers on street corners, itinerant evangelists taking advantage of captive audiences on buses, and crowded tin buildings in rural areas effusive with congregants seemingly tapping into ubiquitous spiritual power. The greater challenge comes in understanding the diversity of such churches, whether they conform to the *classic* Pentecostal model from America, represent a continuation of older independent Prophet/Spirit churches, serve as a re-interpretation of global, charismatic Christianity, or constitute a distinct entity altogether. In some cases, each of these options represent a distinct possibility, while in other instances, there is a blending of the above; for such reasons, Allan Anderson prefers speaking about "Pentecostalisms" as it recognizes a broad spectrum, comprising local and global characteristics.[1]

REDEEMED GOSPEL CHURCH: MODERNITY AND TRADITION

The task of situating the RGC within this wider tapestry of Pentecostalism is equally challenging. Like the broader movement, the RGC represents many different elements with interlocking global and local

---

1. Anderson, *Introduction to Pentecostalism*, 286.

facets that resist neat compartmentalization. There has been considerable discussion within academic circles whether contemporary African Pentecostalism arises from direct contact with the American prosperity gospel, as suggested by Gifford[2] and Mugambi[3]; or is sourced from the internal traditions and worldviews of African culture, argued by such authors as Kalu,[4] Meyer,[5] and Maxwell.[6] A study of the RGC suggests there may be a blend of both. Marshall-Fratani describes a similar picture for Pentecostalism in Nigeria, where global and local elements combine to form "multiple identities" that, in turn, assist practitioners in navigating through modernity.[7] In the case of the RGC, the precise mix of elements may vary depending upon geographical particulars, with urban churches displaying increased degrees of Western import, while rural churches tending to reveal more local initiative. This study, with its emphasis on Ukambani, will likely show greater emphasis upon local elements than might be found in Nairobi or Mombasa churches; yet this point should not be overextended. Through the influence of media and via the extensive interconnecting networks found within Kenyan Pentecostalism as a whole (and the RGC in particular) global influences can work their way to even the remotest rural congregations.

The RGC represents an indigenous African church, yet traces some its origins to three distinct Western influences. During the 1940s, various Pentecostal denominations came to Kenya,[8] including the American-based Pentecostal Evangelical Fellowship of Africa (PEFA), which had amalgamated from three smaller organizations, including Elim Missions.[9] The two founders of the RGC would become active in PEFA churches during their early years of ministry. In the 1950s, the American preacher, T. L. Osborn, undertook evangelistic ministry in Kenya, accompanied by healing services along the coast. He was among the first to bring the American prosperity gospel to Kenya. It is unclear the precise effect Osborn had upon the RGC, but a number of the leaders mentioned

2. Gifford, "Reinhold Bonkke's Mission," 157–82; *African Christianity*.
3. Mugambi, "Evangelistic and Charismatic Initiatives," 111–44.
4. Kalu, *Power, Poverty and Prayer*.
5. Meyer, *Translating the Devil*.
6. D. Maxwell, "'Delivered from the Spirit of Poverty,'" 350–73.
7. Marshall-Fratani, "Mediating," 282.
8. Other missionary endeavors include the Canadian Pentecostal Assemblies of God (PAC) and the Finnish, Full Gospel Churches of Kenya.
9. See Gifford, *African Christianity*, 155–56.

Redeemed Gospel Church: Individualism and Materialism

his influence as an important component in the overall formation of the church. In 1990, Reinhard Bonkke organized a "crusade" in Machakos town. This event would be described by RGC members as the "turning point" of Pentecostalism in Ukambani:[10] where a global actor legitimizes some of the local currents taking place in and around Machakos. These antecedents give the appearance of a foreign Gospel coming into Kenya; however, closer examination reveals a different picture.

A brief overview of the church in Kangundo may illustrate some of the ways local initiative takes place within broader, global currents. Located approximately forty miles northeast of Nairobi, within Machakos District, this small town was among the first targeted by the Africa Inland Mission (AIM) and therefore carries long association with American forms of evangelicalism. Earlier influences from the charismatic movement had little affect on towns such as Kangundo, protected by geographical isolation and the rigorous efforts of mainline churches (such as the AICK) to guard against the encroachment of other ecclesiastical entities. Economic challenges were common within Machakos District, leading to individuals and families occasionally travelling to other parts of the country, or even other nations, to procure better paying jobs. Paul Mutua provides one example. He was born in rural Ukambani within a polygamous family and whose mother died shortly after he was born. His family struggled to send him to school. As a young man, he discovered opportunities available in the hotel business in Kampala, and left Ukambani looking for a better life. Once in Uganda, he heard the Gospel and was saved. In 1964, he met another Mkamba, Arthur Kitonga, who had arrived to assist his uncle, Joseph Kayo, with evangelistic work among the Rwandan Refugee camps. Both served together under the PEFA churches where they preached the Gospel and planted new churches.

In 1973 Idid Amin's reign of terror had grown to such an extent that the two returned to Kenya: Kitonga to Mathare Valley, Nairobi and Mutua to Machakos. Mutua explained to me that he did not intend to begin a new church. He started a revival fellowship in a Secondary School, bordering the District Commissioners office.[11] Both men continued working with the PEFA churches, focusing on preaching the Gospel in the slums of Mathare Valley and throughout most of rural Ukambani, respectively. Joseph Kayo had earlier begun the Deliverance Church and

---

10. Rev. Joseph Nzola, interview by author, Machakos, Kenya, Oct. 18, 2006.
11. Bishop Paul Mutua, interview by author, Machakos, Kenya, Sept. 3, 2007.

was strategic in mentoring these two men upon their return to Kenya. It was not until a year after their return, in 1974, that disagreements with the PEFA churches resulted in the formal beginnings of the church. Both were happiest when evangelizing and hence their initial efforts resulted in the formation of what they called, "Redeemed Evangelistic Association." The notion of an organized church only came later, when governmental pressure necessitated the registering of what had become a notable movement. The church grew rapidly in the following years, swelling to its current figures of approximately two thousand congregations in Kenya, Tanzania, Sudan, Uganda, DRC, Rwanda, Burundi, South Africa, Malawi, and Zambia; eventually extending outside of Africa to India, Jamaica, and the USA.

The two founders continued to guide the church during the early years, but their pathways, though always interconnected, would lead in different directions. Kitonga would eventually receive an honorary degree from South Africa,[12] and travel throughout the world as Chairman for the Evangelical Alliance of Kenya (EAK). Mutua, on the other hand, remains most comfortable in rural Ukambani, where he works with local congregations and introduces new initiatives to impact the region.

During the early 1970s, a fresh wave of Pentecostalism swept across Kenya influencing, in particular, those attending Christian Union's (CUs) in Universities, Colleges, and Secondary Schools. Wilfred Lai and Daniel Matheka (both Wakamba from Kangundo) were heavily influenced from these organizations. At College, they heard the Gospel, became "born again," and experienced a tremendous filling of the Holy Spirit. Returning to their homes in Kangundo they were castigated for associating with Pentecostalism and subsequently expelled from their historic churches. Matheka's family was attending a local AICK congregation; he tells the story of what happened after his conversion:

> We were very bad boys in the village. You go to get saved in school and come home feeling good because all your bad habits [have been dealt with]. Christ has made a difference. Now, I have accepted Christ as my personal saviour and somebody [my church] is [undermining me] saying, "I am destroyed." It became a very big issue.[13]

---

12. Jehovah Jireh School of Ministry, South Africa.

13. Rev. Bishop Daniel Matheka, interview by author, Kangundo, Kenya, Oct. 14, 2007.

Redeemed Gospel Church: Individualism and Materialism

Matheka and many of his friends found no suitable church in which to nurture their Spirit-filled enthusiasm. Only a handful of PEFA churches existed in Ukambani, and none in Kangundo. The charismatic revival had yet to reach most rural areas. Young people would therefore meet in shops, homes, or other available venues so that they could worship with the "freedom" they craved. As their numbers increased, they saw the need to find a more mature person to give them guidance and instruction. They turned to Paul Mutua. Matheka says of the co-founders of the RGC, "They were elderly, most of us were very young. We thought these are the right people to lead us."[14] Finally, five years after the founding of the RGC, the local church in Kangundo officially began. Matheka and Mutua were the two instrumental agents for its inception, and Matheka now serves as Regional Bishop in charge of all RGC churches in Ukambani.

This story of the founding of the Kangundo church illustrates many of the ingredients fundamental to the inception of the Redeemed Gospel Church: including, evangelism, involvement of youth, lay initiative, persecution from historic churches, and uncertain struggles for organization in light of tremendous numerical growth; all combined with interweaving global and local elements. Furthermore, many of these dimensions continue to characterize the church years until today. The unifying theme that captures much of the denomination's history is spiritual power by the Holy Spirit, enabling the church to situate itself and grow within contemporary Kenyan society. This chapter provides the general parameters for interpreting power within the RGC, and explores two facets of it—individualism and materialism—in an attempt to explicate how the RGC contributes to distinct forms of African modernity appearing within Ukambani.

POWER AND THE REDEEMED GOSPEL CHURCH (RGC)

Pentecostal Christianity blossomed during the 1970s and 80s; a period described by John Lonsdale as the "second missionalization" of Kenya.[15] The reasons for this growth are multifaceted. Firstly, historic churches had grown in size and scope, but left some parishioners longing for greater local initiative. A few respondents reported that they attended these churches for family or cultural reasons, and less because they addressed

---

14. Ibid.
15. Lonsdale, "Kikuyu Christianities," 184.

Re-Imaging Modernity

personal needs.[16] Bureaucratization was also a factor. The larger historic churches had developed fixed organizational structures, which in the eyes of many, made them less able to rapidly adjust to broader societal trends. Early leaders of the RGC describe PEFA churches in such ways, as "rigid" and "not open."[17] Hence, many youth found personal needs overlooked by these historic churches (and older Pentecostal denominations), yet addressed within the RGC. Respondents also castigated historic churches for neglecting the work of the Holy Spirit. To the extent that these charges are true, the absence (or diminished emphasis) on the doctrine of the Holy Spirit can leave these historic churches with fewer theological resources in which to *apply* the Gospel for human transformation, influence socio-economic status, bring healing, or protect people from evil spirits: all key issues within an integrative cosmos where spiritual power connects humans with their world. Hence, people pejoratively denounce these churches as "powerless" and "unspiritual."[18]

The post-independent state also contributed to Pentecostalism's rise by failing to bring economic and social progress to Kenyan society. In the absence of an effective (for the people) government and/or civil society, more opportunities became available for ecclesiastical agents. Ogbu Kalu broadens this diagnosis to include many African countries; saying, "The collapse of the state as an agent of modernization enlarged the political space for religious actors and gave fillip to the Pentecostal moral diagnoses for political and economic woes."[19] Thus, the state's inability to address human needs resulted in certain societal voids, yet by emphasizing the power of the Holy Spirit, these newer Pentecostal churches, such as the RGC, furnished congregants with important theological resources in which to personally and corporately face rapidly changing demands within Kenyan society. Theological rationale, thus, undergirds the growth of the RGC. A brief overview of the denomination will show the pervasive nature of spiritual power.

---

16. See Rev. Joseph Nzola, interview with author, Machakos, Kenya, Oct. 18, 2006.

17. Mr. Gideon Musau, Rev. Saul Mutie, and Mr. Justus Musila, interview with author, Machakos, Kenya, Oct. 5, 2006.

18. Ibid.

19. Kalu, *Power, Poverty and Prayer*, 115.

Redeemed Gospel Church: Individualism and Materialism

Powers: Evangelism, Identity and Growth

The church initially arose from the founders' desire to evangelize all nations in light of the imminent return of Jesus Christ. The RGC's vision corresponds to the Great Commission of Matthew 28: "Reaching the Unreached with the Gospel at this end of time!"; or elsewhere expressed, "To reach the lost souls with the Gospel at this end of time!"[20] Hence an eschatological vision for the imminent return of Christ provides these churches, as it did American fundamentalism at the turn of the twentieth century, with theological motivation for personal evangelism. In this way, the RGC's vision (at least on the surface) appears little different from that of the early missionaries. Yet whereas the AICK and other mainline churches would focus upon the "truth" of the Gospel to change lives,[21] the RGC places itself firmly within global Pentecostalism by emphasising the Gospel's "power."

The Holy Spirit functions as the central agent of power within their theological belief system. Power begins with the divine, and moves through humans to the natural realm. (Yet whereas the ABC shows similar ideas, with humans affecting the natural world, the RGC place more emphasis on how humans benefit from material realities, through their unique prosperity gospel). Furthermore, since each human *has* a spirit intrinsic to his or her being, instrumental point of contact is made between spiritual realities and human domains. The presence of ambiguous forces within the cosmos only accentuates the need for tapping into divine power in order to overcome these forces. The Holy Spirit provides important agency for navigating through uncertain (and sometimes hostile) cosmological elements. Later in this chapter, I will explore some of these points, showing how spiritual power orients the denomination according to certain modernity-related themes.

During the early years of the church's formation, the Holy Spirit's power served to authenticate the RGC's emergence into the ecclesiastical scene. The 1970s were times of great tension between Pentecostal and non-Pentecostal churches. The AIM/AICK (along with RC and ACK) had enjoyed near monopoly of religious activity in Ukambani since the late nineteenth century, disrupted only by the periodic rise of AICs such as the Africa Brotherhood Church (ABC) or the African Christian Church

---

20. http://www.redeemedgospel.org/ [accessed Jan. 5, 2008].

21. In ch. 3 I explored some facets of how historic churches such as the AICK utilize God's *truth*, under the label of *rationalism*.

and Schools (ACCS). Other than PEFA churches, few Pentecostal options were available in Ukambani. People were looking for alternatives to what they perceived to be restrictive regulations attached with mission-based Christianity, and the seemingly "powerless" teachings associated with these churches. During the mid-1970s (and extending for more than a decade), historic denominations mounted prolonged attack against Pentecostal ecclesiology, accusing these churches of "sheep stealing" and charging them with being "less biblical" (or even heretical) due to the inordinate emphasis placed upon the third Person of the Trinity. Into this tension-filled context, early RGC leaders testified that the power of the Holy Spirit was essential to demonstrate the church's legitimacy: often displayed through physical manifestations, such as healing, miracles, exorcism, or speaking in tongues. One elder spoke about those early days: "Unless there was that power," he said, "it would've been very difficult. Power to stand and say that [one] was saved."[22] Outward signs especially appealed to youth who struggled with feelings of powerlessness. As historic churches began to see their numbers fall away, polemics against Pentecostalism increased. Meanwhile, leaders within the RGC (and other Pentecostal churches) began to draw sharp distinctions between the faith confessed by adherents within the historic churches (often disparagingly calling them "nominal" Christians) and the salvation experienced by those with the infilling (also called "baptism") of the Holy Spirit; using the phrase "born again" to refer to the latter.[23]

Perhaps resulting from these conflicts, as well the worldview affirmations that attest to an integrative and spirit-filled cosmos, the RGC (and subsequent Pentecostal off-shoots[24]) grew rapidly from the 1980s to the present. Currently, almost one third of all RGC congregations reside

---

22. Gideon Musau, interview by author, Machakos, Kenya, Oct. 5, 2006.

23. This differentiation has led to widespread use of both words *saved* and *born again* to express personal faith in Jesus Christ. These words are usually stated in this order, trying to emphasis the legitimacy of a person's salvation (i.e., "I am saved and born again").

24. More recent development in Ukambani shows the rapid rise of Pentecostal churches, which are, in turn, reacting against established Pentecostal denominations, claiming that churches such as the RGC are too restrictive or limiting. An example would be a new church in Machakos called Worship without Walls that rose from the work of two disgruntled Pentecostal pastors (one coming out of the RGC). Many of these newer churches eschew the word *church* in their name in favor of *fellowship*, *chapel*, or some other appellation that seeks to convey an ecclesiastical entity more *open* and *free*.

within Ukambani, significantly more than any other region within Kenya. The message of spiritual power found fertile soil amongst the Akamba.[25]

From its humble origins as a marginalized denomination, the church has grown to possess significant "popular" power. Bishop Kitonga represents one of the most prominent faces within Christian circles. He frequently hosts dignitaries at his large, Huruma church and travels abroad through extensive networks of international "partnership." Rev. Wilfred Lai, from Kangundo, was an early disciple of Arthur Kitonga. He subsequently quit his work in the banking sector, and began Jesus Celebration Centre in Mombasa, which now boasts a membership of over twenty thousand people. Lai also become one of the main promoters of worldwide missions and his church in Mombasa is largely responsible for new ecclesiastical ventures begun by the RGC throughout the continent and in other parts of the world. Kitonga has likewise mentored non-RGC leaders such as Bishop Margaret Wanjiru of Jesus is Alive Ministries. These two ministers (Wanjiru and Lai), along with other well-known preachers, have weekly television programs on The Family Channel or other Kenyan broadcasting networks. The popularity of Pentecostalism further places it on center stage in Kenyan politics, illustrated by Bishop Wanjiru running (and winning) a parliamentary seat and Pastor Pius Muiru of Maximum Miracle Ministries vying for Presidential office during the 2007 elections.[26] The growth of the RGC (and other like-minded denominations) clearly reveals a shift in power where Pentecostalism has moved from marginalized church to majority religion in Kenya.

During the early years of the RGC's formation, the power of the Holy Spirit served to legitimize ecclesiastical expression, showing, by miracles or other visible representation the authenticity (and relevance) of the church to impact personal lives. In recent years, the teachings have continued to highlight the Spirit's power, but through larger, international spotlights (and broadened to highlight *wealth* as one of the visible representations of the Spirit's power). By combining the power of the Holy Spirit with teachings on the Great Commission, the RGC moves between local and global stages. In emphasising "all nations," the

---

25. I am not suggesting that the Akamba are unique in this regard, only that the message of spiritual power, as represented through these newer Pentecostal churches, has become a defining characteristic of Akamba Christianity since the 1970s.

26. Although Gifford notes how the media was particularly negative towards these two ecclesiastical leaders entering the political realm (see *Christianity, Politics, and Public Life*, 167).

church transcends ethnic or national identities, allowing the denomination to simultaneously move into Western Kenya, Zambia, or India, while benefiting from this trans-national identity. The word *international* frequently appears in various paraphernalia of the church, usually enticing people to hear an international evangelist or global speaker. Yet the *personalness* of the Spirit to indwell individual lives (seen in greater detail later in this chapter) allows the church to contextualize its message within local settings. Anderson states, "Like the churches before them, the new churches have a sense of identity as a separated and egalitarian community with democratic access to spiritual power, whose primary purpose is to promote their cause to those outside."[27] Evangelistic (and missiological) priority, therefore, takes the personal expression of the Holy Spirit's power into broader, global currents, allowing the RGC to express Gospel realities into the world, and incorporate global and local characteristics within their ecclesiastical identity: moving comfortably between Akamba, African, and American stages.

This is possible because the RGC places itself within the broader purview of global Pentecostalism, unified around the role of the Holy Spirit to bring spiritual power into human existence. Despite being an indigenous or African initiated church, the RGC has historically rejected any association with other AICs, and, at least explicitly, with African traditions. The older practices related with traditional religion were perceived to be motivated by demonic activity and all Akamba rituals implied some association with evil spirits. Personal holiness and strict codes of moral ethics led the RGC to break with these traditions. The Holy Spirit's presence in a person's life required rejection of anything sinful. In an interview with Bishop Mutua, I asked if he could explain any traditions that under girded the rise of the RGC; his response illustrates some of the sharp discontinuity between Christianity and African traditions, as well as highlights the church's broader identification with global Pentecostalism. He said,

> [The RGC was] not started on any African traditions because they [the early leaders] received the Pentecostal call; they were just building on the Pentecostal right from the start. When the Pentecost [vision] came, that is when the church began, when they were filled with the Holy Spirit; that is the foundation of the RGC. Not any other tradition.[28]

27. Anderson, "Evangelism," 27.
28. Bishop Paul Mutua, interview with author, Machakos, Kenya, Sept. 3, 2007.

Hence it is Pentecostalism, and not African traditions, that in the minds of the early leaders provided the rationale for ecclesiastical identity. However, this ardent stance appears to be changing. Many people in the church are beginning to see the importance of maintaining some connection with older values and practices, such as associating with non-believing family members (something discouraged in former times, because *born agains* should not relate with *non-born agains*), participating in family weddings, and/or upholding latent values such as respect for elders, hard work, and responsibility. Bishop Mutua has recently begun requiring anyone marrying within his church to follow the Akamba practice of bride price. One pastor shared with me the result of this new thinking:

> We are trying to see how you can remain a Mkamba, a "born again" Mkamba and cause impact in your society, and try to relate to the people, and bring the word of God to their context, . . . but without looking at them like a holier than thou kind of personality who cannot interact with the rest of society.[29]

This perspective comes as a result of transitioning from a little known and often castigated movement to majority religion in Ukambani. Success often breeds the need to re-evaluate how the church interacts with society, especially in light of how spiritual power relates with broader currents operating within the world.

Powers: God and Humanity

In working out a theology of the RGC, it is important to note that despite the strong prominence give to spiritual priorities, God's power extends into "non-spiritual" points of reference, including all aspects of humanity. Theological and cultural resources link God with humans (through the Holy Spirit) providing signature expression to their beliefs (yet often mediated through the "man of God"). This framework provided earlier justification for their evangelistic fervor: where signs and wonders testified to the authenticity of salvation offered to people in danger of finding themselves without God in the last days. More recently, the integrative cosmology furnishes the rationale for their *popular* power. The entire world is "open" to spiritual agents; God's victory is proclaimed to individuals, families, and entire nations; divine power operates within politics, and even applies to larger global systems. The RGC refer to this

---

29. Pastor Josphat Musee, interview with author, Machakos, Kenya, Mar. 8, 2007.

as a holistic gospel, yet where the motivations for integration come from different theological resources than seen with other denominations covered in this study.

As early as 1975, the church began the *social welfare program* designed to cater for people living in poverty around Nairobi's Mathare Valley slums. Similarly, and around the same time, Mutua started a number of initiatives in Machakos aimed at HIV/AIDS orphans, street kids, and others left destitute. God's presence (viewed primarily through his power) relates to wholeness (or newness) of human life, accomplished through the indwelling of the Holy Spirit. Hence when someone becomes *born again*, he or she essentially becomes *a person* with all the rights and privileges accorded to a recipient of God's Spirit. "You need the Spirit to be a complete person," Bishop Mutua shouts to his Machakos congregation. He then proceeds to explain that just as there are disabled persons, so there are people who are disabled in relation to their "spirits." He implores the *washiriki* to "replace the part that is missing" as well as urging them to pray, "Lord, I want to be complete."[30] Evangelism amounts to the re-creation of humanity through the infilling of the Holy Spirit, where God's power is appropriated in individual lives.

The Spirit's presence, however, remains unstable throughout a person's life, subject to great oscillation and flux. Bishop Mutua explained that people, and even pastors, do not "maintain" the presence of the Holy Spirit in their lives.[31] Sin lessens the Spirit's power; evil spirits distort the "completeness" of humanity. Therefore, the denomination hosts yearly leadership conferences where pastors who have neglected the Spirit's work come together in order to become "anointed": where, by the laying on of hands, the Spirit is essentially transferred from one person to another (usually by the pastor or bishop). Local congregations likewise host "anointing services," so that *washiriki* can become "whole" once again.

As I probed deeper into their beliefs, the Holy Spirit became apparent as the source and guarantee of human identity. A preacher asks, "Do you have a living God inside of you?"[32] This question illustrates the importance of God's presence within human nature, accomplished through the infilling of the Holy Spirit. God's nature is understood by his power, which in turn, generates life. The entire landscape of the church,

30. RGC Eastleigh, Machakos, Kenya, Oct. 15 2006.
31. Bishop Paul Mutua, interview with author, Machakos, Kenya, Sept. 3, 2007.
32. Redeemed Gospel Church, Machakos Worship Centre, Machakos, Kenya, Feb. 25, 2007.

therefore, revolves around images and representations of God's power. Churches are decorated with regal colors: reds, purples, and golds. Congregants sing about the majesty of God in almost every chorus: "You are mighty, you are able;" "I'm going to conquer, conquer in the Spirit;" "The Lion of Judah has broken every chain, has given us power;" *Ni nani kama wewe Bwana* (x2) (Who is like you Lord?); and, *Tunaomba uwezo wako* (we pray for your power).[33] Martyn Percy talks about the role that worship songs contribute for the construction of reality within Vineyard churches: "Through passion, passivity and power, the emotivated fundamentalist community stands over and against the world, by articulating ideological states of being, in which full love and full power become realized."[34] African Pentecostal churches utilize worship songs in many of the same ways, especially in light of pervasive feelings of helplessness experienced by people living within a world of unpredictable forces. By entering a church with its images and messages of power, congregants draw on spiritual power emanating from the divine to construct human identities and needed agency for navigating within the world.

God's kingship provides an example of this. One local congregation announces in their welcome flyer, "Feel free in our midst as we join together to worship the King of Kings and the Lord of Lords";[35] another church has an inscription written on their offering envelopes, "This freewill Kingly offering is an expression of my LOVE & OBEDIENCE to God."[36] A pastor stands and announces to the congregation, "People call him a King, but they have not yet seen his authority; he will bring all other kings under his Kingship."[37] An eschatological vision for the triumphant return of Jesus Christ provides a future identity for the people of God; meanwhile, by the Holy Spirit, this victory is realized within the present day community of believers. People participate with God's power, whether by songs, tithing, healing, through evangelism (or, by material prosperity). Hence when a preacher announces, "My walk with him has been victory, to victory, to victory"[38] he is saying much more than that he

---

33. RGC congregations prefer the use of English or Swahili within their ecclesiastical practices; rarely, if ever, using Kikamba except in conversational dialogue.

34. Percy, *Power*, 77.

35. Redeemed Gospel Church, Machakos Worship Centre, Machakos, Kenya, Sept. 17, 2006.

36. Redeemed Gospel Church, Maranatha Chapel, Kenya Israel, Kenya, Feb. 25, 2007.

37. Ibid.

38. Justus Musila, Machakos Worship Centre, Machakos, Kenya, Feb. 25, 2007.

has conquered sin; but is rather referring to a regal identity that places him triumphantly (successfully) within the modern world.

Powers: Pastors and Ecclesiastical Hierarchy

Spiritual leaders fulfill strategic roles in these congregations as they represent God, and transmit divine power to others. For this reason, the pastor is the sole spiritual authority within the church. He (or she) appoints the elders, and can dismiss any lay leader. The pastor has the "God-given mandate"[39] to lead the church and visibly represents God's authority within the congregation. One pastor explained to me the rationale for this perspective, arguing that you "can't have two powers in a church."[40]

Because of this, the RGC often struggle with currents related to the "sacralisation"[41] of ecclesiastical leaders. Ontological associations between God and humans provide pastors, by virtue of their nearness to God, with heightened or privileged access to divine power. Most churches have one prominent chair located atop the podium reserved for the "man of God;" when the preacher is introduced, the entire congregation stands to their feet as the pastor approaches the pulpit, resembling what reformed congregations might do during the reading of the Word of God. Rev. Wilfred Lai promotes this kind of mentality. He admonishes people to "sit at the feet of preachers," and cautions them: "don't treat them as ordinary people."[42] The pastor is notably different from other spiritual leaders in the church (such as elders) as the latter are appointed by humans, while the pastor remains the sole authority *ordained by God*. When conflicts occurs between pastor and *washariki*, appeal is made to God's Word, citing passages such as "Do not touch my anointed ones; do my prophets no harm" (1 Chr 16:22, KJV); or "No weapon formed against you shall prosper. . . . This is the heritage of the servants of the LORD" (Isa 54:17, NKJV). The pastor occupies central position within the congregation. He or she should know everything happening within the church and provides the agency by which congregants tap into spiri-

---

39. Pastor Josphat Musee, interview with author, Mar. 8, 2007, Machakos, Kenya.

40. Rev. Saul Mutie, interview with author, 5 October 2007, Machakos, Kenya.

41. Bediako, "Unmasking the Powers," 207–29. I am using the word "sacralization" in much the same way as Bediako, referring to dangerous associations that leaders have with sacred power, which often leave pastoral authority with limited or no accountability. The RGC would not necessarily see this as a problem, although I have heard numerous concerns regarding the lack of accountability given to spiritual authorities.

42. As heard on Family Glory, Sept. 24, 2006.

tual power. Touch (and oil) is central to this transferral of power, building upon traditional practices within African communities. Every year, Bishop Mutua lays hands on each of his local leaders, revitalizing them for the church's ministry.

Similar notions transfer to non-ecclesiastical realms, based upon biblical interpretations given to passages such as Romans 13. Paul Gifford illustrates some of these predispositions, citing back to the days of the former President Moi, where Bishop Kitonga came to the President's defense during a period of great political upheaval, announcing, "People should shut up, accept the present leadership and prepare to go to heaven."[43] More recently, Kitonga shared similar sentiments on behalf of the current President, Mwai Kibaki, where he praised the President for his leadership and quipped, regarding his detractors, "Those opposed to your leadership might not even get eternal life."[44] One of the dangers with such sentiments is that they easily lead to unrestrained political license; where, for example, Kitonga's own sacred power transfers onto Moi, Kibaki, or any other state leader and endows them with divine authority. Pastoral authority mediates God's power to the community. When Kitonga issues these kinds of declarative statements, he is doing more than making some casual moral judgment on the opposition; rather, the pastor is creating a form of reality where political leaders participate with God (sometimes regardless of their moral shortcomings).[45]

Despite these proclivities, however, the RGC tempers some of its sacralization by means of a growing focus upon organizational structure and some of the specific ways they orient spiritual leadership within local congregations. The church experienced tremendous numerical growth over the first thirty years of its existence. However, during the same period, their expansion proceeded faster than the leadership could develop. This created numerous challenges. In the early years, the RGC appointed pastors solely based upon their calling. They viewed the presence of the Holy Spirit as sufficient for pastoral service and, hence, theological education unnecessary due to the anointing of the Spirit in the minister's life. This had been the case for the two founders (although Bishop Kitonga would eventually receive some theological education at Kaimosi Bible Institute in Western Kenya, and later at Nairobi Pentecostal Bible College).

43. Cited in Gifford, "Some Recent Developments," 529.
44. Mugo Njeru, *Daily Nation*, Oct. 30, 2006.
45. Gifford says something similar regarding the declarative use of words within Pentecostal preaching (see *Christianity, Politics*, 173ff.).

Furthermore, the rapid growth of the church combined with the scarcity of trained pastors often did not allow the RGC to be very selective in their choice of pastors. A lay leader might announce that he or she had a "calling," organize some evangelistic meetings, lease a building, and begin a local congregation. More recently, formal education has become valued. The denomination currently works with American-based, "Vision International University" to offer unaccredited distance-based ministerial training programs.[46] Presently, they have twenty-seven students studying between their Machakos and Mombasa campuses. Many RGC have likewise attended NEGST; while the Pan Africa Christian University (PACU) recently received a governmental charter and highlights the entrance of a Pentecostal University into the Kenyan Higher Education scene. Much has been made of the *charismatization* of the historic churches, but the recent emphasis upon theological education (and growing bureaucratization of the denomination) shows the reverse can be the case: where importance given to credentials and certificates of formal theological institutions is gradually bringing changes within churches such as the RGC, and highlighting the need for training centers that cater for what may be termed the *mainlinization* of Pentecostalism. Most of the leaders interviewed in this study expressed this as the greatest need within the church.

Men and women are eligible to serve as pastors, although female ministers remain scarce in rural regions within Ukambani. The title *Pastor* may refer to an elder, someone with the gift of preaching, or a person assuming spiritual guidance over a local congregation. One group of women told me that their pastor's wife was also a pastor. Unlike some churches where this would mean that she was the pastor of women, the RGC do not see such limitations. Matheka's wife regularly preaches and is viewed as a source of spiritual power for the entire congregation. Once someone has *proven* his or her calling to be true (usually based upon visible representations of spiritual authority, such as tongues, prophesy, and/or power over demons—more recently, by visible representations of wealth), that person is eligible for ordination and awarded the title, *Reverend*, which represents a highly esteemed designation: signifying God's choice of the individual, and thus endowing them with significant spiritual power over/for the congregation.

---

46. See http://www.vision.edu/.

Redeemed Gospel Church: Individualism and Materialism

The numerical growth of the church has likewise accentuated the need for an organizational structure with clear lines of authority and accountability. Presently, the church is divided into five regions, with an overseer in charge of each. Bishop Kitonga serves as the Presiding Bishop, assisted by Bishop Mutua. Neither is responsible for a region but assumes leadership over the executive council, comprised of themselves, along with five regional bishops (Rev. Wilfred Lai, coastal; Rev. Daniel Matheka, eastern; Rev. Abasai Mwaka, central; Rev. Mark Kegohi, western; and Rev. John Jacob Thathi, Mt. Kenya). Each of these regional leaders has a subregional leader who assists with the various administrative duties, and who, in turn, oversees area leaders (pastors who are responsible for seven congregations).

This structure extends considerable power to the local church level. Hypothetically, this is not limited to the pastor, but flows as well through lay leaders and congregants. While the pastor remains the sole authority within the church, his or her main responsibility is to serve as a conduit of power to the people. In this way, the RGC guards against some of the sacralizing tendencies mentioned earlier. The pastor functions as the medium by which spiritual power moves down the hierarchy, and extends to each individual person. When I asked leaders and congregants if the pastor had "more power," they usually laughed and explained that it relates to responsibility. One elder shared that "power begins with the pastor,"[47] but then expounded how it moves downward through the various levels of leadership (elder, deacon, lay leader, usher, etc.) so that all persons experience and participate in its benefits (usually material in nature). Once again, the role of the Holy Spirit remains critical for this movement. Since all believers are filled/baptized with the Holy Spirit, each person has spiritual power emanating from God. The pastor is not the source of the power (although there remains the danger that people may perceive this to be the case), but represents the primary agent responsible for ensuring that the entire congregation relates with God's power in conformity to the dictates of the Bible.

While the pastor acts as the *sole authority* within the church, he or she is technically responsible to the area leader. If elders, deacons, or other congregants have a problem with a local pastor, they can write a letter of complaint to the area leader. Interestingly, Bishop Matheka explained that while he serves as a local pastor (in addition to his duties as regional

---

47. Pearson Katenge, interview by author, Kangundo, Kenya, Oct. 14, 2007.

bishop) he sits under the authority of an area leader. An overview of what they do with tithes and offerings further highlights these structures. Local churches retain 90 percent of their offerings for their own development and growth. These funds pay salaries, mobilize evangelistic endeavors, and/or construct buildings. Among the remaining 10 percent, half is collected by the area leaders and goes to the regional Bishop's office, while the other half goes to the executive council, and is made available to Kitonga and Mutua for global ministry endeavors.

These initial sketches of power provide the foundation for examining, in greater depth, two facets of modern societies: individualism and materialism. I should immediately offer a disclaimer that both words would be repugnant to those within the denomination, and appear very different than those varieties typically associated with Western societies. This is to argue, as I have elsewhere, that African churches are instrumental in growing their humanity within the modern world, particular to their own needs and context; or, in other words, where visions of modernity arise from the cultural and theological resources available to ecclesiastical communities.

INDIVIDUALISM

A number of studies have explored correlations that may (or may not) exist between individualism and Pentecostalism, especially as pertains to forms appearing within African societies. Birgit Meyer has done so most directly. She argues that "conversion to Pentecostalism entails a kind of conversion to modernity, insofar as the process of breaking with individual and collective pasts enable converts to become 'autonomous selves,' free individuals in possession of their own subjectivity."[48] Meyer's comments highlight the need for looking at freedom and autonomy in relation to individualism. Her observations also engender the question: to what extent does the particular kind(s) of individualism experienced within the RGC correlate with Western notions of the autonomous self?

Freedom and the Individual

The RGC offers *washiriki* individual expression of Gospel realities, through their distinct theological beliefs: specifically focusing on *freedom* through the indwelling of the Holy Spirit. Anderson similarly identifies

---

48. Meyer, "Commodities," 286.

the notion of freedom as intrinsic to Pentecostalism's holistic understanding of salvation: "If freedom is always the result of receiving the Spirit, then true freedom or liberation is an integral part of Pentecostal experience."[49] This was certainly born out from my research. Most respondents (and all youth) said they were attracted to the church because of the freedom that it offered.

Evangelism begins the process of emancipation as it marks the moment when an individual moves from captivity under the power of Satan to deliverance by the power of God. As this happens, the person receives a new identity. Yet the defining characteristics of this identity immediately differ from the kind normally associated with Western autonomy, in that it corresponds to freedom *from* Satan, and freedom *to* God (within the context of a new family of believers). For this reason, evangelism is often pictured as a battle, where words such as *crusade, deliverance,* and *victory* feature prominently. Furthermore, freedom is not restricted to some spiritual sense but places the individual within a new world order where he or she benefits (usually materially) from divine power. Pastor Lai preaches to the congregants, "God knows you and has something for you;" "you are more than conquerors;" "God is with you;" and "All things are possible with you;" or where he preaches against sin as that which "inhibits your potential and destiny."[50] These statements reveal that the kind of freedom associated with conversion (being born again) releases the individual into a life-long series of victories within the Christian life, inclusive of spiritual and material gain. Personal choice remains critical for salvation, reinforcing individual agency throughout the entire process.

Most respondents referred to their life prior salvation as "slavery" to Satan and conversion as the moment when they experienced real freedom. Becoming born again signifies deliverance to the point where they can act for themselves, through the power of God, within a world of evil and unpredictable forces. Marshall-Frantani similarly connects Pentecostal conversion with elements of individualism from her study of Christianity in Nigeria. She says, "The model of agency implicit in the born-again conversion depicts a lone individual struggling to achieve selfhood in a world full of evil forces which seek his undoing at every turn."[51] For

---

49. Anderson, *Introduction*, 269.
50. As heard on the God Channel, Sept. 24, 2006.
51. Marshall-Fratani, "Mediating," 285.

the RGC, these traditional notions of spirits are constantly re-expressed within distinctly modern categories. Demons and evil spirits pervade all facets of the modern world, from family systems, to the political state, and extend even into larger global systems. Preachers talk about the need for redeeming technology "from the world;"[52] or where sermons address the evils of the US, World Bank, or IMF in creating a "spirit of poverty" in Africa.[53] One pastor admonished his people to "guard your hearts against the deception of modernization" and where "we should not be swallowed by the world in an age of modernity."[54] These sentiments show how personal agency involves more than victory over sin, but extend into broader categories within the global world. Marshall-Fratani affirms similar ideas for Pentecostalism in Nigeria:

> In this sense, it is not so much the individualism of pentecostal conversion which leads to the creation of modern subjects, but the ways in which its projection on a global scale of images, discourses and ideas about renewal, change and salvation opens up possibilities for local actors to incorporate these into their everyday lives.[55]

The context for her discussion was Pentecostalism's use of media. The RGC also take advantage of this means for communication, but where it is largely limited to large urban congregations that broadcast sermons, or air "crusades," but with limited (or no) production in Ukambani (although viewed everywhere). In these rural areas, preaching appears to be the primary venue for empowering individuals with agency within the modern world. Congregants are constantly reminded of their power ("you are more than conquerors"); preachers relate this to individual sins and larger social problems: talking openly about pornography and/or poverty. Church seminars address topics of sexuality, dating, music, drugs and alcohol, and other matters with specific interest to the youth. One youth leader told me, "We don't want the world in the church, but the church to go to the world."[56] This kind of perspective requires the collective agency of all believers.

52. Redeemed Gospel Church, Kangundo, Kangundo, Kenya, Oct. 14, 2007.
53. Ibid.
54. Redeemed Gospel Church, Maranatha Chapel, Kenya Israel, Kenya, Feb. 25, 2007.
55. Marshall-Fratani, "Mediating," 290.
56. Maurice Matheka, interview by author, Kangundo, Kenya, Oct. 14, 2007.

Redeemed Gospel Church: Individualism and Materialism

To accomplish this, born agains must be incorporated into local congregations. The RGC are particularly effective in this regard, as they take new converts along the pathway of integration into church membership. The process begins by how they market themselves. Greeters stand in the doorways and enthusiastically welcome people as they come into church services. Visitors are publicly celebrated, sometimes with thunderous applause. At the conclusion of the service, all visitors meet with the pastor and are served *chai* (tea) and other special snacks. Bishop Mutua says, "Churches are like hotels in which the customers go for their meal. If the food is not cooked well, they can choose to go to another hotel."[57] When someone becomes saved or wants to join a church, the first step would be for them to meet with the pastor (less often another church leader) to discern the validity of the salvation. If the pastor approves, the person attends an *employment* class where they discover their spiritual gifting. The pastor is usually involved in this process as he or she has greater discernment to see such spiritual things. From this class, the person is immediately placed into a ministry within the church, under the watchful eye of more mature believers. This happens in quick succession due to the great confidence they have in the Holy Spirit's power. Pastoral authority guides the entire process. Therefore, Marshall-Fratani's image of a "lone individual" needs certain modification to fit within the strong community-orientation and pastoral-mediating characteristics of the RGC.

While the Holy Spirit brings God's power into human lives, these powers are not fully developed in the young convert. Growth comes through the community and particularly via relationship with spiritual leadership. However, there remains a personal element as well. In the words of one leader, "a person needs to desire the Holy Spirit in order to have it."[58] Throughout the life of the believer, personal agency relates to seeking the infilling of the Holy Spirit. When someone stops, even temporarily along this process, he or she runs the danger of becoming *nominal*, which for the RGC appears synonymous with being *unsaved*. If a person ceases to attend church, or begins associating with unsaved friends, he or she may be in danger of *backsliding*; furthermore, the same may be true for cases of persistent sin, spirit oppression, or simply when the person does not show the required passion for God. When such things occur,

---

57. Bishop Paul Mutua, interview by Maurice Twahirwa, Eastleigh, Machakos, Feb. 1, 2009.

58. Rev. Joseph Nzola, interview by author, Machakos, Kenya, Oct. 18, 2006.

the person can redouble efforts to seek the Holy Spirit by becoming more involved in the Christian community, praying more passionately, reading the Bible with greater intentionality, or, if the problem becomes acute, request to participate in an anointing service. These ceremonies are not for everyone, but specifically for those in need of special spiritual assistance (as determined by the pastor). Spiritual touch is vital for these services as the power of the Holy Spirit moves between pastor and congregants, almost *jump starting* the person's growth (and often involves sprinkling oil on the congregant's head).

The entire congregation stands under the authority of the pastor for "tapping into spiritual nourishment from God."[59] This does not mean that everything needs to be approved by the pastor, but the minister functions as the nexus of spiritual appropriation within the community. However, the relationship between individual and pastor remains uncertain at times. Some view the minister as being closer to God, and therefore the conduit through which people receive spiritual guidance. To the extent that pastors are perceived as residing closer to God, they appear to have more power. This is in keeping with traditional perspectives of African cosmology, where proximity to God provides spiritual resources for mediating between divine and human realms. When congregants perceive this (and it is widespread) *washiriki* will ask the pastor for special prayers related to persistent problems: deliverance from recurring sin, unemployment, or other challenging hardships. However, by virtue of the Holy Spirit's indwelling of all believers, the individual does not need to rely upon the pastor in order to pray, worship, read the Bible, evangelize, utilize one's gifting, and/or minister in the congregation. One leader told me, "Traditionally, power was not viewed in the people, but in the leaders." But he proceeded to contrast this with more recent beliefs in the RGC, where "God-given power helps you to make decisions for yourself and over your life" and where it leads to "independence."[60]

The relationship between pastor and congregants tends to be rather ambiguous as the RGC simultaneously emphasize (1) the freedom of the individual, along with (2) heightened authority entrusted to the pastor. An illustration of how these combine involves looking at pastoral prayers. Usually, at some point in the service, the pastor or another leader will begin praying, which signifies for the congregants to join in with

---

59. Dan Ngila, interview by author, Kangundo, Kenya, Oct. 14, 2007.
60. Pastor Josphat Musee, interview with author, Machakos, Kenya, Mar. 8, 2007.

simultaneous audible prayers. Sometimes the members simply echo the words of the pastor ("yes, Lord; please do it as he said, Lord"); other times they adjust or modify their prayers to fit their particular circumstances ("deliver me from my pride, Lord;" "help me to find a job"); or, in some instances, the congregants will pray entirely different prayers unrelated to that of the pastor/leader. The preponderance of individual prayers highlights elements of individualization within RGC congregations (especially compared with mission-founded churches where more emphasis is given to congregational and pastoral prayers). Furthermore, prayers are often intensely personal, evidenced by the use of the first person singular: "help me"; "give me power"; "deliver me from . . ."; and, "I need your Spirit."

Freedom is therefore not only a matter of deliverance from Satan, but signifies individual "powers" residing within "born again" lives. Believers may follow, alter, or deviate from the minister's leading. Parishioners may choose to attend another church if they are not happy with what their minister is doing (implied by Bishop Mutua when he referred to churches as "hotels"). Another example occurs through ecclesiastical *dialogue* taking place within worship services. Congregants are constantly encouraged to *test* the validity of what the preacher is saying, while submitting under the authority of the word of God. The pastor will oftentimes ask people to authenticate his or her statements and/or solicit their immediate answer to some (often rhetorical) question. The minister might request them to read some portion of Scripture on their own, do a Bible study, or memorize Scripture. Yet, these kinds of dialogues carry strong pastoral authority where it is expected that the congregants should believe the accuracy of pastor's statements. Most services flow back and forth between preacher and congregants with lively discourse. A member of the congregation may yell something that contributes to a particular point; the preacher will then ask members a question (often with an obvious answer). Yet with this kind of repartee, submission continues to undergird interactions with pastoral authority, illustrated by members taking notes and/or vociferously agreeing with the speaker at different times. Each believer has the Holy Spirit, but personal powers are mediated through the pastor. Furthermore, the dialogue does not just happen between the congregants and the preacher, but also extends horizontally between members. Most preachers ask *washiriki* to repeat a phrase to their neighbor; for example: "tell the person sitting next to you that he or she has power" and the congregants turn to each other and declare:

Re-Imaging Modernity

"you have power." These rituals (as I am calling them) highlight vertical and horizontal interactions as they relate to the growth of persons; where pastoral authority and individualism find their confluence within local congregations.

Power directly relates with life. The creation account in the book of Genesis shows God "breathing" his Spirit into humans. Bishop Mutua explained to his local congregation, "God created man from the mud—he breathed in him; He gave life to the man, life everlasting. So, in you there is life everlasting."[61] He proceeded to tell them to "hold onto your life" as there is nothing so important. Conversion brings humans back to the original plan of God, where power relates to personhood. Humans are set free from the domain of Satan and relate directly with God's Kingship over the world.

Born agains live out God's power through the fruits and gifts of the Spirit. The fruits relate to the character qualities of personhood. One preacher told his congregants that all the "fruit" were required in order to be whole. His text was Galatians 5:22–23 where he systematically worked through the nine "fruits of the Spirit" showing how each one was essential for believers to achieve their full human potential.[62] These qualities are shared by all believers—anyone indwelled or baptized by the Holy Spirit. By emphasizing shared fruits, the RGC represent an inclusivisitic and integrated community where age, social standing, or gender make little difference. All congregants offer valuable contribution within these churches through the Holy Spirit's democratising power.

However, while the fruits relate to common and interconnected aspects of personhood, the *gifts* of the Holy Spirit provide for particular identities and powers within local congregations. In contrast to the fruits, the gifts are unique and distinguishable from each other. I met with a group of women and listened to them talk about their involvement within a local congregation. First of all, each affirmed she had a gift, and therefore power. The ladies then proceeded to talk about each woman's gifting (within the group) as if it were an obvious and distinguishable aspect of that person's appearance: one was an elder, another led worship singing, while several others had the gift of hospitality.[63] The gifts often related to roles in the church, whether caring for visitors, teaching Bible Studies,

61. Redeemed Gospel Church, Eastleigh, Oct. 15, 2006.
62. Ibid.
63. Monica Kethenge, Mary Munthe, Josephine Wanza, Beatrice Mutuku, Patricia Muisyo, Lilisan Kyalo, interview with author, Kangundo, Kenya, Oct. 14, 2007.

ushering, leading music, or doing evangelism. Women are involved in all areas and can pastor a congregation, serve as an elder, or fulfil any other role within the church. This seems possible because of their strong emphasis given to common humanity (by the fruits) and particular individualities (via the gifts). Through the former, they are united into local congregations without any societal (gender, age, or socio-economic) discrimination; and by the latter they stand out as persons with distinct powers that contribute to the collective whole.

Autonomy

A conspicuous word heard throughout the RGC is *autonomy*. In order to understand this concept according to the meaning(s) intended by people within the denomination, it is necessary to return to the origins of the church. From the very beginning, the founders did not set out to establish a church. Instead, their passion was for evangelism. They viewed the structures within PEFA churches as limiting and restrictive, and wanted something more conducive for fulfilling the Great Commission. Hence, when the church actually began, great care was taken to empower local congregations with what they needed in order to minister to their communities.

In order to accomplish this, 90 percent of the tithes and offerings are allocated to remain with local congregations in order to equip them with the material resources necessary for fulfilling their vision. In addition to this, the organizational structure privileges local initiative by allowing congregations freedom for innovative acts of outreach through this autonomy where, for example, decisions do not need approval by hierarchical superiors. This has led to enormous growth by churches such as Rev Lai's Jesus Celebration Centre, which, in addition to a congregation of twenty thousand people, has planted churches in India, South Africa, and the U.S. and begun other programs designed to reach its Mombasa community. Yet even smaller, rural churches benefit. The Kangundo church has recently begun four smaller congregations and was able to purchase the land, construct buildings, hire pastors, and begin services within a short period of time. Other congregations utilize their funds for development or relief operations within local communities. This has been one of the directions taken by Bishop Mutua in his Eastleigh congregation.

Bishop Matheka explained that the concept of autonomy came from Henry Venn's indigenous principles of "self-supporting," "self-governing," and "self-propagating."[64] Whether this was actually in the minds of the founders is not certain, but the general idea of equipping local congregations with leadership, funds, and vision for reaching their communities was certainly foundational to the origins of the church. Matheka explains,

> With [our desire of] wanting people to preach to their own areas with the gospel, there was no need of making so many rules to bind the people. The issue was how [to] make the structure so … that it will allow us to meet the vision of reaching the unreached with the gospel. Let every church do what God has called them to do.[65]

All of this becomes possible because of the enormous confidence given to the role of the Holy Spirit. Spiritual leaders are "vision bearers" as they listen to God and consider ways of reaching their communities. Equipped with all the necessary funds, and through the individual powers (giftings) of parishioners, local congregations are free to experiment, innovate, and move courageously into their communities with the Gospel. Their use of "autonomy" thus retains heavily community-oriented themes. While the pastor functions as the "vision-bearer," the entire congregation forms the nexus of available powers. Furthermore, autonomy does not mean separateness, or independence. Local congregations are free to have particular names, such as "Jesus Celebration Centre," "Maranatha Chapel," or "Celebration Centre," but must acknowledge that they are part of the Redeemed Gospel Church on their signboard or in paraphernalia.

This kind of autonomy is not without dangers, however. One pastor told me about many churches where the pastor has abused these privileges, leading to the congregants catering for his or her personal needs. Pastors may drive expensive cars or live in luxurious houses. In some cases, where the abuse is excessive, the church may discipline such a person, but then risks having the entire congregation break away from the RGC to begin a separate church. Furthermore, accountability at the local level is equally challenging. Area leaders are responsible for collecting funds and monitoring seven local congregations. Yet as the church rapidly expands (as it did for the initial thirty years of its existence), keeping up with new church plants presents a formidable task and maintaining clear lines of communication with all the churches is not easy. Furthermore,

---

64. Rev. Bishop Daniel Matheka, interview by author, Kangundo, Kenya, Oct. 14, 2007.

65. Ibid.

the precise reading of "autonomy" may differ between denominational leader and local congregation. The former are more likely to speak of collective unity while the latter may be more inclined to promote the benefits of separateness.

Individualism within the RGC is thus a heavily nuanced concept. It flows from freedom experienced within conversion, and releases born agains from the realm of Satan to victorious living within the domain of God. The local church represents the individual's new family where fruits and gifts of the Holy Spirit function as instrumentalities for uniting believers together, as well as expressing personal agency. All of this is accomplished through the pastor's direct oversight: guiding the flow of powers from God, through the people, so that they (born agains) become whole and complete. This picture appears different from Birgit Meyer's earlier comments, where she likened Pentecostalism to the creation of "autonomous individuals." The RGC's view of autonomy" relates to local congregations not independent persons. Yet within this strong community orientation, *washiriki* retain freedom for individual expression. Congregants are encouraged to express their own gifting, worship however they like, or read the Bible *for themselves*. One respondent summarized by saying, "One of the things that makes this church to grow is this freedom; nobody will interfere with what you are doing as long as you are not sinning."[66] The RGC combines all these elements from their confidence in the Holy Spirit who applies God's power in life-affirming ways (while mediated by the pastor). This leads to a second consideration of power: connecting humans with the material world.

MATERIALISM

Members of the RGC would be suspicious of any identification with Western individualism, but they would vehemently oppose all associations with materialism. They often refer to this as one of the modern spirits that works to destroy African societies. Therefore, while my use of individualism differs significantly from Western readings of the same, the following discussion related to materialism will carry notable differences with forms normally associated with Western culture. This is because the RGC preaches a form of prosperity gospel that actively combines spiritual and material elements: both in this life and the age to come. This point is critical for understanding their rise to ecclesiastical

---

66. Rev. Joseph Nzola, interview with author, Machakos, Kenya, Oct. 18, 2006.

prominence and subsequent contribution to modern, Kenyan society. I will trace some of their main teachings on the subject, connecting them with theological beliefs. This will allow me to present a view of the RGC as it relates to material prosperity that shows some of the unique contributions that ecclesiastical communities are making toward sociological concepts. Lawrence Nwankwo says, "While the Prosperity Gospel was articulated in America, it intersects with the holistic vision of salvation in the primal religions of Africa."[67] Pentecostal churches like the RGC demonstrate they can borrow, change, and instill their own characteristics of such an America import in order to claim it for their own.

Paul Gifford has written broadly on the relationship between emergent forms of Christianity in Africa and the prosperity gospel as it relates to Western varieties of Pentecostalism. There can be no denying that American Christianity plays one important factor in the development of ecclesiastical identity in Africa, especially related to large, urban congregations or other ministries located in strategic locations such as Kibera slums, where a preponderance of American missionaries and short-term teams *partner* with African churches. Gifford accuses these churches of being focused upon "private, personalized and otherworldly"[68] concerns and seemingly uninterested with larger societal problems. The question for this section is to what *degree* has the RGC incorporated the American prosperity gospel into their African worldview? Do they focus exclusively upon "otherworldly" concerns, or might they have something more tangible to offer contemporary society?

The Holy Spirit launches born agains into the world with access to spiritual and material benefits; Bishop Matheka says that "freedom releases you to fly high, the sky is the limit."[69] Conversion marks the beginning of this freedom, but the process continues as believers "become more complete" by opposing evil spirits that wage war against people's potentiality within the world. The Christian community constitutes the primary battlefield for these exercises to take place, and, the physical world functions as the venue for its appropriation. It is for such reasons that Bishop Mutua says, "Freedom needs to bring economic and spiritual growth."[70]

67. Nwankwo, "You Have Received," 56.
68. Gifford, "Prosperity," 380.
69. Rev. Bishop Daniel Matheka, interview by author, Kangundo, Kenya, Oct. 14, 2007.
70. Redeemed Gospel Church, Eastleigh, Machakos, Kenya, Oct. 15, 2006.

Creational Framework

The RGC's theological framework arises from the creation account where God breathed his spirit into humans. Converted human nature, for the RGC, represents the eternal joining of flesh and spirit. Sin, along with the ubiquity of evil spirits within the cosmos undermines the working of God's power within the world; specifically, sabotaging human life (which according to an integrative cosmos, also pertains to how humans benefit from the material world). People are constantly admonished regarding the destructive effects of disobedience. They are told: "sin is that which inhibits your potential or destiny;"[71] or "sin affects your eternal life."[72] The Holy Spirit provides the only means for humans to overcome these evil forces and claim rightful identity as "children of God," which, for the RGC is much deeper than filial identity but the indwelling of God within humans. Since God created the physical world, the very presence of the Holy Spirit within human nature brings material benefit. God equals power. All things remain under his dominion. The presence of God within believers, therefore, means that the world is open to born agains. When leaders within the RGC talk about tithes, offerings, or development, they invoke spiritual power. Even a seemingly spiritual topic such as the fruit of the Holy Spirit may correlate with conspicuously secular points of reference. In my discussions with Bishop Mutua, I asked him about the connection between spiritual power and material prosperity. He responded by stating that riches and prosperity, according to the Bible, are fruits of the Holy Spirit. His interpretation of these fruits appears much broader than the list included in Galatians 5:22–23. He explained, "When you are filled with the Holy Spirit, part of God is inside of you; you cannot miss or lack money, you cannot lack anything good, you become a child of God."[73] God's presence, therefore, brings physical and material benefits to believers. By opposing deleterious forces, humans reap material rewards.

Theology of Liberation

Evil spirits are contemporized within RGC congregations to have global points of referent. Among the many sermons addressing the topic of prosperity, the West (and in particular, America) appears conspicuous as the source of misfortune affecting the continent. A preacher exhorts the

71. As heard on the God Channel, Oct. 24, 2006.
72. Redeemed Gospel Church, Eastleigh, Oct. 15, 2006, Machakos, Kenya.
73. Bishop Paul Mutua, interview with author, Machakos, Kenya, Sept. 3, 2007.

people to "not trust in the World Bank or the US to give you anything." He decries how Africa often serves as the "field for US and European/Chinese exploitation."[74] Other times I heard pastors vilifying the kind of materialism coming from America, or telling people that the church needs to redeem technology from "the world" (meaning the evil spirits that inhabit contemporary societies). These and other such references highlight a kind of implicit "theology of liberation" coming out of these churches.

Some distinctive features of this "theology of liberation" include a depersonalization of oppressive forces, a strong emphasis upon Africa's responsibility for holistic deliverance, and continuity between temporal and eternal domains. These points show that the RGC does not merely capitulate to Western forms of the prosperity gospel, but invests them with their own rationale and meanings. Local agents respond to global currents.

Initially, despite the RGC's forthright polemic against the West regarding its role in Africa's predicament, the actual sentiment toward the West is not as antagonistic as it might appear. The main reason stems from their belief that evil spirits lie behind these problems, thus obviating the West of some (if not all) moral responsibility. Thus, preachers may speak openly against American materialism or pillory the oppressive actions of Western governments, yet warmly welcome visitors from the West with genuine hospitality. Evil spirits are responsible for Africa's travails; individual persons are not culpable for larger societal problems. Furthermore, "Born agains" stand together (regardless of race, nationality or denomination) to inculcate holiness within the world. The unifying work of the Holy Spirit allows them to develop loose partnerships with international churches and other (primarily Pentecostal) organizations. Each autonomous church is free to construct its own associations. A church may receive funds for a new sound system, build an outreach center, or send missionaries to another country. These alliances are informal and constantly changing, not subject to MOU (Memorandum of Understandings) or policy statements; they bend and flex to fit within the contemporary predicament: serving the global and local. However, most churches with such partnerships reside in larger cities. I never heard of any within Ukambani. Bishop Matheka told me that if I were to assist his church, I would be the first Westerner to do so. Unlike some larger urban

---

74. Redeemed Gospel Church, Kangundo, Machakos, Kenya, Oct. 15, 2006.

Redeemed Gospel Church: Individualism and Materialism

churches, congregations in Ukambani rarely (if ever) receive short-term missionary teams from America and thus represent a more indigenous face of African Pentecostalism.

However, one Western visitor stands out for his contribution to Pentecostalism in Ukambani. In 1990, Reinhold Bonkke came to Machakos and conducted a series of open-air evangelistic campaigns where thousands of people witnessed God's power: through salvation, healing, and/or deliverance. One leader involved in organizing this event described it as the "turning point" for the RGC[75]; when Pentecostalism (and the RGC in particular) experienced a measure of legitimacy within the wider community. Up until this point, most Akamba perceived Pentecostalism to be an eccentric form of Christianity with heightened emotion and speaking in tongues; a deviation from their mission heritage. However, these public meetings caused increased interest in Pentecostalism (and the RGC in particular) enabling the church to grow significantly through the next decade. Bonkke's mission to Machakos shows how global agents can serve to authenticate local domains, even as I earlier maintained that local churches modify global currents of theological/social expression.

These comments provide tempered assessment regarding Gifford's association between the African Christianity and the American prosperity gospel. On the one hand, the RGC resists Western influence by opposing evil spirits behind global powers; yet on the other hand, by depersonalizing these forces they are open to *partnerships* with international churches and/or individuals. In one sense, they promote an indigenous prosperity gospel through their holistic conception of an integrated cosmos, but by linking themselves with all born-agains throughout the world, they participate in a global community with a free exchange of personnel and ideas. Rural churches tend to be more isolated and locally sponsored, while large urban congregations display greater influence from global relationships.

Another facet of the RGC's "theology of liberation" emphasizes that they, as African born agains, are the ones responsible for their own welfare by addressing spiritual and physical needs alike. The origins of the Church (in rural Ukambani and urban Nairobi) show that from the very beginnings, the founders viewed the Gospel as foundational for meeting the needs of Africa's poorest people. In 1975, a year after its inception, Kitonga began the development arm of their church. In Mathare Valley,

---

75. Rev. Joseph Nzola, interview with author, Machakos, Kenya, Oct. 18, 2007.

the church feeds children, operates orphanages and undertakes microenterprise projects; in Machakos they offer programs for those with HIV/AIDs, operate a tailoring school for girls unable to complete secondary school, care for street children, work on agricultural projects, build water dams, and encourage people in the congregation to adopt orphaned children. The two founders provide the inspiration for such a holistic Gospel. Kitonga lived in the slums (yet now occupies less modest accommodation), while Mutua raised a street kid within his own family. The prosperity gospel according to the RGC has a strong component of social action and involvement in societal affairs. The poor need deliverance; evil spirits opposed; society strengthened.

The hermeneutical key for this holistic Gospel comes from the way they combine the spiritual and physical. The church's Web site describes the denomination as committed "to meet the needs—both spiritual and physical" of people; or, where as "an independent Pentecostal Church" they have "adopted evangelism, blended with social concern, as a wholistic approach for the total man—body, soul and spirit."[76] Power, therefore, relates to the entire person through the indwelling of the Holy Spirit: appropriating God's presence within the world. When I questioned Bishop Mutua *why* they undertake development projects, he laughed as if the answer was obvious: "The Holy Spirit is God, isn't he? He is the one that enables us to do anything that is godly. We believe it is God; those are his fruits."[77] Godliness thus has distinct material points of reference (and could conceivably refer to anything). Another preacher told congregants that "the only alter call he makes is money," showing how financial giving opens a window to a person's soul and testifies to the genuineness of their salvation. This leads the church to view words such as "prosperity," "wealth," and "abundance" with positive, spiritual connotations (while "materialism" relates to demonic activity). One leader even carried this to the extent of telling the congregation that Jesus was not poor but that he lived in a large house and had a personal treasurer.[78] Maturity in the Christian life means holistic prosperity (within an integrative cosmology). All congregants, therefore, should aspire wealth and success, if they do so through the proper means (obedience to God). Thus, to attend a church service is to see men and women dressed in their finest clothes,

---

76. Par. 2, http://www.redeemedgospel.org/aboutus.html [accessed 4 Jan. 2008].
77. Bishop Paul Mutua, interview with author, Machakos, Kenya, Sept. 3, 2007.
78. Redeemed Gospel Church, Kangundo, Oct. 14, 2007.

Redeemed Gospel Church: Individualism and Materialism

presenting an image (real or imagined) of successful living in the world. A preacher talks about his rise from poverty to the point of owning a Toyota Prado; others testify to victory in Secondary School exams, or securing a new job. Such narratives address felt needs within the congregation and attest to significant powers within the church: situating believers most favorably within the modern world. Spiritual power brings material benefit.

These narratives (often called *testimonies*) tend to privilege few select individuals while leave others trapped within oppressive social conditions. Yet even the latter experience "success" through association with the church as it expands numerically and engages within modern society through strategic mediums such as television and politics. Youth come to the church because it is "doing something," and by virtue that it represents "success."[79] By joining the church, youth experience some of this prosperity. A lay leader explains, "God has deposited a seed of greatness, righteousness, success, and a peaceful life in each of us."[80] This statement shows how such seemingly nonreligious ascriptions such as *greatness* and *success* can combine with spiritual themes of *righteousness* and *peace* to highlight the integrative nature of RGC teachings. Evangelism, social action, and even sociopolitical involvement all relate to God's power within the world.

A final aspect of the RGC's "theology of liberation" involves continuity between temporal and eternal domains, where the *already* of the Kingdom of God reaches out to effect the *not yet*. However, this perspective is not exclusively one-directional, where the former leads to the latter. Members believe they can access treasures stored in heaven for them within the present age. One preacher told the people that the "Gospel opens the door for you to the resources of heaven." It is a sin to be poor, since God has given humans the entire world for their use. The same speaker explained to his congregants that the Garden of Eden was full of great treasures—gold, silver, previous gems—until Adam and Eve disobedience forfeited these. Salvation makes them accessible once again. Then he announced, "The Garden of Eden is coming to Kangundo," to the reverberating applause of those listening.[81] Continuity between the

---

79. Maurice Matheka, interview with author, Kangundo, Kenya, Oct. 14, 2007.
80. Deacon Muia, Redeemed Gospel Church, Eastleigh, Feb. 8, 2009.
81. Redeemed Gospel Church, Kangundo, Oct. 14, 2007.

two ages reflects similarities with traditional African cultures. Nwankwo describes this within broader continent-wide perspective:

> By Africa's wholistic worldview is meant the expectation that the experience of wholeness, that is, long healthy life, wealth, fertility, success, etc., is legitimate and that religion should contribute to its provision. . . . Thus religion is not just about attaining fullness of life in the "other world." Life on earth is supposed to be a foretaste of that fullness of life and a sign of divine favour.[82]

The RGC believe that while riches follow you to heaven, poverty can do the same. This implies that there will be various levels in the afterlife. A preacher warns people that if they allow themselves to be under the "spirit of poverty" they will not have mansions in heaven.[83] Such statements provide heightened spiritual importance to the present task of wealth acquisition.

Biblical admonition continually reinforces continuity between the present and future ages. Preachers often relate Jesus' teachings to future rewards (cf. Luke 18:29–30); or where people should "store up for yourselves treasures in heaven" (Matt 6:20). Historically, evangelicalism (at least in mainline churches) has tended to spiritualize these verses, understanding rewards as unrelated to material gain. The RGC, however, take these verses very literally. Their hermeneutics appear a bit whimsical at times, subject to great latitude of interpretation; however, they are consistent in seeing interconnections between spiritual and material realities, as well as joining the "already" and the "not yet" within the kingdom of God.

Therefore, any reference to materialism within the RGC needs to be heavily qualified. The kind observed in their churches involves dynamic mobility within an integrative cosmos, where Christian maturity implies "successful" living in the present age (as well as the one that is to come). Wealth appears to be one of the contemporary evidences of the Spirit's power. This can lead to dangerous tendencies where spiritual leaders pursue wealth to substantially increase their powers; or where prosperity and success become outward evidences of Christian maturity due to linkages with sacred powers. These churches also overlook the importance of poverty as a sign of the kingdom of heaven; or, as Gifford

---

82. Nwankwo, "You Have Received," 59–60.
83. Redeemed Gospel Church, Kangundo, Oct. 14, 2007.

has noted, tend to associate poverty with sin or spiritual ineptitude.[84] Yet these criticisms should not entail a wholesale rejection of their theology, nor imply that they are unaware of these dangers. While the RGC elevate wealth as (perhaps) the most important fruit of the kingdom of God, they maintain countermeasures within their theological perspective to guard against over-privileging the material. When I asked various church leaders if a wealthy businessman would naturally become an elder in a local congregation, they all denied that this would happen unless the person showed that he or she was spiritual.[85] One pastor told me, "Many churches have died because wealthy persons have responsibility in the church."[86] Their emphasis upon the Holy Spirit tends to democratize power in their churches, allowing women, youth or those from lower socio-economic backgrounds to participate in ways often unthinkable in other churches. Furthermore, their polemic against the West and materialism tends to constantly remind people about the dangers of over-emphasizing money or wealth. One visiting preacher explained to the congregation that he often asks people to bring all their money to the church so that he can stand (literally) on the currency and pray over it. Wealth should be under people's feet and not on their heads, he told the congregants.[87] Examples such as this testify to a form of anti-materialism that is strong in these churches and needs to be included in the broader purview of the RGC's prosperity gospel.

Marshall-Fratani thus speaks of the prosperity gospel as a "morally-controlled materialism, in which personal wealth and success is interpreted as evidence of God's blessing on those who lead a 'true life in Christ.'"[88] Such a statement may also be applied to those forms appearing within the RGC. Material and spiritual elements combine within an integrative cosmos, with humans functioning as strategic agents for the growth of the world, and where evangelism and prosperity seemingly flow together through the power of the Spirit. Since born agains are filled with the Holy Spirit, they use their powers for the growth of the world around them (with personal and corporate benefit). Human communities coordinate

---

84. Gifford, "Prosperity," 375.

85. Mr Gideon Musau, Rev. Saul Mutie, and Mr. Justus Musila, interview with author, Machakos, Kenya, Oct. 5, 2006.

86. Rev. Saul Mutie, interview with author, Machakos, Kenya, Oct. 5, 2006.

87. Redeemed Gospel Church, Kangundo, Machakos, Kenya, Oct. 14, 2007.

88. Marshall-Fratani, "Mediating," 282–83.

divine power (often mediated through the man of God), and the world functions as the context for its appropriation.

CONCLUSION

This chapter illustrates the significance of power for the development of humanity in Africa, as well as highlighting some of the ways that newer Pentecostal churches, such as the RGC, utilize these powers to situate themselves most favorably within the modern world. While I have focused upon such words as *individualism* and *materialism* they are, in fact, distinctly different from Western forms of the same, and, in this regard, testify to undercurrents of anti-modernity that exist alongside modernity in Africa. The church's indigenous origins, interpretation of evil spirits, and strong diatribe against sin provide the foundation for this anti-modern stance. However, spiritual powers also release congregants from traditional oppressive practices (and structures) making it possible for them to function as God's agents within an open world. The denomination further contemporizes evil spirits to enable people to freely engage in modern categories: as individuals and through association with their church. Furthermore, by connecting spiritual and physical components they allow members access to the fruits of modernity: whether wealth acquisition, technology, or engagement within politics. The RGC, therefore, show how it is possible to be anti-modern and modern at the same time, utilizing concepts such as individualism, autonomy, freedom, and materialism in distinct ways through their overarching theology of spiritual power in order to live effectively (and move) within the modern world.

6

Power and the Image of God: A Contextualized Theological Proposal

THE PREVIOUS CHAPTERS HAVE described characteristics of power through study of three denominations in Ukambani, showing how theological material contributes to the development of sociological themes. In this final chapter, I will draw upon these insights to develop the beginnings of a theology of power for contemporary Africa, using the *imago dei* from Old and New Testaments, and framing the subsequent discussion within the voices of the three theological communities.

Cultures are dynamic precisely because they comprise people, who constantly adjust to their surroundings and re-interpret available information into ever-changing contexts. The history of Christianity reveals many of these interactions, showing new avenues for theological development at the points where the Gospel confronts cultural, religious, or socioeconomic realities. Modernity, I am suggesting, presents one of these vistas for theological activity in Africa. Establishing modernity as a theological category, at once, seeks to bridge the chasm often presented in African studies between traditions and modernity, insisting that "multi-directional global flows of people, ideas and goods"[1] highlight the character of porous societies, framed and interpreted, in part, by the powers available to humans. I want to show some of the ways that ecclesiastical communities utilize their knowledge of God in order to fashion their societies: to inculcate generative images of life into contemporary contexts.

During the previous chapters, I endeavored to show innovative theological activity taking place within churches around orientations with divine power. I will use the remainder of this study to build on this

1. Deutsch et al., *African Modernities*, 11.

framework, offering new possibilities for situating power within the image of God concept as found in the biblical narratives. Anthropocentric orientations of power fit well with the internal logic of African Christianity, where divine power relates to human affairs, and enables ecclesiastical communities with vital resources for imaging God within their societies. The following theological development will therefore borrow from the language and cultural resources found within African cosmological worldviews in order to show the viability of locating power within the image of God; where it (1) emanates from God, (2) relates to human growth or personhood, and (3) promotes cosmic fruitfulness. I will treat the image of God less from the vantage point of biblical exegesis and more as a theological resource in which to paint (in broad strokes) prevailing features of power: evidenced first within Christian theology and, secondly, within Akamba theological communities of faith. Therefore, this will be an integrative project.

POWER AND THE IMAGE OF GOD

The story of creation, as recorded in Genesis 1 and 2, begins in much the same way as Akamba legend,[2] with God as initiator, primary agent, and source of life. God creates the natural world (as opposed to Akamba stories in which he begins with spirits), and then proceeds to fashion human beings as the focal point of life. While the order of creation in African cosmology pertains to nearness or proximity with spiritual power, the Bible account places humans last, furthest from the origin of life; nevertheless, as the culmination of God's created process, the climax of creation, agents endowed with power to provide for the previous acts of creation. God creates the world, and then fashions image-bearers, endowing them with responsibility and powers for caring for life in its totality.

The Genesis narrative begins by describing the functional ontology of human beings, along with essential meanings or values given to them from within creation. God says, "Let us make man in our image, in our likeness" (1:26). The words *image* and *likeness* arise out of the language and customs of Ancient Near Eastern culture, building upon each other to communicate complementary themes, with the latter adding clarity and definition to the former.[3] Rulers in the Ancient Near East oftentimes erected images (i.e., monuments or effigies) of themselves within newly

---

2. See Mbiti, *Akamba Stories*, 14–15; cf. Ndeti, *Elements*.
3. Clines, "Humanity," 486.

Power and the Image of God: A Contextualized Theological Proposal

conquered territories, especially when living in distance lands. In 1979, such a statue was discovered in Tell Fakhariyeh where the words image and likeness were used to convey similar meanings as those found in Genesis.[4] The inscription begins with a prayer, in which the ruler beseeches the deity for protection and favor. The supplication then moves to make correlation between the governor's status and that of the deity: essentially portraying the ruler as an earthly manifestation of the divine, with powers "akin to that of the gods."[5] Images in the Ancient Near East often communicated divine import upon the person of the king (or leading authority).[6] It is possible the biblical account draws upon these associations to ascribe similar powers to human rulers. In such a case, God creates images that embody his power; the word likeness further accentuates the use of image in order to provide "assurance that humanity is an adequate and faithful representative of God on earth."[7]

In like manner, Walter Brueggemann calls attention to regal meanings behind the biblical notion of "dust."[8] In Genesis 2:7 the text reads that God "formed the man from the dust of the ground and breathed into his nostrils the breath of life, and the man became a living being." Comparative passages (1 Kgs 16:2; 1 Sam 2:8; Ps 113:7) show the same Hebrew word *dust* being used to express royal sentiment, where kings arise from lowly places to lead their people. Brueggemann employs these broader meanings for better understanding the Genesis passage. He says,

> Adam, in Gen 2 is really being crowned king over the garden with all the power and authority which it implies. This is the fundamental statement about man.... He is willed by God to occupy a royal office. And when he lives in this relationship he knows life.[9]

Ascriptions of power relate directly with life. God raises divine-like kings out of the dust. "Creation is the enthronement of man as faithful regent of his covenant Lord."[10]

---

4. Garr, "'Image,'" 227–34.

5. Ibid., 230.

6. This is further evidenced in Egyptian cultures, where the king is endowed with "divine fluid"; see Clines, "Humanity," 476.

7. Ibid., 495.

8. Brueggemann, "From Dust," 1–18.

9. Ibid., 12.

10. Ibid., 7 n. 16.

These biblical insights introduce the possibility for looking at creation, and particularly the image of God, through power-related lenses. To represent God means that God has an image. To exercise regal dominion intimates power. To "have" power signifies something about the *kind* of power that humans represent. "Genesis affirms the dignity and worth of humanity, and elevates all humans—not just kings or nobles—to the highest status conceivable, short of complete divinization."[11] However, certain parameters guide this identity. Humans are not God, and the temptation account in Genesis chapter 3 shows that any attempt to usurp God's sovereignty by becoming "like God" (v. 3) stands outside the bounds for what God intends. The image of God *reflects* divine character, rather than hijacking God's nature for personal interest. To the extent that Adam and Eve sought to become like God as a replacement for their humanity, they became less than God created them to be, resulting in expulsion from the Garden and curses upon their powers. Humans, therefore, image God derivatively.[12] They do not *possess* an image, but receive one from accurately representing the divine within the created order. As people faithfully embody God's power within the full array of life experiences, they grow in conformity to that image.

Perhaps the best way of explaining human nature from within the creation account would be to translate Genesis 1:26 in the manner adopted by Clines; where it reads, "Let us make humanity as our image" or "to be our image."[13] The emphasis in this case rests upon what the image images, rather than materialistic components that situate the image as a possession of humanity. The existential character of the image predominates the discussion, indicating "the kinds of things they need to do if they would know God."[14] Men and women are God's representatives on the earth to the extent that they image God with authenticity: expressing the immanence of God's transcendence; the faithful use of divine power.

PARAMETERS FOR IMAGE-BEARING

Situating power within the image of God concept, at once, highlights the need for ethical parameters to guide *how* humans appropriate divine power within the world, while providing a framework for establishing

11. Clines, "Humanity," 447.
12. A point made by McFarland, *The Divine Image*, 4.
13. Clines, "Humanity," 475.
14. McFarland, *The Divine Image*, vii.

those very theological valuations. It has already been shown that African cosmology tends to interpret everything through power-related lenses. On the one hand, orientations with divine power often relate to life growth, and therefore have generative characteristics; on the other, however, dangers exist where certain humans (such as elders, or spiritual specialists) reside in closer proximity to God as the origin (or source) of power, and therefore are perceived by the masses to be *more powerful*. Since power relates to life growth (or personhood), certain ontological hierarchies of power hence appear within human communities: where people nearer to the source(s) of spiritual power seem *more human*, while those farther away appear incomplete or less-than-human (dehumanized). On the surface, a theological response to this quandary might involve dislocating humanity from divine power: essentially creating an impenetrable divide, separating humans from the divine (such as has often occurred within Western evangelicalism). However, this comes with dangers. If humans are disconnected from God's power, they are likewise severed from the source of life, affecting their identity, means of growth, and with implications to power-relations within an integrative cosmos. Therefore, precisely due to proclivities within African societies that tend to integrate spiritual power with the rest of the cosmos (seen earlier in Chapter 2), more work needs to be given to establishing theological guidelines to frame the relationship between humans and divine power.

Initially, the image of God indicates both continuity and discontinuity with divine power. On the one hand, (1) humans represent God's regal agency within the world, and on the other, (2) the image remains derivational in nature: dependent on the source of power. Any attempt to understand how humans interact with God's power, therefore, involves nurturing the concept of divine power (theologically and sociologically) from within the nature of the Godhead, maintaining that humans image God's nature by remaining faithful to the *values and purposes* expressed within the divine community.[15] This highlights the need for sociological expressions of divine power to reach out for theological assistance; further, where theologians should consider how beliefs about God carry sociological implications. It is not enough for theologians to think

---

15. Jürgen Moltmann makes a similar point where he explains the social implications for how humans understand the divine community; for example, where hierarchical views of the Trinity often create the impression of a God who dominates, and therefore, he argues, leading to oppressive coordinates arising within human communities (see Moltmann and Moltmann-Wendel, *Humanity in God*, 91ff.).

theoretically about the image of God as *dominion* but need likewise to give theological valuation to the outworking of God's power: moving from biblical categories to empirical manifestations.

God's agency (precisely, how God uses power) provides the starting point for the discussion, which then leads to implications for how God's nature affects human communities. William Schweiker moves in a similar direction. He says,

> The distinctiveness of a biblically informed moral ontology is that to identify ultimate reality as an agent (for example, "God"), that is, to specify the inner meaning of ultimate power as an identity bearing actor, is to assert a value that transcends natural, social, and political power....[16]

Because of inherent linkages between human and divine communities (especially within the context of an integrative cosmos), affirming that *God is power* says something important about the nature of human power. In the context of creation (and re-creation), God's power generates and promotes fruitfulness. All of life flows from this creational principle:

> From this perspective, one does not see the world simply as a web of interdependent processes nor as so many historical monuments to human civilization and barbarism. Rather, the world is seen as a field of action composed of diverse struggles to transform relations of power for the sake of respecting and enhancing the integrity of life. Identifying or naming ultimate power 'God' entails, then, a construal of the world, or a moral ontology, and a set of moral commitments that necessarily focus on the transvaluation of power.[17]

Schweiker argues that God's agency asserts value and meaning into processes related to power. Said in another way, humans function as image bearers by representing God with fidelity to the powers emanating from the divine community. This is not to reduce God into human constructs, but to rehabilitate (or, nurture) human power from within divine constructs:[18] establishing creational parameters for the employment of divine power within the world.

---

16. Schweiker, "Power," 207.

17. Ibid., 208.

18. Moltmann expresses the divine community in dynamic relationship: "for each other and in each other," with implications for what this means for human communities. See Moltmann and Moltmann-Wendel, *Humanity*, 98.

Power and the Image of God: A Contextualized Theological Proposal

Furthermore, by fixing the discussion within the image of God concept, it is possible to argue that all humans have this orientation with the divine, countering hierarchical configurations that suggest some people are more powerful and therefore, in one sense or another, *more human* (alternatively, in some instances, more powerful and therefore less human).[19] Thus, Schweiker's "moral ontology" brings fresh insights into the image of God concept as it pertains to representing God's nature on the earth. Power must promote life in order to accurately represent the divine. God's agency provides the basis by which humans understand power, and are brought into covenant relationship as regal (powerful) agents on the earth: to be in covenant means to utilize power with similar intention and values to the source of the image; to be out of covenant means corrupting the powers.[20] Furthermore, proximity to God's purposes (as evidenced within biblical and Akamba creation narratives) places humans in strategic position to utilize divine powers: poised for the integration of all things.

REIMAGING POWER WITHIN THE IMAGE OF GOD

African cosmological beliefs (whether in traditional or Christianized forms) employ power as an interpretative mechanism for understanding interrelationships between God, humans, and the created world. God alone is power. Humans participate in divine power by tapping into (or engaging with) the powers available within the cosmos. They do so for the fruitfulness of life.

An imaginative retelling of the story of salvation history from within the lenses of power-related imagery would involve an integrative cosmos where God gives central priority to humans, his image-bearers (Gen 1:26–27), for orienting the cosmos to God (without impinging upon his sovereignty). Instead of juxtaposing God from humans, the image of God moves to reveal the divine from within creation, set within discourses of power. Borrowing from the traditions of African religions, this refers to relatedness and source of power proceeding from God, while providing the context for articulating (or, representing) these powers on the earth. Therefore, to speak of the image of God is at once to acknowledge its associations and webs of interaction. "God separates, creatures separate,

---

19. See Okesson, "Are Pastors," 19–39. I argue that power with God can appear to raise some humans nearer to God and therefore less like humans.

20. See Brueggemann, "From Dust," 3.

God makes, creatures bring forth, God ordains, and creatures rule."[21] In the verses that flow from Genesis 1:26–27 this becomes apparent. God blesses Adam and Eve and commands them to "be fruitful and multiply," "fill the earth and subdue it," and "rule over" the creatures (v. 28). The entire world becomes the gift (vv. 29–30) and God proclaims it "very good" (v. 31). Goodness might refer to the individual properties of creation (as might be understood from an atomistic, Western context) or the webs of interaction connecting everything together (more representative of an African cosmos). Certainly, both need affirming: God creates life and provides the means for growing in life by connecting his image with divine power.

When sin enters the story, it does more than affect the individual properties of creation, but distorts the cohesion, the dignity, and most strategically the ontological and existential representations of God's power within the cosmos. Humans are set against God, each other, and nature. They misappropriate the power by misrepresenting the nature of the power. In wanting to become like God, they become significantly less than God created them to be, scorning the gift and abusing the power. Domination, separation, exploitation, sacralization, and oppression become common themes of power in human communities, affecting how people interact with the rest of the created world. Fear, insecurity and self-abasement follow, where humanity twists and contorts through the rejection of the gift of the image of God.

The Incarnation of Jesus Christ reorients the entire cosmos to God through a human image-bearer (2 Cor 4:4; Col 1:15). The previous theme of kingship receives new definition and clarity. To see Christ is to see God (John 14:9–10); no other image can claim such honor. Rather than dislocate divine power from human control, the Incarnation re-extends God's power into the world. God's "moral ontology" receives new expression from within the Incarnation. Divine power is nurtured within human nature. "In Jesus the world is thus confronted with the claim to have been provided with an objective referent, visible and tangible, against which all claims about God may and must be tested."[22] However, instead of adopting the surrounding culture's view of power, Christ reorients humans to God by reimaging God's power for humans (Luke 22:25; John 13:3–17); he does so through fragility, service, and sacrifice. Jesus depends upon

21. Welker, "Creation," 442.
22. McFarland, *The Divine*, 25.

Power and the Image of God: A Contextualized Theological Proposal

the Holy Spirit for every moment of his life, whether in birth (Luke 1:35), growth in childhood (Luke 2:40),[23] or subsequent ministry (baptism, temptation, proclamation, healing, death and resurrection). Derivative authority defines Jesus' "image": emanating *from* the Father (Matt 28:18; John 3:35; 13:3; 17:2) and enacted *by* the power of the Holy Spirit. However, nearness to God (John 13:3) never impinges upon Christ's humanity, as if to sacralize it, or undermine its authenticity. On the contrary, divinity, in the life of Christ, provides the very gateway for redefining humanity: the re-expression of divine powers. Paul writes in Philippians 2:6–7,

> *Precisely because he was in the form of God* [italics mine] he did not consider being equal with God grounds for grasping. On the contrary, he rather poured himself out by taking the form of a slave, by being born in the likeness of human beings, and by being recognized as a man.[24]

Nearness to God does not create a super-human, but a real man, invested with full human nature (c.f. Heb 2:14–17). J. D. G. Dunn says something similar:

> It would seem then that Adam and *kyrios* Christology as statements of Christ's cosmic lordship are best understood, not as any sort of threat to the unity of God or as a diffusion of the one God's sovereignty over creation, but rather in terms of God's purpose to share his authority as Creator with man the crown of his creation, man the image of God destined from the first to share in his fuller glory.[25]

The image of Christ, therefore, reveals divine power *within* human nature, without either compromising the moral ontology of God, or jeopardizing the goodness of creaturely humanity.

The Incarnation does more, however, than redefine human nature, it also reorients divine power for life growth. God's power never raises humans from their creaturely status (as if needing to be sacralized) but

---

23. The phrase "filled with wisdom" (Luke 2:40) intimates the work of the Holy Spirit by drawing upon Old Testament notions of divine wisdom (Prov 1:2, 7), mirroring similar sentiments made for John the Baptist (Luke 1:80) and therefore expressing a complete dependence upon the power of the Holy Spirit in the life of Jesus Christ; see Hawthorne, *Presence and the Power*, 97–109.

24. This translation was proposed by Hawthorne, *Philippians*, 75.

25. Dunn, "Was Christianity," 328.

rests comfortably within human constructs, with effect to the spaces within an integrative cosmos.[26] Kingship is given to humans, but with ethical parameters that govern the use of powers in relation to God's nature (through the image of God). Adam and Eve scorned the powers by wanting to be more than they were created to be. With the Incarnation of Jesus Christ, God once again establishes his image on the earth, defined in terms of ethical and moral values that pertain to the use of divine power. Power is for humanity, and generates life.

With Christ's death and resurrection (through the power of the Holy Spirit), the localized, culturally embedded Jesus of Nazareth becomes universalized through time and space in the glorified Person of Christ (still fully human), and represented through the lives (quite literally, *humanities*) of the People of God. Jesus' life forms the focal point of salvation, such that the Apostle Paul says, "We shall be saved through his life!" (Rom 5:10) or where believers "reign in life" (Rom 5:17). Yet the means of appropriating that salvation involves the work of the Holy Spirit insofar as he applies the glorified humanity of Christ into the lives of believers, who are the Body of Christ. The Holy Spirit is called the "Spirit of life" (Rom 8:2; cf. John 6:63) because he raised Christ from the dead (1 Pet 3:18; cf. Rom 8:11) and offers that life to humans (2 Cor 3:18).

Power language serves valuable means to express spiritual realities within the New Testament church, mobilizing the People of God toward life (defined by Christ's humanity). Luke explains how a frightened group of disciples receives the "power of the Holy Spirit" to become Christ's witnesses throughout the earth (Acts 1:8). The Apostles testify "with great power" pertaining to the resurrection of the Lord (Acts 4:31). Paul appeals to the Spirit's power for legitimizing his ministry to the Gentiles (1 Cor 2:4). The Gospel is referred to as the "power of God" (Rom 1:16), and the nature of the Kingdom: "not a matter of talk but of power" (1 Cor 4:20). Finally, John describes the eschatological People of God as a "kingdom and priests" (Rev 1:6), with "authority over the nations" (2:26), and who "will reign for ever and ever" (22:4). Kwame Bediako highlights the importance of power-language for expressing Gospel realities in Africa. He says,

---

26. The temptations experienced by Christ in the wilderness were precisely for the purposes of undermining Jesus' human nature: tempting Christ to take shortcuts around his humanity (whether satisfying hunger by changing stones into bread, publicly displaying spiritual authority over angels, or claiming sovereignty over the nations—albeit by bending the knee to spurious powers).

Power and the Image of God: A Contextualized Theological Proposal

> Primal religions generally conceive of religion as a system of power and of living religiously as being in touch with the source and channels of power in the universe; Christian theology in the West seems, on the whole, to understand the Christian Gospel as a system of ideas. And yet, when the apostle Paul described the Gospel, that is what he wrote: "I have complete confidence in the Gospel; it is the power of God to save all who believe...." Surely, this calls for a new idiom.[27]

The image of God I am proposing furnishes such an idiom, where power concepts are expressed within an integrative framework, supplying important ethical parameters to guide the outworking of divine power within human constructs.

God is the source of all power (to borrow from African cosmological language), seen in its clearest form in Jesus Christ. Humans function as image-bearers by being "conformed to the likeness of the Son" (Rom 8:29); which at once says something important about the nature and expression of power. God reveals divine power through the Incarnation. Initially, this informs us that human nature is not something people need to escape, or try to overcome in order to properly represent God; on the contrary, it is only through humanity that divine power can be properly manifested. Vinoth Ramachandra argues something similar, "Our humanity is not something that comes between us and God. On the contrary, it is precisely in our humanity that we are called to be bearers of the divine glory, the means by which God is made known."[28] Sacralizing tendencies that appear (in different forms) within African ecclesiology (whether conceived along the lines of neo-patrimonialism;[29] or Christian deification[30]) run the risk of demeaning humanity by elevating sacred leaders in closer proximity with God, where they "have" (as a substance of their being) greater powers. Sacralization,[31] of this kind, opposes the

---

27. Bediako, *Christianity in Africa*, 106; in a similar way, Bediako proposes that this "idiom" can only be understood within the context of Jesus Christ, by the power of the Holy Spirit.

28. Vinoth Ramachandra, *The Recovery of Mission*, 252.

29. Gifford, *African*, 5–6.

30. Okesson, "Are Pastors Human?" 25ff.

31. Once again, I am using "sacralization" to express heightened spiritual powers in relation to the divine, where a leader (in this case) is viewed as residing in closer proximity to God. There are certainly other possible uses of the word, but my general phraseology corresponds to how Bediako expresses the concept within African cosmology (see "Unmasking the Powers," 207–29).

Incarnation, where Christ "did not consider equality with God a thing to be grasped." Furthermore, if few select individuals have "more power" (understood within African contexts as implying "more personhood") the entire image of God buckles under the misrepresentation of God. This immediately means that all notions of gradated importance of being, whether conceived along ethnic, age, gender, socioeconomic, political, or spiritual categories are nothing more than distortions of God's creaturely good offered to humans, and thus in one sense or another direct attacks against God's very nature. In African contexts, where power correlates with being, elevation of certain persons as more-than-human has the corresponding effect of corporate de-humanization (inclusive of the "structures" within societies).

Christ's authority, in its derivation form, shows the existential outworking of the image of God in selfless service to others. God's image is never a right and always a gift. Christ uses his divine powers to wash the disciple's feet (John 13:3), heal people, and teach "with authority" (Matt 7:29). The climactic portrayal of these realities comes through his death. The cross of Christ represents a new form of power entering the world. Not as might be understand in terms of evolved cultural, structural or epistemological forms of organization, but what Miroslav Volf describes as "space" woven into the "networks of power in which the truth of Christ—which is always a truth about power—can be lived out."[32] Christ's humanity saturates the spaces interconnecting creation: revealing life, and providing mechanisms for growing in life.

Humans are oriented first to Christ; concomitantly, to other image-bearers; and always to the world. Human powers (roughly equated with life) are legitimized (or, in African terms "blessed") insofar as they accurately represent Christ: by promoting the growth of others, and working for the flourishing of the world. Theological categories move in distinctly sociological ways. I will show this in three interconnected ways.

Power from God

God's nature establishes a kind of moral ontology that governs the outworking of power within the world. Believers discover their "life is now hidden with Christ in God" (Col 3:3), nestled within the arms of the divine community.[33] Moltmann contends, "The divine Trinity is so inviting

32. Volf, "Theology, Meaning and Power," 109–10.
33. Irenaeus, *Against Heresies* 5.6.1.

Power and the Image of God: A Contextualized Theological Proposal

and so strong that the divine life reflects itself in true human community and takes human community up into itself."[34] This is only possible because of continuities existing between divine and human realms, through the image of God concept; and later crystallized by the Incarnation of Jesus Christ.

The derivational character of the image of God, however, guards against tendencies that situate one image nearer to the source of power, or more like God, than the others. Humans cannot hijack God's nature (power) for personal gain, except by losing themselves in the process. McFarland argues,

> Paul's insistence that believers need to be transformed into Christ's image (Rom 8:28–29; 2 Cor 3:18; Col 3:10) implies that they do not possess this image in themselves. Thus, if they are one in him, it is because he has made them one (Eph 2:14), not because they share some prior unity apart from him. In this way, the effect of the Christian confession of Jesus as the image of God is not to focus attention on humankind, but to prod people to look away from themselves to God as the source and guarantor of their identity.[35]

Humans rediscover their humanity by looking to God (in Christ). This does not create super-humans, but real persons, authenticated through regal powers on the earth. All believers contribute to the image of God in Christ insofar as they accurately represent Christ on the earth.

Ethical parameters, therefore, govern the representation of divine power on the earth. God creates the world, infusing the cosmos with values pertaining to his nature. However, sin distorts the manifestation of power on the earth, by (1) misrepresenting God's nature in the world, and thus leading to distorted conceptions of human power and/or (2) undermining the derivational essence of human power: making it a right or an independent entity. However, by reasserting God's moral ontology as the fundamental basis for human nature, theological ethics brings new definition to the outworking (or representation) of divine power on the earth. Thus raising the question of *who* represents God.

---

34. Moltmann and Moltmann-Wendel, *Humanity*, 98.
35. McFarland, *The Divine*, 6.

Re-Imaging Modernity

Power with Other Image-Bearers

Conformity to the image of Christ re-establishes humans as regal image bearers. This immediately means that the entities and webs of cohesion need to be rehabilitated within the created world: affecting human life and the means of growing in life. Christ orients humans to God by imaging God for humans. Power is thus *from* Christ's life and it is *for* human growth (through the Holy Spirit).

Diversity (or *otherness*), therefore, remains foundational for representing the glorified Christ, since no earthly image has priority over the others. All represent God insofar as they collectively represent the glorified Christ. Andrew Walls raises this point for addressing some of the benefits wrought by missiological and/or globalizing trends; he says,

> The representation of Christ by any one group can at best be only partial. At best it reflects the conversion of one small segment of reality, and it needs to be complemented and perhaps corrected by others. The fullness of humanity lies in Christ; the aggregate of converted lifestyles points toward his full stature.[36]

Otherness serves the image of God precisely by opening human identity to the richness of the glorified Christ, who alone represents God: the "fullness" of the Deity in bodily form (Col 1:19; 2:9; cf. John 1:16). Believers have the "fullness of Christ" (Col 2:10) as a corporate reality: they do not possess it except as they turn toward other image bearers within the Body of Christ (Eph 2:21–22).

Human diversity *delineates* the power of individual persons by constantly pointing believers to the fullness that resides in Jesus Christ, the head of the Body. Only *in Christ* can humans truly know God and, thus, function as regal agents on the earth. And, because the transcendence of God opposes all idolatry of his image along singular frames of reference (i.e., particular persons, and/or ethnic, gender or socio-economic identities), knowing God involves transporting believers *into* the lives of other image-bearers, filling the spaces with the presence of Christ through the power of the Holy Spirit, and opening the self to the other. Miroslav Volf remarks, "We are who we are not because we are separate from others who are next to us, but because we are both separate and connected, both distinct and related; the boundaries that mark our identities are both

---

36. Walls, "Globalization," 74.

Power and the Image of God: A Contextualized Theological Proposal

barriers and bridges."[37] One cardinal affirmation expressed through the image of God concept is that humans are not complete in themselves. To say otherwise, would be to argue that Christ is reducible to human possession: upending the derivational or representational essence of the image of God, and challenging the Creator-creation distinction. Living "in Christ" therefore means being receptive to the generative forces that exist within the cosmos: "exposed to the power of others;"[38] while at odds with any "force" that would undermine God's "moral ontology" of power (highlighting the need for "conflict scenarios"—of various types—to contend with dehumanizing elements within an integrative cosmos).

The other important lesson learned from Christ's image is that God moves into humanity in order to reveal himself; not vice versa: humanity does not approach God. The actions are one-directional. Only after Christ has taken upon himself human nature can there be any thought of moving toward the divine, and only through Christ's humanity can believers "set there minds on things above" (Col 3:1–2). McFarland argues that Christ's image establishes the "point of contact" between humans and God:[39]

> Human existence in God's image is at no point a matter of human beings possessing divine attributes, but exhaustively and irreversibly of God having taken on human ones. We become "participants of the divine nature" (2 Peter 1:4) only because God has in Christ participated in human nature, and thus only by the fact that we—apart from any merit or capacity on our side—share the humanity God has assumed.[40]

The Incarnation simultaneously restores humans to God by restoring humanity to humans. Life flows from the nature of God. All attempts to circumvent that gift by playing the part of God, harnessing divine powers for self interest, or privileging some persons as closer to God, ultimately amounts to rejection of the derivational nature of divine power and, therefore, raises assault against the fundamental goodness of humanity (redefined in Jesus Christ). Once humans are re-oriented to God in Christ, the corporate image casts further light upon the expansive beauty

---

37. Volf, *Exclusion and Embrace*, 70–71.
38. Ibid., 164.
39. McFarland, *The Divine*, 58.
40. Ibid. Dietrich Bonhoeffer says something similar: "Man becomes man because God became man" (*Ethics*, 63).

Re-Imaging Modernity

of Christ; or said in another way: growth "in Christ" comes through generative power relations with other image bearers.[41]

Power for the World

Finally, God's moral ontology of power, embodied with the corporality of the image of Christ, equips faith communities with respective powers in which to represent God for world growth. Humans exist within the epicenter of the cosmos, positioned as regal agents for the integration of all things. The world becomes the central venue for theological activity to take place, as it represents "a field of action composed of diverse struggles to transform relations of power for the sake of respecting and enhancing the integrity of life."[42] On one hand, this creates *conflict scenarios* where humans utilize divine power for contesting rival ideologies or impersonal forces that misrepresent God's character on the earth. On the other hand, regal agents act for the goodness of creation. Representation assumes different directions: humans represent God to the world (promoting goodness) and the world to God (fruitfulness). The first is an act of service, the latter worship.

Creation remains dependent upon human powers in order to receive value-laden orientation with God. When humans neglect or misappropriate the outworking of their powers, alienation[43] ensues. The consequences of alienation are seen most vividly in distorted values that accompany human-nature interaction (examples include, exploitive uses of natural resources; reductionistic conceptions of wealth; or dehumanizing structures).[44] Humans represent God to the world, and the world to God.

---

41. Volf, however, argues that unqualified otherness can lead to destructive harm upon the self; he proposes, therefore, that "the human self is formed . . . through a complex process of 'taking in' *and* 'keeping out'" to prevent otherness from overwhelming the self (*Exclusion and Embrace*, 66).

42. Schweiker, "Power," 208.

43. Marx used this word to describe the effect of capitalism upon human communities; however, Kenneth Cragg describes a similar result for human relations with nature, where, in modern societies, Cragg suggests there "might fairly be called an artificializing, a coarsening, of the human spirit in its handling of the material of experience" (*The Privilege*, 6).

44. The word *wealth* has etymological roots in *well-being*, thus showing that wealth is for humans, and humans for wealth. See *Oxford English Dictionary*, 2nd ed., s.v. "Wealth."

Power and the Image of God: A Contextualized Theological Proposal

Not only does divine power pertain to physical creation but also to socio-economic systems. Kä Mana's theological development applies the entire spectrum of Christ's powers (inclusive of his death, resurrection and exaltation) to African societies, "in order to make the human being responsible for himself and for the world which he has to transform according to God's plan."[45] He discounts the role that "myths" contribute to this process, arguing that they merely "comfort us in our nature and lock us in our history."[46] Instead, he wants to see people turn their eyes upon Africa's future by "re-integration into the horizon of God's creative and renovative Spirit" so that they can subsequently work for the "revitalization of a human society in all its dimensions."[47] Kä Mana describes this in four particular ways: by the "rebuilding [of] the conscience;" "reforging a new spirit;" "reshaping an imagination;" and finally, "restructuring new institutions."[48] In other words, where Christ's life leads people into all aspects of society, with relevant powers for reconstituting the world through the "image-bearing" resources (powers) available to humans.

My own theological thinking follows that of Kä Mana's. I see the image of God propelling humans in active engagement with the world around them, inclusive of *all its dimensions*. Pannenberg describes something similar whereby humans, because of their "radical openness" to God and the world around them, develop a "spiritual culture alongside a material culture."[49] However, this should not imply dichotomized detachment between sacred and secular realities, but instead suggests that theological activity must work for integration, with effect to the spaces or power-relations that give shape to the world. African Christianity develops much of its community and global engagement from *the various ways* that sacred and secular realities interrelate. This will become more apparent in the final section of this chapter.

Believers simultaneously exist "in Christ" and "in the world." Both realms represent power, highlighting the need for integrative activities that promote God's goodness in the world. The Apostle Paul employs this kind of language ("in Christ" and "in Rome"; alternatively, "in God" and "in Corinth") for representing kingdom realities. Volf contends,

---

45. Cited in Dedji, "Ethical Redemption," 264.
46. Ibid., 264–65.
47. Ibid., 265.
48. Ibid., 265–66.
49. Pannenberg, *What is Man?* 22.

> Both "Corinth" and "God," both "Rome" and "Christ" are more than cultural-linguistic systems, more than symbols and corresponding patterns of behavior. "Rome" is also political power and economy; "Corinth" is also drives and desires. To live in Rome or Corinth means to be inserted into the nexus of political and economic interest and powers, to struggle with drives and desires that form one's personality structure. And what does it mean to live "in God?" According to Christian tradition, God undergirds both "semiotic systems" (even those that are necessary to access God!) and the multiple relations of power in which semiotic systems are always involved.[50]

Humans receive input from the totality of their surroundings, inclusive of political and economic realities. Therefore, to be in Christ says something about what it means to be in Rome. Meanwhile, Corinth (or Ukambani) contributes important resources for the broader representation of Christ in the world. Volf brings these points together through summary: "All this amounts to saying that at different levels we need to talk about structures, forces, and experiences when we talk abut Christian faith in the world."[51]

The entire cosmos needs to be humanized by the power of Jesus Christ. Any attempt to locate the power of the Gospel *only* as it pertains to spiritual points of interest, trivializes Christ as well as compartmentalizes humanity; essentially positing a humanity that is far too small to navigate through the modern order:

> Here, then, is a vision of a public theology for public gospel: looking through the spectacles of its own culture, it sees the city whose builder and architect is God; situated in multiple relations of power, it advocates the weakness of the Crucified as a new form of power; dwelling on the margins, it seeks to bring the reign of the triune God to bear on all domains of life.[52]

Theology, consequently, needs to move into categories currently monopolized by the social sciences, economics, and/or political science. The image of God humanizes the world by accurately representing Christ to the world (as worship before God). Western themes of modernity such as progress, development, individualism, and secularization receive new meanings when set within an interpretative framework where divine

---

50. Volf, "Theology," 104.
51. Ibid., 105
52. Ibid., 113.

power relates to life growth, thus making it possible to think theologically about modernity, while helping to interpret emerging forms of African modernity appearing from within the churches.

POWER AND THE IMAGE OF GOD: THEOLOGICAL CONSTRUCTION FROM WITHIN AKAMBA CHRISTIANITY

The final step in this theological development will involve drawing upon resources found in the three theological communities of faith in order to give flesh to these incipient ideas: showing how churches orient God's power for life, inclusive of sociocultural domains of production. Besides demonstrating the practical outworking of power within the ecclesiastical communities, this final section calls attention to the diversity of theological beliefs held in Ukambani. Brief mention will be given to various ecclesiastical *theologies*, with greater attention focused upon the collective representation of divine power (seen in its diversity) for generating life growth. I will structure the following section upon the points previously covered in this chapter, to show how divine power provides ecclesiastical communities with hermeneutical resources in which to engage in their modern world: *from* God, *with* others, and *for* the world.[53]

Power from God

God is the source of power. All of the churches sing songs, offer prayers, and partake in other ecclesiastical activities that *lift up* or *exalt* God. His elevated status then relates to human accessibility. God's transcendence leads to immanent life concerns. These points were highlighted in Chapter 2.

Sacred-Secular

Integration is a key component in the churches, especially pertaining to sacred and secular domains. The AICK display the greatest amount of dichotomy between these elements, wanting to see them side-by-side: as two viable ways of viewing reality. Yet due to the fact that the church legitimizes both elements, conflicts frequently arise between pastors and church elders (alternatively between those advocating *professionalism*

---

53. These are not the only ways of communicating these integrative realities; it would also be possible to speak of power *for others, with God* and *from the world*. I am merely borrowing those forms most conspicuous within African, and, to a degree, Christian language.

and those, *holiness*). Most congregations privilege education, wealth, and secular experience, while pastors feel relegated to a diminished(ing) role in church and society. Limited spheres for pastoral influence often result in less opportunity for spiritual values to affect material dealings, for example, where development corresponds exclusively with church building construction; or where elders function in business-related roles (rather than fulfilling spiritual roles). However, ministers reassert (re-sacralize) themselves within contemporary contexts by pursuing theological education and through preaching opportunities. Secular credentials associated with an accredited University further legitimize spiritual authority: allowing limited mobility between these domains. Likewise, by arguing for the viability of both sacred and secular currents, it is possible to see some integration taking place; for example through apologetic preaching, or in cases where the AICK operates as a territorial church.

The ABC maintains the highest degree of integration, with sacred and secular seemingly fused together into a comprehensive picture of community transformation. Less emphasis is given to differences between the two realms, and more upon what they achieve: "changing a place religiously." Spiritual priorities make a difference in local communities; secular realities authenticate divine blessings. People are not just "hearers of God's Word," but do what it says.

The RGC, on the other hand, envision spiritual realities spreading out over (on top of) the material: sometimes transforming, other times conflicting, and still in other instances legitimating (or reinterpreting) the material dimension. All aspects of human life feel the effect of divine power, leading to a "spiritualized" reading of the cosmos. Dangers ensue, where virtually any proposal can be justified based upon spiritual interpretations, and where the pastor provides central locus for these hermeneutical processes (with limited or no accountability from others). The advantages of this spiritualized encounter are such that the Holy Spirit furnishes church members with commensurate powers and confidence to move into any facet of the contemporary world: whether confronting societal evils (World Bank or socioeconomic disparity) or, actively promoting global missions. Born agains see themselves as *winners*. Anything is possible. The dangers, however, are such that humans benefit *from* the physical world, rather than actively seeking its growth. Hence, they borrow and oppose certain characteristics of the American prosperity gospel. The RGC simultaneously display a predisposition for the benefits of modernity, while also encouraging an anti-modernity

Power and the Image of God: A Contextualized Theological Proposal

posture in how they oppose materialism and/or other global features of Western societies.

Theological Distinctions

Doctrinal affirmations, whether explicitly or implicitly held, are one of the primary ways churches utilize God's power for human application. Each of the churches stands within the historic tradition of evangelicalism, but lend specific weight to particular doctrines which equip them with the means of engaging within the contemporary world: the AICK emphasising the Bible, the ABC creation, and the RGC the Holy Spirit. Yet even among shared beliefs, differences stand out. For example, the person and work of the Holy Spirit remains central within all the ecclesiastical communities, but with varying degrees of application. The RGC view the Holy Spirit as the interpretive and mobilizing agent connecting spiritual and material realms. He is the immanence of God, granting life and empowering humans to limitless possibilities: from evangelism to missions, social construction to political engagement. The ABC understands the Holy Spirit as their primary guide. In the face of historic needs for self-reliance, the doctrine of the Holy Spirit proved essential for taking this small, oppressed, and seemingly obscure group of Akamba believers out from amidst colonialism to its current status of a large, well-organized church (involved in Kenya, Tanzania, DRC, and Rwanda). Prayers are often heard in their churches beseeching the Holy Spirit for assistance: "Guide your people and bless us" or "Help us and guide us."[54] The AICK view the Holy Spirit as the agent of Scripture: inspiring and illuminating God's Word in order to enact salvation, change human behavior, and contest any rival ideology in the world. Parishioners petition the Holy Spirit to "Feed us from your Word."[55] The work of the Holy Spirit convicts people of sin and leads them toward Christ (understood broadly to affect how believers interact with the world).[56]

Doctrinal affirmations, therefore, provide churches with various resources for applying divine power into human points of reference. All of

---

54. ABC Bomani, Mar. 29, 2009.
55. AICK Bomani, Sept. 28, 2008.
56. However, since less emphasis is given to Christ's humanity, the AICK struggle to appropriate Christ's nature within everyday constructs: leading to tendencies that supernaturalize the Christian life.

Re-Imaging Modernity

the churches covered in this study share similar belief systems, but with different areas of emphasis and/or application.

SACRALIZATION[57]

Pastoral authority mediates God's power to the *washiriki* (fellowshippers). This creates tendencies where parishioners view the pastor as closer to God, imbibing more divine power and, therefore, to one degree or another, with more identity (especially where power relates to being). The danger with this, as previously mentioned, is that if power begins with God, then nearness to the divine indicates (explicitly or implicitly) heightened personhood: where the minister, depending on how it is interpreted, is either more or less human.[58] This makes it hard for pastors to work for the humanization of their churches and society, since they experience a certain dislocation from humanity itself. These churches likewise hesitate to appropriate Christ's humanity within their ministry, and with further effect to ecclesiastical structures. People want to become more like God and, therefore, to some extent, less like themselves.

Sacralization has many different shapes and forms in the churches. The RGC holds the most accentuated, widespread variety of it, with pastors functioning as God's representatives on earth, embodying elements of divine power within their person. Touch, oil, and/or nearness serve as important instruments for its carriage. All believers (those truly born again) have the Holy Spirit, but the tenuous and porous nature of sinful humanity necessitates that pastors actively work to ensure that their members are constantly *filled with the Spirit* and prepared for service. Pastoral blessings jumpstart a believer from spiritual complacency and/ or provide the fundamental powers to equip someone for a leadership position in the church. Church services oftentimes take place everyday of the week, in order to help believers *maintain* God's power within their lives. Bishop Mutua of Eastleigh holds special services for all his leaders, where he prays for them one-by-one, mobilizing members for powerful ministry within the church (and community). After someone receives pastoral blessing, they become an agent of spiritual authority. One youth leader described what this means for him. "The youth see me as a spiritual person and whenever I am with them they respect me so much. I use

---

57. See note 31, this chapter.

58. In the case where it is less, this means that the pastor is more like God and less like other humans.

the pulpit to rebuke them so often because I can share a lot with them as I preach to them."[59]

The AICK demonstrate the greatest amount of contested space for pastoral authority to operate, relegating ministers to overtly spiritual domains (often with narrowing spheres of influence). Pastors preach and elders take care of business. *Non-spiritual* elements increasingly assume heightened importance within the churches, whether announcements, development, or other financial concerns. However, the lines separating these are not as defined as they may appear. Pastors are constantly looking to develop their secular powers (through higher education, purchase of vehicles, or material possessions), while lay leaders vie for spiritual authority (certificates from Bible colleges and/or preaching opportunities). Dichotomies of this kind provide a degree of accountability for pastoral authority but still with tendencies that accentuate the spirituality of the pastor, where people view him or her as more like God and/or having all the biblical answers. One lay leader prayed (before the preaching): "God, help your minister give us understanding that comes from on high."[60] *Washiriki* believe pastors have privileged access to God as a result of their "high" spiritual "calling."

The ABC understands the pastor as the hub around which everything in the church must revolve. Sisters and lay leaders accomplish various ministerial duties, but under the direct oversight of the minister, who can transfer a sister or remove a deacon from the church council. Pastoral powers guide, organize, develop, and mobilize the community; they plan all activities, make important decisions, train lay leaders, chair committees, and organize development work. Pastors manage finances, advise people about agricultural methods, talk about preventative health care, and preach. The integrative nature of the sacred-secular brings a moderating role to the overt spirituality of the pastor. He is seen less as the man of God and more as the supreme authority for ecclesiastical (and community-related) affairs.

Sacralization, thus, remains a danger for all the churches, but with varying degrees of intensity (or application). Anytime communities relate to God through a sole, human representative the tendency exists for power to become exclusively attached to that singular image-bearer; or, for other people to access God through the same. This results in

---

59. Peter Kyondo, interview by Maurice Twahirwa, Machakos, Kenya, Feb. 8, 2009.
60. AICK Bomani, Dec. 21, 2008.

propensities for ecclesiastical structures to assume different forms of sacralization, and hence become less focused on corporate humanization. When this happens, God's nature is essentialized, and the very nature of humanity misrepresented (in church and society). However, churches can also use their *theologies* as a means of revealing divine power *for* the people, and therefore (as the previous chapters have shown) where the doctrines of God's Word, the Holy Spirit, and/or creation can mediate some of the sacralizing tendencies and assuage some of its harmful effect.

Conflict Scenarios

Another important element in the churches relates to how divine power opposes rival forces within an integrative cosmos. A common chorus heard in all the churches has a refrain that says, "Higher, higher raising Jesus higher; lower, lower, making Satan lower." These kinds of dualism are widespread throughout all three churches, yet with particular manifestations specific to each.

Newer Pentecostal churches source their internal logic from traditional frameworks of spiritual power.[61] The RGC envision evil spirits permeating all societal evils; including demons of corruption, sexual immorality, greed, pride, and covetousness. The indwelling of the Holy Spirit confronts spiritual forces in these domains, and overpowers them. All spaces within the cosmos are potential battle lines; everything needs to be spiritualized. One minister highlighted the pervasiveness of these spiritual encounters by stating, "Satan enters in every situation of an individual believer."[62] Most parishioners are not strong enough to oppose these spiritual forces, underscoring their dependency upon pastoral powers for overcoming the kind of conflict scenario posited by these churches.

This paradigm has proven particularly attractive within contemporary African Christianity, evidenced, in part, by the mushrooming of newer Pentecostal churches throughout the continent. However, this remains *only* one kind of conflict scenario. Studies in African Christianity sometimes differentiate between magical, enchanted worldviews of Pentecostal churches and the Enlightenment traditions of the mainline

---

61. See Kalu, *Power, Poverty and Prayer*, 104ff.

62. Rev. Kasula Mutisya, interview by Maurice Twahirwa, Machakos, Kenya, Feb. 8, 2009.

or historic denominations.[63] However, this leaves many questions unanswered. For example, what about churches that do not fit comfortably within either of these categories? The ABC, for example, resists both *enchanted* and *enlightened* classifications, but still offers its own version of spiritual conflict. Youth learn in their catechism that they must give their entire lives to Christ (through the church); failure to do so opens them to the actions of Satan, who comes to "steal, kill and destroy." All parts of human existence represent contested spaces, including body, money, time, relationships, and work. By giving everything to God, believers are choosing the abundant life; when they fail to present everything to God, they open themselves to Satanic corruption. These teachings were particularly effective in the early days of the church when they experienced great opposition from colonial and missionary agents. Conflict scenarios present the need for divine power in the face of contested spaces. For the ABC, this relates to human life in its totality.

Another problem posed by dichotomies between Pentecostal and historic churches is that by differentiating between the two, as such, we may interpret passivity in the latter, where it may be inferred that Africans uncritically accepted the Enlightenment values of early missionaries. I sought to show in Chapter 3 how these traditions were twice reformulated (once by the missionaries, and thereafter by the Africans). The result is a different kind of conflict scenario, with less (overt) emphasis given to spiritual forces and more opposition with global, religious ideologies. The secular world, cults, world religions, and liberal forms of Christianity all provide an opposing "other" to the central tenets of the Bible. Members of the AICK study God's Word in order to know the truth and stand against rival belief systems pervasive within the contemporary world. Yet similar to the RGC, church members are not strong enough, nor adequately equipped with requisite spiritual knowledge to resist these kinds of oppositions. Apologetics forms the central defense (and even attack) against colliding beliefs. Pastors take special courses in how to confront these kinds of oppositions. They study Greek and Hebrew in order to bring special spiritual powers to play against various ideologies. Sermons provide pastors with a strategic forum to confront misguided teachings that corrupt or distort the Gospel, mobilizing the church for active engagement within the contemporary world.

63. See Gifford, *African*, 328–29.

Re-Imaging Modernity

Pentecostal churches, therefore, provide one attractive means of employing divine power in the face of spiritual forces; yet the other churches do as well, albeit without as overtly a spiritualized encounter. The ABC positions church members (expressed in their corporality) against the Devil for the purposes of community development. The AICK utilize preaching and apologetics in order to equip members to stand against rival secular/religious ideologies. In all the churches, continuities between spiritual and material domains provide the underlying framework for interpreting these kinds of conflict scenarios, but through a wide range of application: from highly spiritualized readings of the cosmos to more secular, globalized encounters.

Interpretations of the Bible

God's Word occupies a central role in all the churches. The Bible moves *washiriki* inwards and outwards through the Holy Spirit: into hearts and out into communities. Pastoral preaching confronts members with their sinfulness, and compels them to act as God's agents of salvation in the world, through evangelism, missions, or community transformation. Manifestations differ from church-to-church, with the AICK more focused upon inward parts of human nature, the RGC confronting evil forces in an ambiguous cosmos, while the ABC equips believers with resources to engage in their local communities.

The Great Commission, as found in Matthew 28, features prominently in each of the denominations, showing continuity (and reinterpretation) from a shared missionary heritage. All of the churches cite their central purpose as pertaining to the Great Commission. The ABC has the words, "go ye into all the world" written on their logo, underneath a symbol of the Holy Spirit. The RGC feature a cross standing over the globe, with the words "reaching the unreached with the Gospel." The AICK begin their constitution with the words, "God's word is the authority for the Great Commission, which He has chosen to share with His people, the Church."[64] Their logo is an outline of Africa, with a cross superimposed over the continent. These symbols reveal the outward focus of the Gospel.

Yet not all equally engage in trans-cultural endeavors. The AICK tend to associate missions with Western personnel, viewing it as something that the AIM (or other Western missions) undertakes. The ethnic nature of the AICK sometimes inhibits these kinds of cross-cultural

---

64. Africa Inland Church, *Constitution*, 1981, 1.

activities. Scarcity of funds at the local and national church level further discourages the sending of missionaries. The ABC and RGC are the most active in these kinds of activities (ironically, having the least historical contact with Western missions). Both have been energetic in planting churches throughout East Africa, with the RGC moving into India, South Africa, and Jamaica. Prevalence of funds at the local church (RGC) or Central Church Council (ABC) makes it easier for these denominations to mobilize resources for missionary activity. Their theology of the Holy Spirit (RGC) and holistic Gospel (ABC) further furnishes members with confidence to proceed globally with the message of Jesus Christ.

Sermons provide another vantage point by which to explore various trajectories of God's Word in the churches. The style of preaching in AICK and ABC share points of similarity, following an expository approach where the text of Scripture is treated in systematic method (often, with verse-by-verse progression). The AICK reveal "critical"[65] readings of the text, where authorial intent, historical background, "original meaning," and word studies bring the passage from its historical antecedent into the contemporary stage. Specific application is made to individual lives, where pastors admonish members regarding sin, forgiveness, obedience, and/or financial giving (becoming more common). *Critical* readings of Scripture appeal to parishioners wanting academically informed insights from theologically trained ministers. People generally believe AICK sermons to be "more biblical" than those from other churches, since they maintain a tighter sense of loyalty to the literal meaning of the text (and come from ministers who have attended Bible college). Pastors are usually the only ones equipped with the requisite theological knowledge necessary for interpreting Scripture. Sermons in AICK assume a directive, convicting, and/or apologetic nature: they seek to change behavior by condemning sin, decrying moral laxity, and attacking societal problems.[66] Pastors assert their spiritual authority through sermons, and, when they do this, they are said to be "hammering the Gospel."

The ABC differs from the AICK in having much looser interpretations of Scripture, exemplifying what has been termed "pre-critical"[67] readings of the Bible. Deacons and other lay leaders assume regular pul-

---

65. Anum, "Ye Ma Wo Mo!" 8–9.

66. This is in contradistinction to the common stereotype of the AICK being silent on political or socioeconomic matters. Their primary stage for involvement is through preaching, and this occurs in local church contexts.

67. Anum, "Ye Mo Wo Mo!" 8–9.

pit responsibilities. The liturgy consists of one or two Scripture readings, with the sermon following these. Rather than dealing with authorial intent or other critical interpretative mechanisms, preachers in the ABC use storytelling, commonplace examples, and focus on personal and corporate application (working these in and out of the text). They frame God's Word in relevant categories, preaching on "Growing in Divine Wisdom," "Knowing God's Will," "Perfect Peace in the Midst of Danger," or "Rebuilding the already Broken Walls." Sermons use God's Word to guide members through the trials and travails of life. People will oftentimes pray, "Bless us through your Word," or where they appeal to the Spirit: "we want to hear from you."[68] Applicational components receive greater weight in ABC sermons, especially related to a wide range of human experiences: from relationships to finances, whether godliness or development. Preachers assume a less directive (more shepherding) style of communication. God's Word helps people navigate through the vicissitudes of life.

The RGC display the loosest of all styles. Paul Gifford regards Pentecostal preaching as "performance" in which the historical Word of God becomes a "contemporary document"[69] and enacted on a stage. Pastors appropriate God's power into the lives of parishioners: speaking authoritatively into personal domains of existence. God's truth pertains to all facets of contemporary existence, from growing in righteousness to finding a husband or wife; from sexual temptation to the World Bank. Nothing is too mundane or trivial. The role of the preacher is to mediate these truths, and help make the kinds of personal application necessary. Sermons assume a dialogical tone. Conversation moves back and forth between the pastor and members. Preachers ask rhetorical questions and wait for responses from the parishioners. They implore the *washiriki* to "go study God's Word for yourself,"[70] then tell the listeners what the Bible says. When ritualized in this manner, God's Word becomes personalized. The pastor is the "effecter of Scripture,"[71] the one whose authority relates to applying the Bible into all facets of human existence. One minister explained: "a broken pulpit is a broken congregation."[72] Pastors mediate the

68. ABC Bomani, Mar. 29, 2009.
69. Gifford, "The Bible," 206.
70. Maranatha Chapel, 25 February 2007.
71. Gifford, "The Bible," 214.
72. John Mutiso, interview with Samson Nungwana, Machakos, Kenya, Feb. 11, 2009.

Power and the Image of God: A Contextualized Theological Proposal

words of God into individual lives; without this, people feel unmoored and adrift within a hostile world.

Power with Other Image Bearers

The practical outworking of divine power relates to mobilizing theological communities for life growth. The transcendence of God leads to immanent life concerns. In traditional Akamba societies, divine power orients community members toward peaceful coexistence and with affect to cosmic fruitfulness. The same applies to evangelical communities of faith, but with different points of manifestation.

Hierarchies

The three churches display contrasting hierarchies of power, with the ABC representing the strongest top-down ecclesiastical structure, with mixed representation of clergy and laity at all levels. The RGC has the greatest diffused power, with local congregations displaying the primary signature of power within the denomination (but where authority remains exclusively in the hands of pastors). The AICK operates on what appears to be a top-down hierarchy, but where most of the power is located at the district level (one point removed from the local congregations) and with combined representation of clergy and educated laity. The key component that differentiates the organization of power in the churches pertains to the location of money. Very specifically, where do tithes and offerings go?

For the AICK, funds go directly to the district office. The DCC is then supposed to distribute these resources to the region, area, and finally the central church office. However, districts often hoard monies for themselves. While on paper the central church council provides the policy-making arm of the church and organizes all affairs related to areas, regions, districts, and local churches; in practice, districts determine the implementation of policy since they are the ones in control of finances.

In contrasting manner, RGC congregations retain 90 percent of offerings, sending only 10 percent to the diocesan headquarters. Pastors decide how they want to use those monies, whether in development, evangelism, church planting, purchase of vehicles, or building large church structures. People equate this with freedom. Local churches are free to do what they like, and grow where they want. This explains one facet of the growth of the RGC in Kenya and around the world. When churches decide on a certain direction (and local pastors have great latitude in this regard) they have funds to support their work.

For the ABC, all tithes and offerings go directly to the central church office and with direct oversight by the presiding bishop; this includes money generated from the Kibwezi farm or other agricultural projects. When the governing council of the ABC makes a decision as pertains to the use of finances, the entire church complies.

Access to money, as seen above, tends to orient human communities, which then allows the churches to use these resources for societal endeavors. Ecclesiastical hierarchies, and their policies pertaining to the distribution of tithes and offerings, give different expression to *how* churches position themselves as agents in society, and with commensurate resources that facilitate these processes.

Otherness (Difference and Inclusion)

Another theological component of the churches concerns how members complement and demarcate each other's powers: how they use diversity and otherness to offer richer and more elaborate representations of God's image on earth.

The ABC and AICK reveal the greatest discord between traditional and modern values, with older people favoring hymns, order, respect, and ethnic languages; while younger people yearn for choruses, lively musical accompaniment, freedom (usually interpreted as *doing what they want to do*), and increased participation in the churches. The AICK has gradually become more receptive to toward meeting the needs of both groups, while the ABC remains reluctant to follow (mainly because of commitments to traditional values, and how these are interpreted within biblical categories). One compromise for the AICK has been the inclusion of a youth service, which comes before or after the traditional service. This has the advantage of attracting youth, but keeps them isolated from older members (with each attending the service of their choice). Differences of ecclesiastical preference are acknowledged, but without effect to the spaces existing between people.

Ethnic identities are most conspicuously encouraged within AICK churches. Rural congregations in Ukambani operate exclusively in Kikamba: through prayers, sermons, hymns, and Bible reading. Even town churches have an early service in English[73] to cater for educated profes-

---

73. Yet even in English-speaking services, people will intersperse Kikamba into the ecclesiastical discourse (through hymns or prayers).

Power and the Image of God: A Contextualized Theological Proposal

sionals and youth, and a later (main) service that highlights the use of Kikamba. Ethnic identities remain one of the heritages given by AIM missionaries who were active in Bible translation and the development of rural communities.

The ABC uses a combination of Kiswahili and Kikamba. Their notion of brotherhood necessitates wide and diverse representation of believers (though, in reality, most of their churches still exist in Ukambani and are made up of Akamba Christians). Kiswahili facilitates the development of brotherhood by linking people together under a common language. However, changes have taken place such that in 1991 they changed their name to Africa (rather than the previous *African*) Brotherhood Church to allow for the incorporation of the Canadian Baptists or any other person wanting to become a member of their church, and have added English services in town settings. The church adopts an inclusive stance. All people are welcome: polygamists, unwed mothers, people with physical disabilities, different ethnic identities, women, and anyone who might struggle to find a church home. They further send Akamba pastors to other regions in Kenya, and Luo pastors to Ukambani. Diversity is embraced for what it contributes to the congregation. All persons have something to give: whether mangoes, a song, a poem, or a particular skill. Sermons and other ecclesiastical teachings continually draw upon resources found in creation in order to provide for this inclusiveness. God blesses humans, who then bless others. All people are involved in this transaction (through creation) and have something to contribute. However, certain "modern" differences (of perspective) have been known to clash with the ABC's traditional and hierarchical structure. This has been particularly the case for how they deal with values (such as freedom), or adapting to various facets of rapidly changing societies. Church leaders maintain high regard for traditional values of respect and honor, but struggle to appropriate the same into contemporary contexts. Youth feel the church hesitates in meeting their needs.

The RGC experiences little of the tension between modern and traditional values, since from its inception the church specifically catered to youth and those discontented with mainline churches (and tended to vilify traditional values as demonic). The primary languages used by the RGC are English and Kiswahili, and they actively use these to promote trans-ethnic identities. Historically, like other newer Pentecostals, they place more emphasis upon loyalty to born-agains than kinship relations, creating tension with unsaved family members. Slowly, this is beginning to change. Yet, members still privilege other born-agains in business dealings and develop identities based upon their involvement within the church. One young lady said that this was one of the most distasteful things she experiences in her church; members will hug each other in the presence of an unbeliever and not show similar signs of affection for the person outside the church.[74] Diversity is embraced as long as it resides within the congregation (among born-agains). Their doctrine of the Holy Spirit accounts for these predispositions. All believers have the fruits of the Holy Spirit, exhibiting spiritual similarities that bind believers together; however, each believer possesses a different spiritual gift. The RGC interpret gifts loosely, where they may relate to musical ability, ushering, technology, or some other talent recognized by the pastor. The Holy Spirit thus uses similarities and differences (fruits and gifts) for equipping born-agains with what they need to live in the world (yet mediated through pastoral authority).

Sacralizing tendencies within each of the denominations continue to guide (and restrict) the outworking of diversity in the churches. Pastoral authority nurtures sacred powers within the congregations (through spiritual gifts, biblical knowledge, or community-related activities). However, by requiring everything to go through the man of God (in some cases, quite literally touching him or her), diversity becomes essentialized through a single human agent. This leads to tendencies where the pastor represents all members before God. People stand before the pastor, who stands before God. Sacralization undermines diversity by making all members dependent upon a solitary image, and sabotages unity by linking all members together through one human representative. True otherness resists these kinds of limitations. Christ's presence in a believer's life offers authentic (yet localized) representation of God on earth. The role of pastoral authority should be to coordinate the powers for maximum edification, resulting in corporate growth. As long as the pastor holds more spiritual power, the derivational nature of the image of God is at risk, affecting the church's ability to authentically represent God in (and for) the world.

Power for the World

Finally, the entire cosmos requires faithful representation of God in order to flourish. Human agents utilize their powers to infuse meaning and

---

74. J. Kioko, interview with George Kiasyo, Kakuyuni, Kenya, Dec. 2008.

value into creation: humanizing creation by faithfully acting as God's regal agents for the growth of the world around them (broadened here to include the kind(s) of modernity represented by these churches).

Conservatism of Values

All the churches contribute to a broad, sweeping religious/moral conservatism within modern Kenyan society. Evangelical churches represent some of the most active agents in promoting these values, and are increasingly becoming more vocal against corruption and political wrangling within the coalition government.[75] People often place greater trust in churches than political leaders to instill moral and biblical values (often understood synonymously) within local contexts. Politicians, from their side, seek to mitigate some of these contrasts by drawing upon biblical themes within their political discourses. They become cosy to church leaders in order to create the appearance they stand on the side of God. These realities are particularly important within Ukambani, where traditional values oftentimes are interpreted as synonymous with the Bible. One of Kenya's ministers attended the graduation ceremonies of AICK's Nduluka Bible Institute, and proclaimed, "There is no bigger vocation than the Bible," and, "The Word of God overrides everything."[76] He went on to state that he was going to require all local council members to attend a two-week Bible training at the College. In Ukambani, ecclesiastical language provides propitious means for enhancing conservative credentials and promoting traditional values.

Church and Politics

Preachers frequently speak out openly against corruption, avarice, and lack of integrity from local to national stages yet are cautious about not "naming names" and making reproaches too specific or personal (especially when dealing with political leaders). Sacralizing currents often inhibit the RGC from openly confronting political leaders. Linkages between God and leaders (sourced from within cosmological traditions, and reinforced from within biblical categories; e.g., Rom 13:1, NKJV)[77] prevent pastors from challenging sociopolitical powers. Yet this should

---

75. See "You Have Failed Us, Kibaki, Raila Told," *The Standard*, Feb. 20, 2009, 1, 6.

76. Hon. Mutula Kilonzo, Nduluku Bible Institute, Mar. 15, 2008.

77. The RGC, like many other Pentecostal churches, use the King James Version (KJV) or, more frequently, the New King James Version (NKJV).

not imply a disengagement from the political realm. The presence of the Holy Spirit motivates born-agains into all societal domains. Believers overcome evil forces (quite literally, demons) associated with corruption, disunity, and political wrangling. In such ways, members of the RGC assert themselves within political processes, but with care to "submit to the authorities" (Rom 13:5). They oppose *forces* but demur from attacking leaders (showing some contradiction between the two). In some cases they blame demons behind societal ills, and thus obviate political accountability.

The ABC maintains high regard for leaders, but grounds it upon traditional values of *honor* and *respect*. They refuse to challenge any authority openly (political or ecclesiastical) and deliberately pray for all leaders in their weekly services: ritualized by methodically working through their ecclesiastical hierarchy (bishop, canons, pastors, sisters, deacons and lay leaders), moving to political realms (world leaders, president, cabinet ministers, MPs, etc.) and concluding their intercessions by remembering "all church leadership throughout the world."[78] Similar to the other churches, they openly denounce corruption or any other moral greed within society, but avoid direct attacks against leaders for fear of disrespecting them.

Meanwhile, the AICK base their relative silence in regard to political matters from the separation of sacred and secular (church and state) they inherited from the early American missionaries. People believe church leaders should deal with spiritual matters and leave politics to those with different callings. Increased emphasis (in church and society) upon secular priorities (such as development and education) leaves the AICK wanting with regard to theological resources in which to navigate through sociopolitical domains of engagement. They are frequently taciturn in such matters, uncertain what role they should adopt.

The above characteristics communicate similarities in the churches pertaining to opposition (or lack thereof) to political fraudulence yet where each of the ecclesiastical communities source their *silence* (in some cases, complicity) from different theologies: whether sacralization (RGC), honor (ABC), or dichotomization (AICK), thus giving different expression to church-state interactions.

---

78. ABC Bomani, Jan. 18, 2009.

Power and the Image of God: A Contextualized Theological Proposal

Money and Wealth

Evangelicalism in Ukambani builds upon traditional values of power and wealth in order to orient some of its society-wide impact. The following section traces some of the main contours of money in the denominations, with the preface that financial conflicts and abuse are conspicuous elements in all the churches. My intentions are not to romanticize any of the churches (or vilify others), but identify some of the main values undergirding the use of money in local congregations (understood explicitly and implicitly).

The AICK view wealth from the role that educated laity contribute within their ecclesiastical structure, and viewed, most conspicuously, through emphasis given to "development" (understood almost exclusively through church structures). The denomination has successfully navigated through its historic struggles with the AIM and education-related conflicts in order to have one of the few private chartered Universities in the country, with a corresponding preponderance of educated laity holding important leadership positions from local to national levels. The AICK attaches great importance to education. Degrees signify status, which generates wealth-acquisition. Educated laity function as the primary actors within church councils due to their money, yet sometimes without the ethical values that formerly undergirded "wealth" in traditional societies. Money serves personal interests, and relates to corporate affairs by how rich people affect the status of local congregations. One way they accomplish this is by erecting sizeable church edifices. Pastors are poorly paid, but the church has some of the most impressive church buildings of any denomination in Ukambani. People look at the size of the church structure and draw conclusions about the spiritual capacity of the denomination to make a difference in human lives. They also remember who "built the church" (quite literally, the individuals who gave money or land for the building) and ascribe honor (power) to these people, and their families.[79]

The ABC provides a more holistic orientation by relating finances with community development. They exhibit less individualism of wealth, and more corporate ownership. Children in the ABC learn they must give all their money to the church; otherwise, Satan will come and steal it

---

79. This shares similarities with Akamba traditions where people want to be remembered for successive generations so that they would remain among the living dead and not become *aimu* (spirits).

from them. At the time of baptism, members publicly devote all aspects of their person to God, inclusive of money. These kinds of interconnections are ritualized through weekly offerings. After giving generously, congregants corporately declare, "God bless us, and grant us more." Church money goes into local communities in order to "change a place religiously" (which includes all aspects of human goodness). In these kinds of ways, the ABC orients wealth to welfare, humanizing money through association with traditional values. However, tensions sometimes exist between the central church office and local congregations. The presiding bishop (along with the governing council) arbitrates on the distribution of resources, leaving local congregations feeling helpless in the overall hierarchy.

Money in the RGC provides physical manifestation to spiritual realities, thus incorporating Western prosperity teaching into traditional frameworks of continuity between sacred and secular domains. Financial giving reveals a window to a person's soul and corresponds to spirituality. Pastors typically stand beside the offering basket (placed at the front of the sanctuary). Parishioners go forward, hand the money to the pastor, and receive a blessing (usually through touch). During this time, the doors of the church are closed (or even locked!) to prevent anyone from leaving. Preachers tell people that it is a sin to be poor, and that their problems relate to lack of faith or abiding sin. Bishop Mutua admonishes the people, "Don't eat your offering," "place your offering in your hands, raise it,"[80] and then blesses the money for God's purposes (which relates at the same time to human prosperity). Wealth displays contemporary manifestation of spiritual power. Continuities exist between temporal concerns and future glory. Faith in this life relates to wealth in the age to come; generosity in the present world leads to abundance in heaven.

Global Networks of Affiliation and Partnership

All of the churches give evidence of formal or informal affiliations with global (mostly North American) partners. Among the three denominations, the AICK struggles the most to develop these kinds of partnerships, since the AIM provides no support to local congregations and only sporadic assistance to the national church (and even then, only to specific ministries within the denomination). Local congregations receive funds from the West when they happen to know a former member who resides

---

80. RGC Eastleigh, Oct. 15, 2006.

Power and the Image of God: A Contextualized Theological Proposal

in the states, and who might be willing to link the churches together. However, this is rare. The ABC has a formal Memorandum of Understanding (MOU) with the Canadian Baptists, which relates to financial and personnel assistance associated with various development projects. The RGC invites American-based evangelists for area crusades. The presence of "international evangelists" or "world-renowned international speakers" adds credibility to local congregations, and provides some of the basis for future partnerships.

Global otherness remains particularly attractive to all the churches, not only due to potential financial benefits but also because of the exchange of ideas, personnel, and other resources. The RGC use the word *international* to lend spiritual credibility to local congregations. A recent circular from the Eastleigh congregation announced a seminar entitled, "Family Under Attack" presented by "an international speaker." (The person highlighted was, ironically, Kenyan). The RGC see themselves spiritually linked with other born-agains, while the ABC understand something similar through the notion of brotherhood. Both denominations value diversity so long as it does not compromise the fundamental values of the church. The AICK often feel disadvantaged with regards to global resources, having fewer partnerships in Ukambani. The one exception pertains to educational commitments. Scott Theological College has a number of Western personnel, and limited access to overseas funding.[81] These kinds of linkages help boost the credibility of the institution within East Africa and around the world.

Development—Spiritual Landscape

All the churches organize themselves for development, but with very different meanings depending upon the theological valuation imparted by the particular denomination. The RGC use the words *evangelism* and *development* with almost seamless unity due to the ways they integrate spiritual and material affairs, yet where spiritual priorities tend to predominate the encounter (almost hijacking material matters with religious expression). Most people in their churches expect evangelistic efforts to transform all aspects of human life, while development (such as their involvement with street children, education, or water projects) provides a

---

81. The Kenyan Commission for Higher Education specifies that Western lecturers need to account for less than 30 percent of all faculty personnel. STC likewise relies primarily on local income for its operating expenses.

means for sharing the Gospel with unbelievers. Development, therefore, follows the Gospel, with material benefits serving to legitimize spiritual power.

Their theology of the Holy Spirit provides central impetus to fashion these spiritual realities, which in turn affects all aspects of an integrated cosmos. Confidence in the Spirit's power propels humans throughout the world. One local preacher made the statement, "Eighty percent Christianity [in the country] should mean *less than* twenty percent corruption, because we should be influencing others around us."[82] The Gospel does not just relate to Christian (born again) lives but also affects the "spaces" around believers (inclusive of sociocultural realities). Bishop Mutua likewise proclaimed, "Freedom needs to bring economic and spiritual growth;"[83] and Bishop Lai of Jesus Celebration Centre commented, "If people were saved, we wouldn't have corruption; we wouldn't need prisons."[84] Their hermeneutic of the Holy Spirit enables members to connect spiritual power with social, economic, and material development (although one may question the degree they are actually doing so). They envision a kind of millennial kingdom completely consumed by spiritual realities, and authenticated by material prosperity. Born-agains benefit from the world, with less emphasis given to values and ethics for how they should cause the world to flourish in regard to spiritual power.

The AICK tends to display a schizophrenic attitude towards development, where each DCC gives unique expression to sacred and secular dynamics. Some districts, like one I visited in Kalamba, show active and intentional engagement in community transformation, inclusive of agricultural schemes, income-generating projects for youth, and educational development for future church leaders. The chairman of the DCC, Rev. Kioko Mwangangi told me that "Christianity has such an influential force for the community; it touches every part, including: animals, people, positions, hygiene, and other community matters."[85] He models these practices on his own farm, and invites pastors to observe his methods. Other DCCs reveal a more restricted reading of development, attaching it exclusively with church building construction, or the purchase of musical instruments. This narrowed perspective, however, implies more

82. Justus Musila, Machakos Worship Centre, Feb. 25, 2007.
83. Bishop Mutua, Eastleigh, Oct. 15, 2006.
84. *Family Glory*, Sept. 24, 2006.
85. Rev. Kioko Mwangangi, interview with author, AIC Kalimani, Kenya, July 16, 2008.

Power and the Image of God: A Contextualized Theological Proposal

than it initially appears, since church buildings function as public centers or hubs of social interaction within local communities. Even though the AICK publicly disavows any involvement in national politics, they tend to be very active in grassroots politics, with lay leaders oftentimes deeply enmeshed in all facets of local governance (formal and informal). Other denominations sometimes complain about the "political" nature of the AICK in Ukambani, and how entrenched it has become in local communities. The size of church edifices, likewise, corresponds to public status: the bigger the building, the more political and spiritual clout the church possesses in the community.

The ABC has the most organized, widespread, and intentional form of development of any other the churches. Theological underpinnings coming from Genesis provide members a means of engaging in all facets of society. They actively engage in micro-credit schemes, water storage, agricultural technologies, health care, nutrition, educational activities for those with physical disabilities, food protection, development of roads and infrastructure, tree planting, and other projects that give flesh to their holistic gospel. The ABC does not require community members to attend their churches in order to benefit from these services. The Gospel naturally compels them into material affairs. Similar to the AICK, the ABC shies away from involvement in political matters, but (unlike the AICK) they actively participate with the NCCK and other ecumenical organizations, thus extending their realm of influence across ecclesiastical boundaries. Their interpretation of the Great Commission likewise provides authority for exporting their "holistic gospel" to other nations around the world (particularly Rwanda, DRC, and Tanzania). They view the entire world as the arena for theological activity, and religious transformation as naturally affecting socio-economic growth.

All the churches studied in this book utilize divine power to affect life growth, inclusive of spiritual and material realities. Theological distinctions lend particular shapes to *how* the churches undertake social construction, with attendant values undergirding the relationship between sacred and secular. The previous chapters demonstrated how modernity-related concepts symbolize these kinds of linkages: posturing theological communities as agents of growth within an integrated world. Divine power equips human communities to act as agents of modernity. It should be noted that the churches rarely involve themselves in large-scale political or economic undertakings, and, due to their theological proclivities, often hesitate in confronting governmental abuses. However, this should imply that they are unconcerned with these problems, or that spiritual power is divorced from world-shaping exercises. More work needs to be given to developing these kinds of resources to better position the churches generatively, as agents of modernity within the contemporary world.

CONCLUSION

All of the churches utilize divine power for life growth, inclusive of socio-economic domains of production. The above assessment has largely focused upon the positive contributions of the churches (with brief mention to dangers, as they exist). This should not indicate a blind-sightedness to larger problems, especially related to mismanagement of resources, court cases, corruption within ecclesiastical hierarchies, and/or privileging of power along ethnic, gender, age, socio-economic, or sacralistic lines of distinction. I have merely wanted to offer a more generative picture for how the churches are engaging in the world, while developing a theological valuation that can help faith communities with ethical parameters for the employment of divine power: safeguarding humans (and the world) from abuses related to God's power, and propelling believers to function as agents of life. All aspects of an integrated world need to be "humanized" by the corporate image of Jesus Christ; the world becomes the arena for public theology, and modernity one of its primary discourses.

Conclusions

THIS STUDY POSITS THAT God has an image on earth, and as such, that that image relates to the broad expanse of humankind who function as regal agents in the world. Humans draw upon divine powers, in a sense, to continually fashion human societies according to the image of God. Churches, furthermore, contribute a leading role in this process as they invoke divine power for the purposes of organizing and ordering themselves within the contemporary world. I have sought to make connections between this outworking, and what may roughly be called modernity: showing linkages between theological ideas and sociological constructions.

Resultant forms of African modernity rarely express themselves with similar characteristics to Western varieties, being largely sourced from spiritual domains, with more fluid dynamics between sacred and secular realities, and/or predicated upon the re-interpretation of African traditional values into modern categories. African societies experienced the Enlightenment indirectly, at best. Any form of Western modernity coming to the continent, therefore, has already been mediated (modified) no less two times: once by the missionary (or other agent) and thereafter by Africans. This should not indicate that modernity, such as it arises in Africa, is of inferior quality to that in the West,[1] as if suggesting that Western constructs stand as "eternal monolith[s] to which successive generations bow in reverent obeisance."[2] Humans are interpretive agents.

---

1. Or, suggesting that only one (rigid, unyielding, and eternal) variety of modernity appears in Western societies.

2. Gyekye, *Tradition*, 229; Gyekye uses these words to caution against eternalizing African traditions. I borrow the same words for how Western forms of modernity tend to stand as the permanent measure against which all other forms must be compared.

Re-Imaging Modernity

They act and react to global, cultural flows. And, what is more, humans undertake these processes through theological resources. I am proposing that divine power provides Africans with valuable expression of sociological concepts, especially as it allows them to see themselves as powerful agents within an integrative cosmos: to *answer back* to global themes.

By looking at ecclesiastical communities and how they orient themselves along modernity-related themes, I am suggesting a number of important points. Firstly, theology and sociology need to deepen dialogue with each other, even at the risk of occasionally being misunderstood. Sociological methods provide essential insight into *how* (and *why*) ecclesiastical agents think about theologically nuanced subjects, underscoring the importance of context in the hermeneutical process. Qualitative research, in particular, gives attention to some of the voices frequently overlooked within theological convention, including those of women, children, and the broader expanse of *washiriki*. These people, no less than professional theologians, think about God and make connections between divine and human communities; they explore how God's nature relates to the world around them. Their thoughts, aspirations, prayers and longings are eminently theological.

What is more, as people come together and make mutual affirmations regarding God, themselves, and the world, they likewise bring impact to their societies (precisely through their theological imagination). Religious beliefs nourish ecclesiastical practices, which in turn affect the development of social context. Moltmann[3] and others have suggested something similar, nudging and prodding theological method in the West to expand into newer, distinctly modern categories. Sociological methods raise awareness to issues that matter most to people; these may or may not be expressed within traditional systematic categories, and often involve new vistas for theological reflection. "Power" and "modernity" represent two such prospects, and in the case of African societies, with interlocking trajectories.

Churches organize themselves according to power, and draw upon theological constructs to posit themselves powerful. In chapter 2 I sketched some of the predominant images of power, through cultural and theological analysis; then in chapters 3, 4, and 5, I showed how ecclesiastical communities employ divine power for the development of modernity-related themes. All of the churches examined in this book

3. For example, Moltmann, "Progress and Abyss," 3–26; Moltmann, "Theology," 1–21.

seemingly tap into God's power. The Great Commission propels ecclesiastical agents into the world. The Bible stands against contemporary forces. Humans receive the Holy Spirit, which then catapults them into the world with spiritual and material application. Gospel realities affect the world, bringing holistic transformation. God is powerful, and humans actively appropriate God's power for the purpose of social transformation, whether navigating through ambiguous spiritual forces, governing human communities, or interacting with the world around them. In such ways, divine power lends itself to sociological categories.

Modernity-related themes hence coalesce from *how* ecclesiastical communities employ divine power. There can be little doubt that modern and distinctly Western categories matter to Africans. Even a casual perusal of Christianity on the continent reveals a wide variety of images that feed off Western points of reference (e.g., ecclesiastical discourses, songs, books, or even seemingly non-religious carriers, such as *matatu*). Rather than handling modernity as a historically or sociologically conditioned concept (yet not denying that it can serve these purposes), I view it through the lenses of theological discursive: a category open to ecclesiastical communities, and predicated upon the employment of divine power. Precisely because humans are the image of God, they image God's nature for the world. Ecclesiastical communities are the primary actors in this process and appropriate divine power in generative (and oppressive) ways, and always in *dialogue* with global flows. Western constructs (i.e., modernity) are therefore not determinative to African societies, but revelatory of human aspirations within a modern world.

Churches, I argue, occupy central role in this process. Kwame Bediako says something similar for understanding Majority World contributions to theological methodology:

> Because of the strong element of "the experience of community" in the theologies of the South, these theologies have a distinct inclination to being "ecclesial" theologies, which is not to say that they are confessional or denominational. Rather, this simply expresses the way in which the theologies of the South are rooted in the churches, and are produced from within the churches, to the extent that they proceed on the basis of seeking to understand and articulate the longings and aspirations of the communities they represent.[4]

---

4. Bediako, *Christianity in Africa*, 162; similarly, Paul Bowers proposes that African theology must focus upon the "present Christian community of Africa, with the

Such a *praxis* theology takes seriously the contributions of people within congregations, especially related to how spiritual (theological) resources lend themselves for social construction. Bediako even argues that African churches with their "primal imagination" may, if given opportunity, speak into Western contexts struggling with various facets of their modernity-related heritage.[5] While he wants to avoid intimating that this "experience of the community" amounts to mere denominationalism, important differences do exist between the various ecclesiastical communities, and these dissimilarities are essential for displaying the broad panorama of African responses to the Gospel. The three denominations examined in this book provide rich tapestry to theological expression. Similarities assert common themes within African ecclesiology, while differences reveal a "hermeneutical community,"[6] or what Kevin Ward describes as "global Christian identity in a pluralist world."[7]

The presence of these similarities and differences further brings to light the stark reality that not all the forms of modernity listed in the previous chapters represent healthy or robust varieties. Sociologists will rightfully critique these manifestations and the underlying presuppositions that give rise to how ecclesiastical communities employ divine power within the world. Sometimes the churches succumb to broader society-wide trends and fail to appropriate their theological resources for the purposes of critiquing social or economic exploitation (or, with affect to civil structures). Other times, theological motivations become part of the problem, as in the case of sacralization or what Gifford refers to as "neo-patrimonialism."[8] Theologians need to attend carefully to these concerns, even when sociologists appear to intrude, as it were, upon explicitly theological frames of reference. Yet theologians should likewise engage in sociological dialogue. For example, just because power occupies privileged position within African societies, this does not mean that human agents *tap into* God's nature in healthy ways. Biblicism may, depending on the ways that it is used, function to elevate pastoral identity over (or at the expense of) the *washiriki*. The infilling of the Holy Spirit can bypass essential human nature: jump-starting believers with sacred

---

full range of needs and expectations, its requirements and preoccupations" ("African Theology," 122).

5. Bediako, *Christianity*, 262.
6. Hiebert, "Critical Contextualization," 288–96; *Anthropological* 75–92.
7. Ward, "Africa," 235.
8. Gifford, *African Christianity*, 5ff.

power. Traditions may, at times, merge with biblical themes and impart sacrosanct meaning to ecclesiastical communities. Quite simply, ample evidence exists within contemporary ecclesiastical (and non-ecclesiastical) domains to suggest that divine power can easily become misused and function as a weapon against the masses,[9] or serve as an impediment to human growth.

A theological assessment of power, therefore, aids in the overall discussion by showing that humans image God by imaging his power in the world; they do so, likewise, by maintaining fidelity to the *values, ethics, and purposes* of divine power as seen within the divine community. Power comes from God, and must image divine intent. This means that humans use their powers for life, and do so through service, giving, sacrifice, and creative acts of agency. Human power is therefore power from God, and predicated upon the ways of God. Laurenti Magesa expresses something similar for African communities:

> In African religion, therefore, power is ultimately "power of God" and its proper use, known as authority, constitutes "power as of God." To the person in authority, the ever present and most important concern is how to use the power of God granted to him or her through the community, to enhance the life of the community, as God would do.[10]

These comments underscore the importance of God's nature for representations of power within the world (what Schweiker refers to as God's "moral ontology"). Rather than subverting power relations—which appear so vital within African ecclesiology—greater effort needs to be given to developing ethical (and precisely, theological) parameters to guide the appropriation of divine power within the world: with attention to the entities and the "spaces" existing within an integrative cosmos. I have sought such an enterprise through the image of God concept.

African varieties of modernity, such as were highlighted in Chapters 3, 4, and 5 reveal a more integrated and nuanced role for the sacred in contributing to modernity-related themes. Humankind exists within the center of an integrative cosmos, with relevant powers emanating from the divine for shaping the world around them. Recent studies in post- (or liquid) modernity, as well as the growing literature connecting religion (or the sacred)[11] with contemporary societies, suggests that more, not less,

---

9. See for example, Monga, *The Anthropology*, 127–37.
10. Magesa, "'Power' in African Religion," 317.
11. Peter Berger and Harvey Cox represent two important sociological voices

Re-Imaging Modernity

attention should be given for understanding how human communities utilize the divine for social construction. Some scholars are thus beginning to call Western societies back to a reintegration of sacred and secular realities. Max Stackhouse and Don Browning are among those advising theological ethics to "reengage the authorities and regencies of modernity and revitalize their inner spirit."[12] These authors explain how, in days past, sociological currents were more connected with their "spiritual and moral roots" but in modern times have become dislocated from these sources of sacred power, leaving them "vulnerable to spiritual and moral emptiness or superficiality, to manipulation by narrow interests, and thus to potential threats to the human future."[13] Ecclesiastical communities in Ukambani view themselves as agents of the divine. They tap into divine power in order to shape the world around them. Modernity, therefore, is not something that humans need to reject, but reshape. Vinoth Ramachandra appeals for such a reassessment:

> No one, whether Christian or non-Christian, who cares about such human emancipation can rejoice in the "end of modernity" chorus emanating from certain quarters of the Western world. But we also stand in great need of discernment lest we identify the "spirit of the age" with the Holy Spirit, the Spirit of truth who mediates the reality of the risen Lord in the midst of historical change and uncertainty. If, indeed modernity is the prodigal son of the Christian narrative, then what would the return of the prodigal—the "recapitulation" (apokata-lassein, Eph 1:10) of modern society in Christ—involve?[14]

Humans create modernity, and not the other way around. If the Gospel of Jesus Christ relates to "life," then modernity falls within the scope of theological reflection. Human transformation, Ramachandra suggests, will involve the "recapitulation" (drawing upon Irenaeus' use of the word) of human society: the remaking of the modern order.[15]

---

calling attention to the role of the sacred within the modern world (see Berger, *Desecularization*; Cox, *Fire from Heaven*).

12. Stackhouse and Browning, *God and Globalization*, 3; see also 29.

13. Ibid.

14. Ramachandra, "Learning from Modern European Secularism," 39.

15. I am not offering a postmillennial view of eschatology, advocating a neo-Constantinian order, nor inferring that the recapitulation of Christ represents a total remaking of modern society, as if assuming that modernity represents a singular and unified way of looking at reality. I am merely working along the lines offered by these denominations, suggesting that ecclesiastical communities in Africa are deeply

Conclusions

My focus has been to call attention to the positive contribution of the churches in Ukambani as they reimage modernity. Divine power represents a central theme in each of the denominations. Differences between the churches (whether in terms of doctrinal development and/or application) reveal elements of flexibility and adaptability: two important attributes in a destabilized and constantly morphing human ethos. At times, I have highlighted areas of deficiency or misappropriation of power within the churches, but these have served less central to my overall thesis. I do hope, however, that in the midst of examining the different ecclesiastical communities, and laying their theologies as it were side-by-side, that valuable insights could be gained in how to strengthen the churches through the image of God concept; and in so doing, buttress the appropriation of power within modern, Kenyan society.

Humans image God derivatively. Power is not a right, but a gift flowing from the divine into human image-bearers, and with application (construction) for the modern world. Theology cannot afford to neglect the issues that matter most to humans, and these often fall along sociological themes. Kä Mana understands Christian theology in a similar light: to create a "power of reconstruction" that seeks "to integrate and to accommodate others by reforming oneself, to transform by re-orienting the world in which one lives."[16] Humanization, according to Kä Mana, indicates a reorientation to Christ for the purposes of affecting the "entire constellation of people's patterns of thought in order to motivate those who were objects of life to become subjects of their destiny, with Christ as an ultimate guide."[17] Power *from God* must serve as *power as of God*. Transformation "*in Christ*" necessitates that divine power work to affect the entities and spaces that guide human agency within the modern world.

---

committed to orienting theological resources along sociological trajectories, and that these kinds of endeavors are not only valid, but essential.

16. Cited in Dedji, "Ethical Redemption," 266.
17. Ibid., 269.

Bibliography

Abraham, K. C. "Theology in the Context of Globalization." *Voices from the Third World*, 21.1 (1998) 135–252.

———, ed. *Third World Theologies: Commonalities and Divergences*. Maryknoll, NY: Orbis, 1990.

Abrahamsen, Rita. "African Studies and the Postcolonial Challenge." *African Affairs* 102 (2003) 189–210.

Adeyemo, Tokunboh, ed. *Africa Bible Commentary*. Grand Rapids, MI: Zondervan, 2006.

Africa Inland Church. *Constitution*, 1981 ed. Kijabe, Kenya.

———. *Constitution*, rev. 2005 ed. Kijabe, Kenya.

"The African Brotherhood Church." *Ecumenical Review* 24.1 (Jan. 1972) 145–59.

African Brotherhood Church: 40 Years of Service: 8-4-1945 to 8-4-1985. Translated by Moses Mollombe. Machakos, Kenya: Eastern Printing Works, 1985.

Agu, Charles. *Secularization in Igboland*. New York: Peter Lang, 1989.

AIM Archives. *BGC*, 20.12 (Dec. 14, 1933).

———. *Hearing and Doing*, Apr.–May 1902.

———. *Hearing and Doing*, Jan. 1896.

———. "Joint Meeting of the AIM, GFF, CMS, for the admission of ABC in the CCK." Nairobi, Kenya: Mumbuni, 1957.

The Akamba Christian Brotherhood: The Aim of Forming this Association, n.d.

Anderson, Allan. "Evangelism and the Growth of Pentecostalism in Africa." University of Birmingham. Apr. 11, 2000. Online: http://artsweb.bham.ac.uk/acanderson.

———. *An Introduction to Pentecostalism*. Cambridge: Cambridge University Press, 2004.

———. "Pentecostal Pneumatology and African Power Concepts: Continuity or Change?" *Missionalia* 19.1 (Apr. 1990) 65–74.

Anum, Eric. "Ye Ma Wo Mo! African Hermeneuts, You Have Spoken At Last: Reflections on Semia 73 (1996)." In *Reading Other-Wise: Socially Engaged Biblical Scholars Reading with the Local Communities*, edited by Gerald O. West, 7–18. Atlanta: Society of Biblical Literature, 2007.

Anyanwu, Simaon O. "The Notion of the Human Persons in African Traditional Society: Its Relevance to Christianity and Modern Society." *Jos Studies* 2.1 (June 1991) 3–16.

Bibliography

Appiah, Kwame Anthony. *The Ethics of Identity*. Princeton: Princeton University Press, 2005.

Aquinas, St. Thomas. *Summa Theologiae: A Concise Translation*. Edited by Timothy McDermott. Allen, TX: Christian Classics, 1989.

Arens, W., and Ivan Karp, eds. *Creativity of Power: Cosmology and Action in African Societies*. Washington: Smithsonian Institution Press, 1989.

Asante, Emmanuel. *Towards an African Christian Theology of the Kingdom of God: The Kingship of Onyame*. Lewiston, NY: Mellen University Press, 1995.

Atieno-Odhiambo, E.S. "Democracy and the Ideology of Order in Kenya." In *The Political Economy of Kenya*, edited by Michael G. Schatzberg, 177–201. New York: Praeger, 1987.

Ayandale, Emmanuel. "Mission in the Context of Religions and Secularization: an African Viewpoint." *Lutheran World* 20.3 (1973) 263–78.

Bahemuka, Judith Mbula, and Joseph L. Brockington, eds. *East Africa in Transition: Communities, Cultures and Change*. Nairobi: Acton, 2001.

Barkan, Joel D. "The Rise and Fall of a Governance Realm in Kenya." In *Governance and Politics in Africa*, edited by Goran Hyden and Michael Bratton, 167–92. London: Lynne Reinner, 1992.

Barth, Karl. *Church Dogmatics*. Edited by G. W. Bromiley and T. F. Torrance. Vol. III/I. Edinburgh: T. & T. Clark, 1958.

Bauman, Zygmunt. *Liquid Modernity*. Cambridge: Polity, 2000.

Baur, John. 2000 *Years of Christianity in Africa: An African Church History*. Nairobi: Paulines, 1994.

Bebbington, David W. *The Dominance of Evangelicalism: The Age of Spurgeon and Moody*. Leicester: InterVarsity, 2005.

———. *Evangelicalism in Modern Britain: A History from the 1730s to the 1980s*. Grand Rapids, MI: Baker, 1989.

Bediako, Kwame. *Christianity in Africa: The Renewal of a Non-Western Religion*. Maryknoll, NY: Orbis, 1995.

———. "Unmasking the Powers: Christianity, Authority, and Desacralization in Modern African Politics." In *Christianity and Democracy in Global Context*, edited by J. Witte, 207–29. Boulder CO: Westview, 1993.

Behrend, H., and Ute Luig, eds. *Spirit Possession, Modernity and Power in Africa*. Oxford: James Currey, 1999.

Benney, M., and E. Hughes. Editorial preface to "Of Sociology and the Interview." *American Journal of Sociology*, 62 (1956) 137–42.

Benson, G. P. "Ideological Politics versus Biblical Hermeneutics: Kenya's Protestant Churches & the Nyayo State." In *Religion and Politics in East Africa*, edited by Holger Bernt Hansen and Michael Twaddle, 177–99. London: James Currey, 1995.

Berger, Peter, ed. *The Desecularization of the World: Resurgent Religion and World Politics*. Grand Rapids, MI: Eerdmans, 1999.

———. "Religion and the West." *The National Interest* (Summer 2005) 112–19.

———. *The Social Reality of Religion*. London: Faber and Faber, 1969.

———. "Sociological and Theological Perspectives." In *Theology and Sociology: A Reader*, edited by Robin Gill, 93–100. New York: Paulist, 1987.

Berman, Bruce J. "Nationalism, Ethnicity, and Modernity: The Paradox of the Mau Mau." *Canadian Journal of African Studies*, 25.2 (1991) 181–206.

Black, Matthew. "The Pauline Doctrine of the Second Adam." *Scottish Journal of Theology* 7 (1954) 170–79.

Blaxter, Loraine, Christina Hughes, and Malcom Tight. *How to Research*. Milton Keynes: Open University, 2006.
Bonhoeffer, Dietrich. *Ethics*. Translated by Eberhard Bethge. London: SCM, 1955.
Borowitz, Eugene B. "The Autonomous Self and the Commanding Community." *Theological Studies* 45.1 (1984) 34–56.
Bosch, David J. *Transforming Mission: Paradigm Shifts in Theology of Mission*. Maryknoll, NY: Orbis, 1991.
Bowers, Paul. "African Theology: Its History, Dynamics, Scope and Future." *Africa Journal of Evangelical Theology* 21.2 (2002) 109–25.
Bratton, Michael. "Beyond the State: Civil Society and Associational Life in Africa." *World Politics* 41.3 (Apr 1989) 407–30.
———. "Toward Governance in Africa." In *Governance and Politics in Africa*, edited by Goran Hyden and Michael Bratton, . Boulder, CO; London: Lynne Rienner, 1992.
Browne, Herman. *Theological Anthropology: A Dialectic Study of the African and Liberation Theology*. London: Avon, 1996.
Browning, Don. *A Fundamental Practical Theology: Descriptive and Strategic Proposals*. Minneapolis, MN: Fortress, 1991.
Brueggemann, Walter. "From Dust to Kingship." *Zeitschrift Für Die Alttestamentliche Wissenschaft* 84.1 (1972) 1–18.
Brunner, Emil. *Man in Revolt: A Christian Anthropology*. Translated by Olive Wyon. London: Lutterworth, 1939.
Bryman, Alan. *Social Research Methods*. 2nd ed. Oxford: Oxford University Press, 2004.
Bujo, Bénézet. *African Theology in its Social Context*. Maryknoll, NY: Orbis, 1992.
———. *Foundations of an African Ethic: Beyond the Universal Claims of Western Morality*. Translated by Brian McNeil. New York: Crossroad, 2001.
Camps, Arnulf. "Missiology and Secularization." *Exchange* 21 (Apr 1992) 49–56.
Carrithers, Michael, Steven Collins, and Steven Lukes, eds. *The Category of the Person: Anthropology, Philosophy, History*. Cambridge: Cambridge University Press, 1985.
Chabal, Patrick, ed. *Political Domination in Africa*. Cambridge: Cambridge University Press, 1986.
Chabal, Patrick, and Jean-Pascal Daloz. *Africa Works: Disorder as a Political Instrument*. Oxford: James Currey, 1999.
Clines, David J. A. "Humanity as the Image of God." In *On the Way to the Postmodern, Old Testament Essays, 1967–1998*, edited by David J. A. Clines, 2:447–97. Journal for the Study of the Old Testament, Supplemental Series 293. Shefield, UK: Shefield Academic Press, 1998.
Cochrane, James R. "Theology and Faith: Tradition, Criticism and Popular Religion." In *Doing Theology in Context: South African Perspectives*, edited by John W. de Gruchy and Charles Villa-Vicencio, 26–39. Maryknoll, NY: Orbis, 1994.
Cohen, David William, and E. S. Atieno Odhiambo. *Burying SM: The Politics of Knowledge and the Sociology of Power in Africa*. Portsmouth, NH: Heinemann, 1992.
Cohen, Jeremy. *"Be Fertile and Increase, Fill the Earth and Master It": The Ancient and Medieval Career of a Biblical Text*. Ithaca, NY: Cornell University Press, 1989.
Coleman, Simon. *The Globalisation of Charismatic Christianity: Spreading the Gospel of Prosperity*. Cambridge: Cambridge University Press, 2000.
Comaroff, John L., and Jean Comaroff. *Of Revelation and Revolution: The Dialectics of Modernity on a South African Frontier*. Vol. 2. Chicago: University of Chicago Press, 1997.

Bibliography

———, eds. *Modernity and Its Malcontents: Ritual and Power in Postcolonial Africa.* Chicago: University of Chicago Press, 1993.

Comaroff, John. "Governmentality, Materiality, Legality, Modernity." In *African Modernities: Entangled Meanings in Current Debate*, edited by Jan-Georg Deutsch, et al., 107-34. Oxford: James Currey, 2002.

Conradie, E. M. "On the Integrity of the Human Person and the Integrity of Creation: Some Christian Theological Perspectives." In *The Integrity of the Human Person in an African Context: Perspectives from Science and Religion*, edited by C. W. du Toit, 107-51. Pretoria, SA: Research Institute for Theology and Religion, University of South Africa, 2004.

"Constitution and Rules of African Brotherhood Church," n.d.

Corin, Ellen. "Refiguring the Person: The Dynamics of Affects Symbols in an African Spirit Possession Cult." In *Bodies and Person: Comparative Perspectives from Africa and Melanesia*, edited by Michael Lambeck and Andrew Strathern, 82-102. Cambridge: Cambridge University Press, 1998.

Cox, Harvey. *Fire from Heaven: The Rise of Pentecostal Spirituality and the Reshaping of Religion in the Twenty-First Century.* Reading MA: Addison-Wesley, 1995.

Cragg, Kenneth. *The Privilege of Man: A Theme in Judaism, Islam and Christianity.* London: Athlone, 1968.

Cross, Sholto. "Independent Churches and Independent states: Jehovah's Witnesses in East and Central Africa." In *Christianity in Independent Africa*, edited by Edward Fashole-Luke et al., 304-15. London: Rex Collings, 1978.

Cummings, Robert J. "The Early Development of Akamba Local Trade History, c. 1780-1820." *Kenya Historical Review* 4.1 (1976) 85-110.

Day, Philip. "Secularization in Africa," *AFER* 14 (1972) 332-36.

Dedji, Valentine. "The Ethical Redemption of African *Imaginaire*: Kä Mana's Theology of Reconstruction." *Journal of Religion in Africa* 31.3 (2001) 254-74.

———. *Reconstruction and Renewal in African Christian Theology.* Theology of Reconstruction Series. Nairobi: Acton, 2003.

Degenaar, Johan. "The Changed View of Man." *Journal of Theology for Southern Africa* 6 (Mar. 1974) 41-64.

Delanty, Gerard. *Modernity and Postmodernity: Knowledge, Power and the Self.* London: Sage Publications, 2000.

Denzin, Norman K., and Yvonne S. Lincoln, eds. *Collecting and Interpreting Qualitative Materials.* Thousand Oaks, CA: Sage, 1998.

Deutsch, Jan-Georg, Peter Probst, and Heike Schmidt, eds. *African Modernities: Entangled Meanings in Current Debate.* Oxford: James Currey, 2002.

Devisch, Rene. "Treating the Affect by Remodelling the Body in a Yaka Cult." In *Bodies and Person: Comparative Perspectives from Africa and Melanesia*, edited by Michael Lambeck and Andrew Strathern, 130-56. Cambridge: Cambridge University Press, 1998.

Dorsten, Linda Eberst, and Lawrence Hotchkiss. *Research Methods and Society: Foundations of Social Inquiry.* Upper Saddle River, NJ: Pearson Education, 2005.

du Toit, C. W., ed. *The Integrity of the Human Person in an African Context: Perspectives from Science and Religion.* Pretoria, SA: Research Institute for Theology and Religion, University of South Africa, 2004.

Dunn, James D. G. "'A Light to the Gentiles': The Significance of the Damascus Road Christophany for Paul." In *The Glory of Christ in the New Testament: Studies in Christology*, edited by L. D. Hurst and N. T. Wright, 251-66. Oxford: Clarendon, 1987.

---. "Was Christianity a Monotheistic Faith from the Beginning?" *Scottish Journal of Theology* 35.4 (1982) 303-36.
Dupre, Louis. *The Enlightenment and the Intellectual Culture of Modernity*. New Haven: Yale University, 2004.
Edwards, Jonathan. "A Dissertation on the End for Which God Created the World." In *The Works of Jonathan Edwards*, revised by Edward Hickman, pp. 94-120. Edinburgh: Banner of Truth, 1974.
Eichrodt, Walther. *Man in the Old Testament*. Translated by K. Smith and R. Gregor Smith. London: SCM, 1951.
Ellis, Stephen, and Gerrie ter Haar. *Worlds of Power: Religious Thought and Political Practice in Africa*. London: Hurst, 2004.
Evans-Pritchard, E. "The Divine Kingship of the Shillunk of the Nilotic Sudan." In *Social Anthropology and Other Essays*, edited by Evans-Pritchard. New York: The Free Press, 1962.
Fasholé-Luke, Edward, Richard Gray, Adrian Hastings, and Godwin Tasie, eds. *Christianity in Independent Africa*. London: Rex Collings, 1978.
Featherstone, Mike. "The Body in Consumer Culture." In *The Body: Social Process and Cultural Theory*, edited by Mike Featherstone et al., 187-96. London: Sage, 1991.
Ford, David F. "Theology." In *The Routledge Companion to the Study of Religion*, edited by John R. Hinnels, 61-79. London: Routledge, 2005.
Foster, Robert J. "Making National Cultures in the Global Ecumene." *Annual Review of Anthropology* 20 (1991) 235-60.
Foucault, Michel. *Power/Knowledge: Selected Interviews and Other Writings 1972-1977*. Translated by Colin Gordon et al. Brighton, UK: Harvester, 1980.
Frederiksen, Bodil Folke. "Popular Culture, Gender Relations and the Democratization of Everyday Life in Kenya." *Journal of Southern African Studies* 26.2 (2000) 209-22.
Friedman, Galia Sabar. "Church and State in Kenya, 1986-1992: The Churches Involvement in the 'Game of Change.'" *African Affairs* 96.382 (1997) 25-52.
---. "The Power of the Familiar: Everyday Practices in the Anglican Church of Kenya." *Journal of Church & State* 38.2 (1996) 377-96.
Garr, W. Randall. "'Image' and 'Likeness' in the Inscription from Tell Fakhariyeh." *Israel Exploration Journal* 50 (2000) 227-34.
Geertz, Clifford. "Thick Description: Toward an Interpretive Theory of Culture." In *The Interpretation of Cultures: Selected Essays*, edited by Clifford Geertz, 3-30. New York: Basic Books, 1973.
Gehman, Richard. "The Africa Inland Mission: Aspects of Its Early Years." *Africa Journal of Evangelical Theology* 23.2 (2004) 115-44.
Germond, Paul. "Theology, Development and Power: Religious Power and Development Practice." *Journal of Theology for Southern Africa* 110 (July 2001) 21-31.
Giddens, Anthony. *Conversations with Anthony Giddens: Making Sense of Modernity*. Stanford, CA: Stanford University Press. 1998.
Gifford, Paul. "Africa's Inculturation Theology: Observations of an Outsider." *Hekima Review* 38 (May 2008) 18-34.
---. *African Christianity: Its Public Role*. London: Hurst, 1998.
---. "The Bible in Africa: A Novel USage in Africa's New Churches." *Bulletin of the School of Oriental and African Studies* 71.2 (2008) 203-19.
---, ed. *The Christian Church and the Democratisation of Africa*. New York: Brill, 1995.
---. *Christianity, Politics, and Public Life in Kenya*. London: Hurst, 2009.

Bibliography

———. "Prosperity: A New and Foreign Element in African Christianity." *Religion* 20 (1990) 373–88.

———. "Reinhard Bonnke's Misson to Africa, and His 1991 Nairobi Crusade." In *New Dimensions in African Christianity*, edited by Paul Gifford, 157–82. Nairobi: All Africa Conference of Churches, 1992.

———. "Some Recent Developments in Africa Christianity." *African Affairs* 93.373 (1994) 513–34.

Gikandi, Simon. "Reason, Modernity and the African Crisis." In *African Modernities: Entangled Meanings in Current Debate*, edited by Jan-Georg Deutsch et al., 135–57. Oxford: James Currey, 2002.

Gill, Robin. *Prophecy and Praxis: The Social Function of the Churches*. London: Marshall Morgan & Scott, 1981.

———. *Social Context of Theology*. London: Mowbrays, 1975.

———. *Theology and Social Structure*. London: Mowbrays, 1977.

———. *Theology and Sociology: A Reader*. London: Chapman, 1987.

———. "Three Sociological Approaches to Theology." In *Social Context of Theology*, edited by Robin Gill, 3–14. London: Mowbrays, 1975.

Gitari, David. "Church and Politics." *Evangelical Review of Theology* 28.3 (2004) 220–31.

Gration, John A. "The Relationship of the Africa Inland Mission and Its National Church in Kenya between 1895 and 1971." PhD diss., New York University, 1974.

Gulliver, P. H., ed. *Tradition and Transition in East Africa: Studies of the Tribal Element in the Modern Era*. London: Routledge & Kegan Paul, 1969.

Gyekye, Kwame. *Tradition and Modernity: Philosophical Reflections on the African Experience*. Oxford: Oxford University Press, 1997.

Harries, Patrick. "Missionaries, Marxists and Magic: Power and the Politics of Literacy in South-East Africa." *Journal of Southern African Studies* 27.3 (2001) 405–27.

Harris, Hermione. "Continuity or Change? Aladura and Born Again Yoruba Christianity in London." In *Christianity and Social Change in Africa: Essays in Honor of J. D. Y. Peel*, edited by Toyin Falola, 307–34. Durham, NC: Carolina Academic, 2005.

Harrison, Beverly. *Making the Connections: Essays in Feminist Social Ethics*. Boston: Beacon, 1985.

Hastings, Adrian. *African Christianity: An Essay in Interpretation*. London: Geoffrey Chapman, 1976.

———. *A History of African Christianity: 1950–1975*. Cambridge: Cambridge University Press, 1979.

Haugerud, Angelique. *The Culture of Politics in Modern Kenya*. Cambridge: Cambridge University Press, 1995.

Hawthorne, Gerald F. *Philippians*. Word Biblical Commentary 43. Waco, TX: Word, 1983.

———. *The Presence and the Power: The Significance of the Holy Spirit in the Life and Ministry of Jesus*. Dallas, TX: Word, 1991.

Haynes, Jeff. "Popular Religion and Politics in sub-Saharan Africa." *Third World Quarterly* 16.1 (1995) 89–108.

———. *Religion and Politics in Africa*. Nairobi: East African Educational Publishers, 1996.

Hearn, Julie. "The 'Invisible' NGO: US Evangelical Missions in Kenya." *Journal of Religion in Africa* 32.1 (2002) 32–60.

Hengel, Martin. *Christ and Power*. Belfast: Christian Journals, 1977.

Bibliography

Henriksen, Jan-Olav. "Creation and Construction: On the Theological Appropriation of Postmodern Theory." *Modern Theology* 18.2 (2002) 153–69.

Herskovits, Melville J., and William R. Bascom, eds. *Continuity and Change in African Cultures.* Chicago: University of Chicago Press, 1959.

Hiebert, Paul. *Anthropological Reflections on Missiological Issues.* Grand Rapids, MI: Baker, 1994.

———. "Critical Contextualization." *Missiology* 12.3 (1984) 288–96.

Himmelfard, Gertrude. *The Roads to Modernity: The British, French, and American Enlightenments.* New York: Vintage, 2004.

Hobley, C. W. *Ethnography of the A-kamba and Other East Africa Tribes.* Cambridge: Cambridge University Press, 1910.

Hobsbaum, Eric, and Terence Ranger, eds. *The Invention of Tradition.* Cambridge: Cambridge University Press, 1983.

Hofstede, Geert. *Cultures and Organizations: Software of the Mind.* New York: McGraw-Hill, 1997.

Hooker, Morna D. *From Adam to Christ: Essays on Paul.* Cambridge: Cambridge University Press, 1990.

Horton, Robin. "African Traditional Thought and Western Science." In *Rationality: Key Concepts in the Social Sciences*, edited by Bryan R. Wilson, 131–71. Oxford: Basil Blackwell, 1970.

———. *Patterns of Thought in Africa and the West: Essays on Magic, Religion and Science.* Cambridge: Cambridge University Press, 1993.

House-Midamba, Bessie. "Gender, Democratization & Associational Life in Kenya." In *Readings in African Politics*, edited by Tom Young, 175–81. Oxford: James Currey, 2003.

Hyden, Goran. "Capital Accumulation, Resource Distribution, and Governance in Kenya: The Role of the Economy of Affection." In *The Political Economy of Kenya*, edited by Michael G. Schatzberg, 117–36. New York, Praeger, 1987.

Idowu, E. Balaji. *African Traditional Religion: a Definition.* London: SCM, 1973.

Iioanusi, Obiakoizu A. *Myths of the Creation of Man and the Origin of Death in Africa.* Frankfurt: Peter Lang, 1984.

Ilesanmi, Simeon O. "The Myth of a Secular State: A Study of Religious Politics with Historical Illustrations." *Islam and Christian-Muslim Relations* 6.1 (1995) 105–17.

Irenaeus. *Against Heresies.* Translated and annotated by Dominic J. Unger with further revisions by John J. Dillon. New York: Paulist, 1992.

Isichei, Elizabeth. *A History of Christianity in Africa: From Antiquity to Present.* Grand Rapids, MI: Eerdmans, 1995.

Jackson, Michael, and Ivan Karp, eds. *Personhood and Agency: The Experience of Self and Other in African Cultures.* Stockholm: Almqvist & Wiksell, 1990.

Jacobs, Donald Reiman. "The Cultural Themes and Puberty Rites of the Akamba, A Bantu Tribe of East Africa." PhD diss., New York University, 1961.

Jacobson-Widding, Anita. *Identity: Personal and Socio-Cultural.* Atlantic Highlands, NJ: Humanities Press, 1983.

———. "The Shadow as an Expression of Individuality in Congolese Conceptions of Personhood." In *Personhood and Agency: The Experience of the Self and Other in African Cultures*, edited by Michael Jackson and Ivan Karp, 31–56. Stockholm: Almqvist & Wiksell, 1990.

Bibliography

Jahn, Janhienz. *Muntu: An Outline of Neo-African Culture.* Translated by Marjorie Grene. London: Faber and Faber, 1961.

Jenkins, Philip. *Religion in English Everyday Life: An Ethnographic Approach.* Vol. 5 of *Methodology and History in Anthropology.* New York: Berhahn, 1999.

Johnstone, Patrick, and Jason Mandryk. *Operation World.* Twenty-first century edition. Waynesboro GA: Paternoster, 2001.

Josephides, Lisette. *Bodies and Persons: Comparative Perspectives from Africa and Melanasia.* Ediburgh: University of Edinburgh, 2001.

Jules-Rosette, Bennetta. *The New Religions in Africa.* Norwood, NJ: Ablex, 1979.

———. "The Sacred in African New Religions." In *The Changing Face of Religion,* edited by James A. Beckford and Thomas Luckmann, 147–62. London: Sage, 1989.

Kabasélé, François. "Christ as Ancestor and Elder Brother." In *Faces of Jesus in Africa,* edited by Robert J. Schreiter, 116–27. Maryknoll, NY: Orbis, 1991.

———. "Christ as Chief." In *Faces of Jesus in Africa,* edited by Robert J. Schreiter, 103–15. London: SCM, 1991.

Kagame, Alexis. *La Philosophie Bantu Comparee.* Paris: Presence Africaine, 1976.

Kalu. Ogbu U. "African Christianity: From the World Wars to Decolonisation." In *The Cambridge History of Christianity: World Christians,* Vol. 9: *c. 1914–c. 2000,* edited by Hugh McLeod, 206–18. Cambridge: Cambridge University Press, 2006.

———. *Power, Poverty and Prayer: The Challenges of Poverty and Pluralism in Africa, 1960–1996.* Frankfurt: Peter Lang, 2000.

———. "Review of African Christianity: Its Public Role." *International Bulletin of Missiological Research* 24.1 (2000) 36.

Kanyinga, Karuta. "Leadership and Governance in Post-Colonial Africa." In *East Africa in Transition: Communities, Cultures and Change,* edited by Judith M. Bahemuka and Joseph L. Brockington, 36–46. Nairobi: Acton, 2001.

Kapolyo, Joe M. *The Human Condition: Christian Perspectives through African Eyes.* Downers Grove IL: InterVarsity, 2005.

Karp, Ivan. *Creativity of Power: Cosmology and Action in African Societies.* Washington, DC: Smithsonian Institute Press, 1989.

———. "Power and Capacity in Iteso Rituals of Possession." In *Personhood and Agency: The Experience of the Self and Other in African Cultures,* edited by Michael Jackson and Ivan Karp, 79–90. Stockholm: Almqvist & Wiksell, 1990.

Katibu: Africa Inland Church. Rev. ed. Kijabe, Kenya: Kijabe Press, 2005.

Kempny, Marian, and Aldona Jawlowska, eds. *Identity in Transformation: Postmodernity, Postcommunism, and Globalization.* Westport, CT: Praeger, 2002.

Kenyatta, Jomo. *Facing Mount Kenya: The Tribal Life of the Gikuyu.* London: Secker & Warburg, 1938.

———. *Suffering Without Bitterness: The Founding of the Kenya Nation.* Nairobi: East African Publishing House, 1968.

Knobl, Wolfgang. "Modernization Theory, Modernization and African Modernities." In *African Modernities: Entangled Meanings in Current Debate,* edited by Jan-Georg Deutsch et al., 158–78. Oxford: James Currey, 2002.

Knott, Kim. "Insider/Outsider Perspectives." In *The Routledge Companion to the Study of Religion,* edited by John R. Hinnells, 243–57. London: Routledge, 2005.

Kombo, James Owino. "The African Renaissance as a New Context for African Evangelical Theology." *Africa Journal of Evangelical Theology* 19.1 (2000) 3–24.

Komolafe, Sunday Babajide. "The Changing Face of Christianity: Revisiting African Creativity." *Missiology: An International Review* 32.2 (2004) 217–38.

Krapf, J. L. *Travels, Researches and Missionary Labours*. Cambridge: University Press, 1860.

Kratz, Corinne A. "Genres of Power: A Comparative Analysis of Okiek Blessings, Curses and Oaths." *Man: The Journal of the Royal Anthropological Institute* 24 (1989) 636–56.

Krause, Deborah. "Keeping It Real: The Image of God in the New Testament." *Interpretation* 59.4 (2005) 358–68.

Kreitzer, L. J. "Adam and Christ." In *Dictionary of Paul and His Letters*, edited by Gerald F. Hawthorne et al., 9–15. Downers Grove IL: InterVarsity, 1993.

Kretzschmar, Louis. "Authentic Christian Leadership and Spiritual Formation in Africa." *Journal of Theology for Southern Africa* 113 (July 2002) 41–61.

Kwark, Lawrencia. "The Reinvention of Tradition in African Independent Churches as a Means to Engage Modernity." In *Engaging Modernity: Methods and Cases for Studying African Independent Churches in South Africa*, edited by Dawid Venter, 127–45. Wesport, CT: Praeger, 2004.

Lambeck, Michael, and Andrew Strathern, eds. *Bodies and Persons: Comparative Perspectives from Africa and Melanesia*. Cambridge: Cambridge University Press, 1998.

Lindblom, G. *The Akamba in British East Africa*. Uppsala: Appelbergs Boktryckeri Aktiebolag, 1920.

LiPuma, Edward. "Modernity and the Forms of Personhood in Melanesia." In *Bodies and Persons: Comparative Perspectives from Africa and Melanesia*, edited by Michael Lambeck and Andrew Strathern, 53–79. Cambridge: Cambridge University Press, 1998.

Lonsdale, John. "The Emerging Pattern of Church and State Co-operation in Kenya." In *Christianity in Independent Africa*, edited by Edward Fashole-Luke et al., 267–84. London: Rex Collings, 1978.

———. "Jomo Kenyatta, God and the Modern World." In *African Modernities: Entangled Meanings in Current Debate*, edited by Jan-Georg Deutsch et al., 31–66. Oxford: James Currey, 2002.

———. "Kikuyu Christianities: A History of Intimate Diversity." In *Christianity and the African Imagination: Essays in Honour of Adrian Hastings*, edited by David Maxwell with Ingrid Lawrie, 157–98. Leiden: Brill, 2002.

———. "'Listen While I Read': Patriotic Christianity Among the Young Gikuyu." In *Christianity and Social Change in Africa: Essays in Honor of J. D. Y. Peel*, edited by Toyin Falola, 563–93. Durham, NC: Carolina Academic Press, 2005.

Lonsdale, John, with Stanley Booth-Clibborn and Andrew Hake. "The Emerging Pattern of Church and State Co-Operation in Kenya." In *Christianity in Independent Africa*, edited by Edward Fashole-Luke et al., 267–84. London: Rex Collings, 1978.

Lucier, Ruth M. "Dynamics of Hierarchy in African Thought." *Listening: Journal of Religion and Culture* 24.1 (1989) 29–40.

Luckmann, Thomas. *The Invisible Religion: The Problem with Religion in Modern Society*. New York: Macmillan, 1967.

Mackey, James P. *Power and Christian Ethics*. Cambridge: Cambridge University Press, 1994.

Magesa, Laurenti. *African Religion: The Moral Traditions of Abundant Life*. Nairobi: Pauline, 1997.

Bibliography

———. "'Power' in African Religion." In *Social and Religious Concerns of East Africa: A Wajibu Anthology*, edited by Gerald J. Wanjohi and G. Wakuraya Wanjohi, 313–17. Nairobi: Wajibu: A Journal of Social and Religious Concern, 2005.

Maimela, Simon S. "Traditional African Anthropology and Christian Theology." *Journal of Theology for Southern Africa* 76 (1991) 4–14.

Majibizano ya Africa Inland Church. Kijabe, Kenya: Kijabe Press, 2000.

Marks, Darren C., ed. *Shaping a Theological Mind: Theological Context and Methodology*. Aldershot, UK: Ashgate, 2002.

Marsden, George. "Afterward: Religion, Politics, and the Search for an American Consensus." In *Religion and American Politics: From the Colonial Period to the 1980s*, edited by Mark Noll, 459-470. New York: Oxford University Press, 1990.

———. *Fundamentalism and American Culture: The Shaping of Twentieth Century Evangelicalism, 1870–1925*. New York; Oxford: Oxford University Press, 1980.

Marshall-Fratani, Ruth. "Mediating the Global and Local in Nigerian Pentecostalism." *Journal of Religion in Africa* 28.3 (1998) 278–315.

Martin, David. *Pentecostalism: The World Their Parish*. Oxford: Blackwell, 2002.

———. *Reflections of Sociology and Theology*. New York: Oxford University Press, 1997.

———. John Orme Mills, and W. S. F. Pickering, eds. *Sociology and Theology: Alliance and Conflict*. Brighton: Harvester, 1980.

Masango, Maake. "Leadership in the African Context." *The Ecumenical Review* 55.4 (2003) 313–21.

Masolo, D. A. *African Philosophy in Search of Identity*. Bloomington, IN: Indiana University Press, 1994.

Maxwell, David. "Christianity and the African Imagination." In *Christianity and the African Imagination: Essays in Honour of Adrian Hastings*, edited by David Maxwell with Ingrid Lawrie, 1–24. Leiden: Brill, 2002.

———. "Christianity without Boundaries: Shona Missionaries and Transnational Pentecostalism in Africa." In *Christianity and the African Imagination: Essays in Honour of Adrian Hastings*, edited by David Maxwell with Ingrid Lawrie, 295–332. Leiden: Brill, 2002.

———. "'Delivered from the Spirit of Poverty?' Pentecostalism, Prosperity and Modernity in Zimbabwe." *Journal of Religion in Africa* 28.3 (1998) 350–73.

———. "Post-Colonial Christianity in Africa." In *Christianity: World Christians*, edited by Hugh McLeod, 401–21. Cambridge: Cambridge University Press, 2006.

———. "Review Article: In Defence of African Christianity." *Journal of Religion in Africa* 30.4 (2000) 468–81.

Maxwell, Ian Douglas. "Civilization or Christianity? The Scottish Debate on Mission Methods, 1750–1835." In *Christian Missions and the Enlightenment*, edited by Brian Stanley, 123–40. Grand Rapids, MI: Eerdmans, 2001.

Mayer, Ruth. *Artificial Africas: Colonial Images in the times of Globalization*. Hanover, NH: University Press of New England, 2002.

Mbembe, Achille. "The Banality of Power and the Aesthetics of Vulgarity in the Postcolony." Translated by Janet Roitman. *Public Culture* 4.2 (1992) 1–30.

Mbiti, John. *African Religions and Philosophy*. London: Heinemann Press, 1969.

———. *Akamba Stories*. Nairobi/Oxford: Oxford University Press, 1966.

———. "A Change of the African Concept of Man through Christian Influence." In *For the Sake of the Gospel*, edited by Gnana Robinson, 54–63. Arasarad, India: T.T.S., 1980.

———. *Concepts of God in Africa*. London: Heinemann, 1970.

Bibliography

———. *New Testament Eschatology in an African Background: A Study of the Encounter between New Testament Theology and African Traditional Concepts.* Oxford: Oxford University Press, 1971.

———. "When the Bull is in a Strange Land, It Does Not Bellow." In *God and Globalization: Christ and the Dominions of Civilization,* edited by Max L. Stackhouse and Diane B. Obenchain, 145–70. Harrisburg, PA: Trinity, 2002.

Mboya, Tom. "The Impact of Modern Institutions on the East African." In *Tradition and Transition in East Africa: Studies of the Tribal Element in the Modern Era,* edited by P. H. Gulliver, 89–103. London: Routledge & Kegan Paul, 1969.

McFadyen, Alistair I. *The Call to Personhood: A Christian Theory of the Individual in Social Relations.* Cambridge: Cambridge University Press, 1990.

McFarland, Ian A. *The Divine Image: Envisioning the Invisible God.* Minneapolis, MN: Fortress, 2005.

McMinn, Mark R., and Timothy R. Phillips, eds. *Care for the Soul: Exploring the Intersection of Psychology and Theology.* Downers Grove, IL: InterVarsity, 2001.

Meijer, W. "The Plural Self: a Hermeneutical View on Identity and Plurality." *British Journal of Religious Education* 17.2 (1995) 92–99.

Metzger, Paul Louis. *The Word of Christ and the World of Culture: Sacred and Secular through the Theology of Karl Barth.* Grand Rapids, MI: Eerdmans, 2003.

Meyer, Birgit. "Commodities and the Power of Prayer: Pentecostal Attitudes Towards Consumption in Ghana." In *Globalization and Identity,* edited by P. Geschiere and B. Meyer, 151–76. London: Blackwell, 1999.

———. "Mediating Tradition: Pentecostal Pastors, African Priests, and Chiefs in Ghanian Popular Films." In *Christianity and Social Change in Africa: Essays in Honor of J. D. Y. Peel,* edited by Toyin Falola, 275–306. Durham, NC: Carolina Academic Press, 2005.

———. *Translating the Devil: Religion and Modernity Among the Ewe in Ghana.* Trenton, NJ: Africa World Press, 1999.

Middleton, J., and G. Kershaw. *The Kikuyu and Kamba of Kenya.* London: International African Institute, 1965.

Milbank, John. "The Last of the Last: Theology, Authority and Democracy." In *Shaping a Theological Mind: Theological Context and Methodology,* edited by D. C. Marks, 59–86. Grand Rapids, MI: Eerdmans, 2002.

———. *Theology and Social Theory: Beyond Secular Reason.* Cambridge, MA: Blackwell, 1991.

Miller, Elmer S. "The Christian Missionary: Agent of Secularization." *Missiology: An International Review,* 1.1 (1973) 99–107.

Moi, Daniel T. arap. *Kenya African Nationalism: Nyayo Philosophy and Principles.* London: Macmillan, 1986.

Mol, Hans. *Identity and the Sacred: a Sketch to a New Social-Scientific Theory of Religion.* New York: The Free Press, 1976.

Moltmann, Jürgen. *Man: Christian Anthropology in the Conflicts of the Present.* Translated by John Sturdy. London: SCM, 1971.

———. "Progress and Abyss: Remembrances of the Future of the Modern World." In *The Future of Hope: Christian Tradition amid Modernity and Postmodernity,* edited by Miroslav Volf and William Katerberg, 3–26. Grand Rapids, MI: Eerdmans, 2004.

———. "Theology in the Project of the Modern World." In *A Passion for God's Reign: Theology, Christian Learning, and the Christian Self,* edited by Miroslav Volf, 1–21. Grand Rapids, MI: Eerdmans, 1998.

Bibliography

———. *The Trinity and the Kingdom of God: The Doctrine of God.* London: SCM, 1981.
Moltmann, Jürgen, and Elisabeth Moltmann-Wendel. *Humanity in God.* London: SCM, 1983.
Monga, Célestin. *The Anthropology of Anger: Civil Society and Democracy in Africa.* Translated by Linda L. Fleck and Célestin Monga. London: Lynne Reinner, 1996.
Moore, Robert O. "God and Man in Bantu Religion." *African Ecclesiastical Review* 9.2 (1967) 149–60.
Morad, Steve. "The Founding Principles of the Africa Inland Mission and Their Interaction with the African Context in Kenya from 1895 to 1939: A Study of a Faith Mission." PhD diss., University of Edinburgh, 1997.
Morris, Paul. "Community Beyond Tradition." In *Detraditionalization: Critical Reflections on Authority and Identity*, edited by Paul Heelas et al., 223-249. Malden: Blackwell, 1996.
Mudimbe, V. Y. *The Invention of Africa: Gnosis, Philosophy, and the Order of Knowledge.* Bloomington: Indiana University Press, 1988.
Mugambi, J. N. K. *The Church and the Future of Africa: Problems and Promises.* Nairobi: All Africa Conference of Churches, 1997.
———. "Evangelistic and Charismatic Initiatives in Post-Colonial Africa." In *Charismatic Renewal in Africa: A Challenge for African Christianity*, edited by Mika Vähäkangas and Andrew A. Kyomo, 111–44. Nairobi: Acton, 2003.
———. *From Liberation to Reconstruction: African Christian Theology after the Cold War.* Nairobi: East African Educational Publishers, 1995.
Mugambi, J. N. K., and Mary N. Getui, eds. *Religions in East Africa Under Globalization.* Nairobi: Acton, 2004.
Mulago, Vincent. "Vital Participation." In *Biblical Revelation and African Beliefs*, edited by Kwesi A. Dickson and Paul Ellingworth, 137–57. Maryknoll, NY: Orbis, 1969.
Müller-Fahrenholz, Geiko. *The Kingdom and the Power: The Theology of Jürgen Moltmann.* Translated by John Bowden. London: SCM, 2000.
Munro, J. Forbes. *Colonial Rule and the Kamba.* Oxford: Clarendon, 1975.
Muriuki, Godfrey. "Kenya's Historical Experience: An Overview." In *East Africa in Transition: Communities, Cultures and Change*, edited by Judith M. Bahemuka and Joseph L. Brockington, 135–47. Nairobi: Acton, 2001.
Murphy, N, W. Brown, and N. Maloney, eds. *Whatever Happened to the Soul: Scientific and Theological Portraits of Human Nature.* Minneapolis, MN: Fortress, 1998.
Musopole, Augustine. *Being Human in Africa: Toward an African Christian Anthropology.* New York: Peter Lang, 1994.
———. *A Critical Evaluation of an African View of Humanity in the Writings of John Mbiti.* New York: Union Theological Seminary, 1991.
Mutuku, Peter. "African Brotherhood Church Launches Anti-Poverty Initiative." *The Link* (Feb 2007) 2–3.
Nasr, Seyyed Hossein. *Knowledge and the Sacred: The Gifford Lectures, 1981.* Edinburgh: Edinburgh University Press, 1981.
Ndeti, Kivuto. *Elements of Akamba Life.* Nairobi: East African Publishing House, 1972.
Nesbitt, Eleanor. "British, Asian and Hindu: Identity, Self-Narration and the Ethnographic Interview." *Journal of Beliefs & Values* 19.2 (1998) 189–200.
Ness, David Carroll. "Cultural Transmission among the Akamba of Kenya." PhD diss., Temple University, 1992.
Ng'weshemi, Andrea M. *Rediscovering the Human: The Quest for the Christo-Theological Anthropology in Africa.* New York: Peter Lang, 2002.

Nieder-Heitmann, Jan H. "The Missionary Challenge of Christendom and Modernity in South Africa." *International Review of Mission* 92.365 (2003) 178–91.

Noll, Mark. *A History of Christianity in the United States and Canada*. Grand Rapids, MI: Eerdmans, 1992.

Nwankwo, Lawrence. "'You Have Received the Spirit of Power' (2 Tim 1:7) Reviewing the Prosperity MesSage in the Light of a Theology of Empowerment." *JEPTA* 21 (2002) 56–77.

Nyamiti, Charles. "The Incarnation Viewed from the African Understanding of Person." *African Christian Studies* 6.1 (1990) 3–27.

Okafor, Stephen O. "*Bantu Philosophy*: Placides Tempels Revisited." *Journal of Religion in Africa* 13.2 (1982) 83–100.

Okesson, Gregg A. "'Are Pastors Human?' Sociological and Theological Implications for Ministerial Identity in Africa." *Africa Journal of Evangelical Theology* 25.2 (2008) 19–39.

Okure, Teresa. "Africa: Globalization and the Loss of Cultural Identity." In *Globalization and its Victims*, 67–74. London: SCM, 2001.

Oman, John. *The Natural and the Supernatural*. Cambridge: Cambridge University Press, 1931.

Oosthuizen, G. C. "The AIC and the Modernisation Process." In *Religion Alive: Studies in the New Movements and Indigenous Churches in South Africa: A Symposium*, edited by G. C. Oosthuizen, 223–45. Johannesburg: Hodder and Stoughton, 1986.

Orabator, Agbonkhianweghe E. "Ecclesiology in Crisis: A Contextualised Theological Study of the Church in Africa in the Situation of HIV/AIDS, Refugees, and Poverty." PhD diss., University of Leeds, 2004.

Order of Services of the Africa Brotherhood Church. 4th ed. Translated by Moses Mollombe. Machakos, 2002.

Otto, Rudolf. *The Idea of the Holy*. Oxford: Oxford University Press, 1950.

"Overview of Africa Brotherhood Church," 2007.

Pannenberg, Wolfhart. *Anthropology in Theological Perspective*. Translated by Matthew J. O'Connell. Edinburgh: T. & T. Clark, 1985.

———. *Christianity in a Secularized World*. London: SCM, 1988.

———. *What is Man? Contemporary Anthropology in Theological Perspective*. Translated by Duane A. Priebe. Philadelphia: Fortress, 1970.

Parrinder, E. G. "God in African Mythology." In *Myths and Symbols: Studies in Honor of Mircea Eliade*, edited by Joseph M. Kitagawa and Charles H. Long, 111–25. Chicago: The University of Chicago Press, 1969.

Parson, Timothy H. "No More English than the Postal System: The Kenya Boy Scout Movement and the Transfer of Power." *Africa Today* 51.3 (2005) 61–80.

Pato, Luke Lungile. "Being Fully Human: From the Perspective of African Culture and Spirituality." *Journal of Theology for Southern Africa* 97 (1997) 53–61.

Payne, Roland J. "The Influence of the Concept of the Traditional African Leadership on the Concept of Church Leadership." *Africa Theological Journal* 1 (1968) 69–74.

Peel, J. D. Y. *Religious Encounter and the Making of the Yoruba*. Bloomington, IN: Indiana University Press, 2003.

Percy, Martyn. *Words, Wonders and Power: Understanding Contemporary Christian Fundamentalism and Revivalism*. London: SPCK, 1996.

Peterson, Derek. *Creative Writing: Translation, Bookkeeping, and the Work of Imagination in Colonial Kenya*. Portsmouth, NH: Heinemann, 2004.

Bibliography

Popular Objections, Powerful Answers: The ABCs of Defending the Christian Faith in Africa. Nairobi: NEGST, 2008.

Probst, Peter, Jan-Georg Deutsch, and Heike Schmidt. "Cherished Visions & Entangled Meanings." In *African Modernities: Entangled Meanings in Current Debate*, edited by Peter Probst et al., 1–17. Oxford: James Currey, 2002.

Ramachandra, Vinoth. "Learning from Modern European Secularism: A View from the Third World." *European Journal of Theology* 12.1 (2003) 35–48.

———. *The Recovery of Mission: Beyond the Pluralist Paradigm*. Carlisle, UK: Paternoster, 1996.

Ranger, T. O. "African Traditional Religion." In *The World's Religions*, edited by Southerland et al., 106-114. London: Routledge, 1988.

———. "The Churches, the Nationalist State and African Religion." In *Christianity in Independent Africa*, edited by Edward Fasholé-Luke et al., 479–502. London: Rex Collings, 1978.

———. "The Invention of Tradition in Colonial Africa." In *The Invention of Tradition*, edited by Eric Hobsbawm and Terence Ranger, 211–62. Cambridge: Cambridge University Press, 1983.

———. "Religious Movements and Politics in Sub-Saharan Africa." *African Studies Review* 29.2 (1986) 1–69.

Rasmussen, Larry L. "Power Analysis: A Neglected Agenda in Christian Ethics." In *The Annual of the Society of Christian Ethics*, edited by D. M. Yeager, 3–17. Georgetown VA: Georgetown University Press, 1991.

Rathbone, Richard. "West Africa: Modernity and Modernization." In *African Modernities: Entangled Meanings in Current Debate*, edited by Jan-Georg Deutsch et al., 18–30. Oxford: James Currey, 2002.

Ray, Benjamin C. *African Religions: Symbol, Ritual, and Community*. 2nd ed. Upper Saddle River, NJ: Prentice Hall, 2000.

Reisman, Paul. "The Person and the Life Cycle in African Social Life and Thought." *African Studies Review* 29.2 (1986) 71–138.

Ribgy, Cynthia L., ed. *Power, Powerlessness, and the Divine: New Inquiries in the Bible and Theology*. Durham, NC: Duke University Press, 1997.

Roberts, Richard H. *Religion, Theology, and the Human Sciences*. Cambridge: Cambridge University Press, 2002.

Robertson, Roland, and Burkart Holzner, eds. *Identity and Authority: Explorations in the Theory of Society*. Oxford: Basil Blackwell, 1980.

Rutto, Christopher Kiprugut Kogo. "Nandi Identity and Christian Denominationalism: The Concepts of Barriet, Lem, and Kiet in an Interpretation of Nandi Christianity, 1985-1992." PhD diss., University of Birmingham, UK, 2003.

Sabar-Friedman, Galia. "Church and State in Kenya, 1986–1992: The Churches Involvement in the 'Game of Change.'" *African Affairs* 96.382 (1997) 25–52.

———. "'Politics' and 'Power' in the Kenyan Public Discourse and Recent Events: The Church of the Province of Kenya (CPK)." *Canadian Journal of African Studies* 29.3 (1996) 429–53.

———. "The Power of the Familiar: Everyday Practices in the Anglican Church of Kenya." *Journal of Church & State* 38.2 (1996) 377–96.

Sampson, Philip, Vinay Samuel, and Chris Sudgen, eds. *Faith and Modernity*. Oxford: Regnum, 1994.

Sandgren, David. "Kamba Christianity: From Africa Inland Mission to African Brotherhood Church." In *East African Expressions of Christianity*. edited by Thomas Spear and Isaria N. Kimambo, 169–95. Oxford: James Currey, 1999.

Bibliography

Sanneh, Lamin, and Joel A. Carpenter. *The Changing Face of Christianity: Africa, The West, and the World*. Oxford: Oxford University Press, 2005.
Sanneh, Lamin. *Encountering the West: Christianity and the Global Cultural Process: The African Dimension*. Maryknoll, NY: Orbis, 1993.
———. *Piety and Power: Muslims and Christians in West Africa*. Marknoll, NY: Orbis, 1996.
Saayman, Willem A. "Some Reflections on the Development of the Pentecostal Mission Model in South Africa." *Missionalia* 21.1 (1993) 40–56.
Schweiker, William. "Power and the Agency of God." *Theology Today* 52.2 (1995) 204–25.
Setiloane, Gabriel M. *The Image of God Among the Sotho-Tswana*. Rotterdam: A. A. Balkema, 1976.
Shaw. Rosalind. "The Invention of 'African Traditional Religion.'" *Religion* 20.4 (1990) 339–53.
Sheriffs, Deryck. "'Personhood' in the Old Testament? Who's Asking?" *Evangelical Quarterly* 77.1 (2005) 13–34.
Sherlock, Charles. *The Doctrine of Humanity*. Downers Grove IL: InterVarsity, 1996.
"A Short Memo on Modernism at the Request of Some African Christian Leaders." AIM Archives, Nairobi, Kenya. July 1962.
Shorter, Aylward. *Inculturation in Africa*. Chicago: CCGM, 2005.
———. *Toward a Theology of Inculturation*. London: Geoffery Chapman, 1988.
Shorter, Aylward, and Edwin Onyancha. *Secularism in Africa: A Case Study: Nairobi City*. Nairobi: Paulines Africa, 1997.
Shweder, Richard A., and Edmund J. Bourne. "Does the Concept of the Person Vary Cross-Culturally?" In *Culture Theory: Essays in Mind, Self, and Emotion*, edited by R. A. Shweder and R. A. LeVine, 158–99. Cambridge: Cambridge University Press, 1984.
Smith, Edwin W., ed. *African Ideas of God: A Symposium*. London: Edinburgh House, 1950.
Snyder, Katherine A. "Being of 'One Heart': Power and Politics among the Iraqw of Tanzania." *Africa* 71.1 (2001) 128–48.
Stackhouse, Max L., and Don S. Browning. *God and Globalization: The Spirit and the Modern Authorities*. Vol. 2. Harrisburg PA: Trinity, 2001.
Stackhouse, Max L., and Diane B. Obenchain, eds. *God and Globalization: Christ and the Dominions of Civilization*. Vol. 3. Harrisburg PA: Trinity, 2002.
Stambach, Amy. "Spiritual Warfare 101: Preparing the Student for Christian Battle." *Journal of Religion in Africa* 39 (2009) 137–57.
Stanley, Brian, ed. *Christian Missions and the Enlightenment*, edited by R. E. Frykenberg and Brian Stanley. Studies in the History of Christian Missions. Grand Rapids, MI: Eerdmans, 2001.
———. "Conversion to Christianity: Colonization of the Mind?" *International Review of Mission* 92.366 (2003) 315–31.
Strayer, Robert W. *The Making of Mission Communities in East Africa*. London: Heinemann, 1979.
———. "Mission History in Africa: New Perspectives on an Encounter." *African Studies Review* 19.1 (1976) 1–15.
Sundkler, Bengt, and Christopher Steed. *A History of the Church in Africa*. Cambridge: Cambridge University Press, 2000.
Sussman, David. "The Authority of Humanity." *Ethics* 113.2 (2003) 350–66.

Bibliography

Taylor, Charles. *A Secular Age*. Cambridge, MA; London: Belknap, 2007.

———. *Sources of the Self: The Making of Modern Identity*. Cambridge: Cambridge University Press, 1989.

Taylor, John V. *The Primal Vision: Christian Presence amid African Religion*. London: SCM, 1965.

Tempels, Placides. *Bantu Philosophy*. Paris: Présence Africaine, 1959.

Throup, David. "Render unto Caesar the Things that are Caesar's: The Politics of Church-State Conflict in Kenya 1978–1990." In *Religion and Politics in East Africa*, edited by Holger Bernt Hansen and Michael Twaddle, 143–76. London: James Currey, 1995.

Tuma, Tom. "Major Changes and Developments in Christian Leadership in Busoga Province, Uganda, 1960–1974." In *Christianity in Independent Africa*, edited by Edward Fashole-Luke et al., 60–78. London: Rex Collings, 1978.

Turner, Harold W. "A Model for the Structure of Religion in Relation to the Secular." *Journal of Theology for Southern Africa* 27 (1979) 42–64.

———. "The Place of Independent Religious Movements in the Modernisation of Africa." *Journal of Religion in Africa* 2 no.1 (1969) 43–63.

———. "The Primal Religions of the World and their Study." In *Australian Essays in World Religions*, edited by Victor C. Hayes, 27–37. Adelaide: Lutheran Publishing House, 1977.

———. *Religious Innovation in Africa*. Boston: G.K. Hall, 1979.

Ukamba Christian Literature Joint Committee. *Mbathi Sya Kumutaiia Ngai*. Kijabe: A.I.C. Kijabe, 1984.

Vahakangas, Mika, and Andrew A. Kyomo, eds. *Charismatic Renewal in Africa: A Challenge for African Christianity*. Nairobi: Acton, 2003.

Vanhoozer, Kevin. "One Rule to Rule Them All? Theological Method in an Era of World Christianity." In *Globalizing Theology*, edited by Craig Ott and Harold A. Netland, 85–126. Grand Rapids, MI: Baker, 2006.

Vanhoozer, Kevin, Charles A. Anderson, and Michael J. Sleasman, eds. *Everyday Theology: How to Read Cultural Texts and Interpret Trends*. Grand Rapids, MI: Baker, 2007.

Venter, Dawid J., ed. *Engaging Modernity: Methods and Cases for Studying African Independent Churches in South Africa*. Westport, CT: Praeger, 2004.

Vincent, Joan. "Colonial Chiefs and the Making of a Class." *Africa* 47.2 (1977) 140–59.

Volf, Miroslav. *Exclusion and Embrace: A Theological Exploration of Identity, Otherness, and Reconciliation*. Nashville, TN: Abingdon, 1996.

———. "Theology, Meaning and Power." In *The Future of Theology: Essays in Honor of Jurgen Moltmann*, edited by Mirolsav Volf et al., 98–113. Grand Rapids, MI: Eerdmans, 1996.

Von Balthasar, Hans Urs. *A Theological Anthropology*. New York: Sheed & Ward, 1967.

Von Rad, Gerhard. *Genesis: A Commentary*. London: SCM, 1972.

———. *Old Testament Theology*. Vol. I and II. Translated by D. M. G. Stalker. New York: Harper & Row, 1962.

Walls, Andrew. "The Eighteenth-Century Protestant Missionary Awakening in Its European Context." In *Christian Missions and the Enlightenment*, edited by Brian Stanley, 22–44. Grand Rapids, MI: Eerdmans, 2001.

———. "Globalization and the Study of Christian History." In *Globalizing Theology: Belief and Practice in an Era of World Christianity*, edited by Craig Ott and Harold A. Netland, 70–82. Grand Rapids, MI: Baker, 2006.

Bibliography

Walt, B. J. van der. *Being Human: A Gift and a Duty: On the Way to a Christian view of Man for Africa*. Potchefstroom, SA: Potchefstroom University for Christian Higher Education, 1990.

Ward, Kevin. "Africa." In *A World History of Christianity*, edited by Adrian Hastings, 192–237. Grand Rapids, MI: Eerdmans, 1999.

———. "Evangelism or Education? Mission Priorities and Educational Policy in the Africa Inland Mission, 1900–1950." *Kenya Historical Review* 3.2 (1975) 243–60.

———. *A History of Global Anglicanism*. Cambridge: Cambridge University Press, 2006.

Weber, Hans-Ruedi. *Power: Focus for a Biblical Theology*. Geneva: WCC Publications, 1989.

Weber, Max. "The Sociology of Charismatic Authority." In *From Max Weber: Essays in Sociology*, translated and edited by H. H. Gerth and C. Wright Mills, 245–52. London: Routledge & Kegan Paul, 1948.

———. *The Theory of Social and Economic Organization*. Translated by A. M. Henderson and Talcott Parsons. New York: The Free Press, 1947.

Welker, Michael. "Creation and the Image of God: Their Understanding in Christian Tradition and the Biblical Grounds." *Journal of Ecumenical Studies* 97.3 (1997) 436–49.

Wesche, Kenneth Paul. "'Mind' and 'Self' in the Christology of Saint Gregory the Theologian: Saint Gregory's Contribution to Christology and Christian Anthropology." *The Greek Orthodox Theological Review* 39.1 (1994) 33–61.

West, Charles C. *The Power to Be Human*. New York: MacMillan, 1971.

Westermann, Claus. *Creation*. Translated by John J. Scullian. Philadelphia: Fortress, 1974.

———. *Genesis*. Translated by David E. Green. Edinburgh: T. & T. Clark, 1988.

White, Leland J. "Theology and Authority: A Cross-Cultural Analysis of Theological Scripts." In *Theology and Authority*, 71–82. Peabody, MA: Hendrickson, 1987.

Whiteley, D. E. H., and Roderick Martin, eds. *Sociology, Theology and Conflict*. Oxford: Blackwell, 1969.

Wink, Walter. *Naming the Powers: The Language of Power in the New Testament*. Philadelphia: Fortress, 1984.

Wolff, Hans Walter. *Anthropology of the Old Testament*. Philadelphia: Fortress, 1974.

Wood, Ralph. *Contending for the Faith: The Church's Engagement with Culture*. Waco, TX: Baylor University Press, 2003.

Wright, G. Earnst. *The Biblical Doctrine of Man in Society*. London: SCM, 1954.

Wright, N. T. *The Climax of the Covenant: Christ and the Law in Pauline Theology*. Edinburgh: T. & T. Clark, 1991.

———. *The New Testament and the People of God*. Minneapolis MN: Fortress, 1992.

Zeleza, Tiyambe. *Rethinking Africa's Globalization*. Trenton NJ: Africa World, 2003.

Zizioulas, John D. "Human Capacity and Human Incapacity: A Theological Exploration of Personhood." *Scottish Journal of Theology* 28.5 (1975) 401–48.

———. "On Being a Person: Towards an Ontology of Personhood." In *Persons, Divine and Human*, edited by C. Schwobel and G. E. Gunton, 33–46. Edinburgh: T. & T. Clark, 1991.

Zuesse, Evan M. *Ritual Cosmos: The Sanctification of Life in African Religions*. Athens: Ohio University Press, 1979.

Index

Africa Brotherhood Church
  (ABC), ix, xiii, xviii, xx–xxii,
  19, 35, 39–40, 44, 62, 69,
  71–6, 85, 87, 107, 115–44,
  151, 200–201, 203, 205–11,
  214–17, 219, 229, 241
Africa "Initiated" Churches, ix, xxi,
  13, 17ff. 111, 115, 154
Africa Inland Church (AICK),
  xiii–xiv, xv, xvii, xx–xxi, 17,
  35–36, 39, 43, 62, 66–76,
  79–114, 118, 147–48, 151,
  199–201, 203, 205–7, 209–
  10, 213–19, 229, 236, 238
Africa Inland Mission (AIM), xiv,
  xxi, xxii, 8–9, 25, 62, 66, 79,
  81, 79–114, 118, 119, 122,
  123, 137, 139, 147, 151, 152,
  206, 211, 215, 216, 229, 233,
  234, 240, 242, 243, 245
African Traditional Religions, xiii,
  11, 53, 119, 141
Agriculture(al), xviii, 40, 84, 123,
  127, 137–38, 140–43, 176,
  203, 210, 219
America, xv, 10, 19–20, 43, 80,
  84, 93, 103, 108–9, 133–34,
  145–47, 151, 154, 160,
  172–75, 200, 214, 216–17
Anthropology, Anthropological,
  xiii, 47, 50, 57, 77, 107

Apologetic, 36, 84, 90, 96, 103–4,
  106–10, 113, 200, 205–7

Bible, Biblical, Biblicism, xxn13,
  5, 31–2, 34, 36, 39–41, 53,
  64, 71, 83, 86–96, 99–114,
  119, 125, 127, 129, 138, 141,
  152, 159, 161, 166–68, 171,
  173, 178, 182–87, 201, 203,
  205–8, 210–25

Canadian Baptist, 40, 130, 133–35,
  137, 211, 217
Choruses, xxiv, 29, 66–71, 77, 90,
  121, 157, 204, 210, 226
Conservative, xiii, xx, 18, 37, 44,
  80, 87–88, 91, 213
Contextual, xiii, xvi, 26, 28, 30–33,
  37–38, 41, 154, 181

Democratic Republic of Congo
  (DRC), 48–49, 80, 122, 128,
  132, 135, 137, 140, 148, 201,
  219
Duka, xxiv, 40, 63, 65

Evangelism, 70, 72, 80–87, 95, 98,
  122, 125, 127, 135, 139–42,
  146–47, 149, 151–52, 154–
  57, 160, 162, 169, 175–76,
  179, 201, 206, 209, 217

247

Index

Evangelicals, Evangelicalism, xv–xxii, 5n17, 8, 18, 25–26, 30–31, 33–34, 44, 62, 67, 71–72, 79–88, 91, 97, 100–101, 103, 108–12, 115, 118–12, 121, 129, 132, 135–36, 138, 141–42, 144–45, 147, 178, 185, 201, 209, 213, 215, 217

Fundamentalistic, 8n30, 79, 151

Gospel, xviii, xx, xxiii, 4, 17, 19, 21–22, 31–32, 34–35, 50, 52, 62, 76, 80, 87, 91, 100–102, 107–9, 118–19, 121–24, 127, 129–30, 132, 137–41, 144–51, 170, 1756, 181, 190, 198, 205–7, 218–19, 223–24, 226

Health, Heal(ing), xviii, 20–21, 67–68, 73, 75, 85, 99, 123, 127, 136–43, 146, 150, 152, 157, 175, 178, 189, 192, 203, 219, 224

Hermeneutic, Hermeneutical, xv, xxiii, 31–33, 46, 50, 144, 176, 178, 199–200, 218, 222, 224

Higher Education, 110–13, 160, 203, 217n81

Holism, Holistic, xviii, 19, 26, 28, 35, 41, 56, 62, 121–24, 133, 136–39, 142–43, 156, 163, 172, 174–75, 178, 207, 215, 219, 223

Holy Spirit, 17, 19, 32, 37, 41, 55, 69, 102, 105, 107, 120–21, 214–15, 129, 131, 134, 138, 141–43, 148–57, 159, 161–62, 165–66, 179, 189–91, 194, 200–202, 204, 206, 212, 214, 218, 223–24, 226

Human, Humanity, xiii, xv–xix, xxiii–xxiv, 1–9, 12, 14, 18, 22–32, 46–62, 64–69, 71–72, 73–77, 79, 84, 87, 99, 101–2, 104–7, 110, 123–24, 129–30, 134–44, 150–51, 154–58, 162, 165–69, 171, 173, 177, 179–227

Image of God, *Imago Dei*, xvii, xix, xxiii, xxiv, 5, 26, 28, 30, 46, 181–98, 199, 223, 225, 227

Kamba (Akamba, Kikamba, Wakamba), ix, xiii–xix, xvi, xxi–xxiii, 20, 26, 34–35, 37, 40, 43, 47, 56–74, 76–77, 80, 85–88, 93, 96, 99, 104–5, 109, 113, 115–16, 118–22, 129, 131–32, 135, 137–40, 143, 147–48, 153–55, 175, 182, 187, 199, 201, 209–11, 215n79

Kenya, xiii, xvi–xvii, xx–xxii, 13, 16, 19–20, 42, 49, 65, 66–67, 79–80, 82, 85–89, 93–94, 104, 108–14, 115, 119, 122, 124, 129, 131–32, 135, 140, 146–50, 153–54, 159–61, 172, 201, 209, 211, 213, 217, 227

Leadership, xiii, xv–xvi, 25, 35, 37, 43, 84, 91, 96, 99–100, 116–17, 119, 125, 127–28, 135, 156, 159, 161, 165, 170, 202, 215–16

Majority World, 30–31, 34, 223

Matatu, xxiv, 30, 40, 63–66, 76, 110, 223

Missions(s), Missionary(ies), xv–i, xx–iii, 4, 8–17, 19–20, 25, 30–31, 44, 62, 66, 70–71, 79–80, 92–97, 100, 102–53, 167, 172–75, 200–201, 205–7, 211, 214, 221

Index

Modernity, xiii, xv–xvi, xviii–xix, xxiii–xxiv, 1–2, 4–14, 16–19, 21–26, 35–36, 43, 45–47, 77–79, 84, 103–4, 115, 129, 143–46, 149, 151, 162, 164, 180–81, 198–200, 213, 219–20, 221–27

Money, xviii, 72, 92–93, 98, 98, 100–101, 116, 122, 125–26, 128, 134–35, 141, 173, 176, 179, 205, 209–10, 215–16

"Moral Ontology," 186–87, 192–93, 195–96, 225

Non-Govermental Organization (NGO), 25, 111, 138, 143–44

Offerings, 97, 121, 126, 135, 143, 157, 162, 169, 173, 209–10, 216

"Ordinary" Readers, 28–29

Parishioner(s), xvii–iii, 33, 71–72, 76–77, 89, 98, 1067, 120–21, 149, 170, 201–2, 224, 207–8, 216

Pastor(s), xvi, xvii, 25, 35, 54, 72–73, 76–101, 105–10, 114, 120–21, 125–29, 135, 137, 139–40, 142, 153, 155–61, 163–71, 174, 179, 199, 201–16, 218, 224

Pentecostal(s), Pentecostalism, xiii, xx–xxii, 13, 19–22, 40, 69, 88, 107, 111, 124, 145–64, 171–72, 174–76, 180, 204–6, 208, 211

Peter Cameron Scott, 80–83

Physical, 4n12, 22, 57, 62, 76, 136, 138–41, 143–44, 152, 172–73, 175–76, 180, 197, 200, 211, 216, 219

Politics, Political, xiii, xix, xx, 3–6, 11–14, 17, 24, 48, 87, 89, 95–6, 98, 100, 110, 112, 118–19, 123, 131, 150, 153, 155, 159, 164, 177, 180, 186, 192, 198, 201, 213–14, 219

Politicians, 54, 213

Power, xiii–xiv, xv–xxi, xxiii–xxiv, 1–7, 9–10, 12–14, 18, 21–26, 28, 30, 35–38, 41–43, 45–71, 73–78, 79–80, 83–84, 87, 89–93, 95–96, 98–108, 110–14, 116, 120, 124–27, 129–31, 134–36, 138–41, 143–44, 145, 149–71, 173, 175–213, 215–27

Prosperity, 20–22, 25, 37, 61, 63, 76–77, 141, 146, 151, 157, 171–79, 200, 216, 218

Rational, Rationalism, Rationalization, 6, 8, 12, 103–14, 151n21

Redeemed Gospel Church (RGC), ix, xiii, xvii, xx–xxii, 20, 22, 35–37, 39–40, 43–44, 69–71, 73–77, 108, 145–80, 200–202, 204–9, 211–14, 216–17

Re-imaging, xvi, 45–46, 57, 187–88

Reflexivity, 7, 30, 42–43

Rwanda, 122, 128, 132, 135, 137, 147–48, 201, 219

Salvation, 32, 67, 71, 102, 105, 119, 132, 134, 139–40, 142–43, 152, 155, 163–65, 172, 187, 190, 201, 206

Salvation Army, xviii, xxii, 118–19, 137

Scott Theological College (STC), ix, xv, 24n99, 37, 39, 88, 99, 101, 105, 111–12, 114, 117

Secular, Secularization, xv–xvi, 3–4, 6, 8, 18, 25, 65, 79, 84–84, 89, 95, 96–114, 126, 136, 138, 173, 197–200, 203, 205, 214, 216, 218–19, 221, 226

249

Index

Sermon(s), xxiv, 29, 36–37, 39, 76, 90–91, 98, 102, 106, 108, 120–21, 140, 164, 173, 205, 207–8, 210–11
Sociology, Sociological, xv, xvi, xix, xxiv, 1, 5, 7, 9, 13, 24, 25–27, 29–30, 41, 43–46, 78, 84, 96, 172, 181, 185, 192, 221–27
Spiritual, xvii, xviii, 4–5, 8, 16, 18, 20–22, 24, 27, 48–50, 55–61, 63–67, 73, 75–77, 80, 83–84, 87–88, 91–92, 95, 98–101, 104–8, 110, 113, 121–25, 127, 129, 134–35, 137–38, 141–44, 145, 149–51, 153–55, 157–61, 163, 165–66, 170–80, 182, 185, 190–92, 197–207, 212, 214–20, 221, 223–24, 226
Songs, 37, 66–73, 76, 97, 120, 157, 199, 223
Spirituality, 18, 20–21, 62, 81–82, 84, 106, 138
Sudan, 148

Tanzania, 72, 80, 128, 132, 137, 140, 148, 201, 219
Theology, Theological, ix, xiii–xiv, xv–xx, xxiii–xxiv, 1–11, 22–41, 44–47, 50–52, 54–56, 62, 66, 77–78, 80, 82, 84, 86–87, 90, 92–96, 98–99, 101–6, 108–14, 119, 126–27, 136, 138–43, 150–51, 155–56, 159–60, 162, 171–75, 177, 179–205, 207, 209–27
Traditions, xiii–xiv, xviii–xix, xxiii–xxiv, 1, 10–5, 19–20, 23, 62–63, 65–66, 84, 87–88, 93, 115, 117–20, 129, 138, 143, 146, 154–55, 181, 187, 205, 213, 215, 221, 225

Washiriki (parishioners), xvi, xviii, 25, 28, 36–38, 44, 75, 156, 162, 166–67, 171, 202–3, 206, 208, 222, 224
West(ern), xvi, xix, xxiii–xxiv, 3–14, 16–20, 23–33, 47–51, 55, 62, 64, 66–67, 78, 80–84, 96–97, 102, 108–9, 118, 120, 122, 124, 128–38, 141, 146, 162–63, 171–80, 185, 188, 191, 198, 201, 206–7, 216–17, 221–26
World, xvii, xviii, xix, xxiii, xxiv, 1, 3, 4, 6–9, 12, 16–17, 22, 24–28, 31–34, 38–39, 46, 48, 50, 52, 54, 56–57, 59–62, 66–68, 70, 72, 74, 79, 81, 83–84, 87, 100, 103–7, 110, 114, 119, 121–24, 129, 132–34, 136, 138–39, 141–44, 148, 150–51, 153–55, 157–58, 162–64, 168, 171–80, 182, 184–88, 192–94, 196–201, 205–6, 209, 212–14, 216–27
Worldview, xv, xvi, xviii, xx, 5, 18, 26, 28, 47–8, 61, 84, 111, 113, 137, 146, 152, 172, 178, 182, 204
World Bank, 23, 164, 174, 200, 208
World Council of Churches, xii, 119

Ukambani, ix, xiii, xv–xviii, xxi–xxiv, 1, 8–9, 19, 25, 34, 41, 44, 46–47, 57, 59, 66, 72, 80, 82, 85–86, 88, 91–92, 96, 104–5, 113, 115, 118, 121–24, 128, 130–33, 135, 137, 145–49, 151–55, 160, 164, 175, 181, 199–211, 213, 215, 217, 219, 226–27

www.ingramcontent.com/pod-product-compliance
Lightning Source LLC
Chambersburg PA
CBHW050343230426
43663CB00010B/1973